This book provides a state-of-the-art account of developments and applications of the social accounting methods that Richard Stone developed and applied during his long and distinguished career, focussing on applications of social accounts in economics and demography, and addressing issues of new formulations and specifications at both national and regional levels.

One theme is economic structure, and particularly issues of structural change, focussing on: changes in final demand composition; fundamental economic structure and hierarchical decomposition, all of these within the context of social accounts matrices. Another theme covers Economic-Demographic Relationships, with special focus on extended input–output models, including consistency problems, linking of macro- and microeconomic approaches and Linear Expenditure Systems.

The importance of Social Accounts Matrices in generating Computable General Equilibrium models, and the enormous potential that both SAM and CGE models have for policy analysis, particularly in the interregional context, is also stressed.

Social and demographic accounting

Social and demographic accounting

EDITED BY

GEOFFREY J. D. HEWINGS
University of Illinois, Urbana-Champaign

AND

MOSS MADDEN
University of Liverpool

CAMBRIDGE
UNIVERSITY PRESS

Published by the Press Syndicate of the University of Cambridge
The Pitt Building, Trumpington Street, Cambridge CB2 1RP
40 West 20th Street, New York, NY 10011-4211, USA
10 Stamford Road, Oakleigh, Melbourne 3166, Australia

© Cambridge University Press 1995

First published 1995

Printed in Great Britain at the University Press, Cambridge

A catalogue record for this book is available from the British Library

Library of Congress in publication data
Social and demographic accounting
    edited by Geoffrey J.D. Hewings and Moss Madden.
        p.   cm.
      ISBN 0-521-46572-9
        1. Demography – Mathematical models.   2. Social accounting –
    Mathematical models.   I. Hewings, Geoffrey.   II. Madden, Moss.
    HB849.51.S65   1995
    330'.011–dc20   94-13047   CIP

ISBN 0 521 46572 9

SE

Contents

viii **Contents**

Contributors

ARNE BIGSTEN   Department of Economics University of Göteborg

MARTIN CLARKE   School of Geography University of Leeds

JOHN H. LL. DEWHURST   Department of Economics University of Dundee

GEOFFREY J. D. HEWINGS   Regional Economics Application Lab. University of Illinois

SARWAR JAHAN   Department of Urban and Regional Planning Bangladesh University of Engineering and Technology

RODNEY C. JENSEN   Department of Economics University of Queensland

MAUREEN KILKENNY   Department of Economics Iowa State University

JONG-KUN LEE   Industrial Analysis Division Bank of Korea

MOSS MADDEN   Department of Civic Design University of Liverpool

JAN OOSTERHAVEN   Department of Economics University of Groningen

ANDREI ROGERS   Institute of Behavioral Science University of Colorado

ADAM ROSE   Department of Economics The Pennsylvania State University

JEFFERY I. ROUND   Department of Economics University of Warwick

MICHAEL SONIS   Department of Geography Bar-Ilan University

DIRK STELDER   Department of Economics University of Groningen

ANDREW B. TRIGG   Faculty of Social Sciences The Open University, Milton Keynes

1 Social accounting: essays in honour of Sir Richard Stone

GEOFFREY J. D. HEWINGS AND MOSS MADDEN

Richard Stone was awarded the Nobel Prize in Economic Science in 1984; in the citation describing his contributions to economics, the Royal Swedish Academy of Sciences commented:

The theoretical analysis of national economic balance problems was perceived by Stone as the starting point and justification for national accounts. Although it was primarily the Keynesian revolution in economics which provided the strongest impulse towards the construction of national accounts systems, these systems may currently be regarded as 'neutral' from both an analytical and ideological point of view. The systems are applied by all analytical streams within economic science and in all types of countries. National accounts have thus created a systematic data base for a number of different types of economic analysis, the analysis of economic structures, growth analysis and, particularly, international comparisons between countries in these respects. (Royal Swedish Academy of Sciences, 1985)

Stone's contributions to social accounting (broadly defined) have extended into many fields and many countries; hence, it would have been impossible to represent these contributions within a single volume. In addition, the impact of his work has extended far beyond his initial conceptions in analytical sophistication, problem area and spatial scales of analysis. The collection of essays in this volume honours the individual for his perspicacity in sensing the importance of accounting frameworks, and recognises the various fields of social science that have been able to build upon and expand his conception of the structure of socio-economic systems. The fields of demography, geography, education and regional science together with economics have cause for association in this celebration, since Stone's original ideas have penetrated in important ways into many of the major branches of these disciplines.

However, no one volume alone can do justice to Stone's contributions; for this reason, the essays here focus on social accounting, addressing issues of new formulations, applications in economics and other fields, specifications at the national and regional levels and a myriad of issues that have

1

arisen from the insights and perspectives provided by the initial formulations of a social accounting matrix. The volume will not cover the ground of Johansen's (1985) broad evaluation of Stone's contributions to economics, but will focus on some specific subareas; the major objective is to provide a forward-looking perspective that addresses some of the major themes and issues of the present decade rather than focussing on a historical treatment of ideas and their development. In a sense, the contribution of the volume may be seen as a complement to Stone's (1986) own assessment of social accounting, but with a focus on regional and demographic issues.

In the remainder of this chapter, the various essays will be placed in the broader context of Stone's work and its application in the fields of regional and demographic analysis. Outside economics, regional science has probably been one of the major consumers of Stone's work. In fact, an earlier assessment of Stone's contributions and their impact in regional science (Hewings, 1990) revealed remarkably little overlap between the impact of his work in economics and in regional science, although it is the case that much of his input in economics has filtered on to regional science in manifestations different from those of its origins. When the larger picture is assembled, it is clear that regional science has much to be grateful for to Stone, and that this sense of gratitude is likely to continue to grow. It is regrettable that this evaluation, assessment and set of essays could not have been completed before Richard Stone's death in 1992.

Economic structure

During the 1950s and 1960s, especially with the emergence of national accounts and input–output tables, there was a great deal of interest in examining the degree to which economies at the same stages of development differed from each other and the extent to which differentiation could somehow be related to development paths. In this regard, the theories and empirical evidence presented by Kuznets (1957) must be regarded as extraordinary in focus and scope. Subsequently other authors, especially Chenery (1960) and Syrquin and Chenery (1989), have provided an impressive sweep of analytical work examining economic structure at the national level. However, Stone (1960), in some of his earlier work, raised the issue about the way in which the structure of regional economies might be revealed and the degree to which this might be based on some distance metric. With customary style, the reader was invited to consider the contribution in the following light:

This paper is concerned with comparing the economic structure of regions on the assumption that we cannot define the concept of economic structure in concrete terms. Those readers who believe that this stage of regional analysis has been passed can have no interest in what is proposed here and would be wasting their time reading this paper; they begin where it leaves off and beyond.

Parenthetically, one cannot help but wonder whether an editor today would allow an author to be quite so forthright in his statements. Essentially, Stone posed the question as to whether it was possible, given a number of variables, to group regions into clusters in which the internal distinctions were smaller than the external ones. Assuming that such a procedure can be found, can one say anything about the criteria used in concrete terms? Drawing on a set of regional accounts that he had developed, Stone (1961a) proceeded to manipulate the data to reveal possible groupings of regions within the United Kingdom.

We can find many similar approaches following this work, although most have been focussed at the urban scale, and there has been little subsequent work focussing on the nature of regional structure and its variation over time and space. A review of measurement possibilities in Hewings et al. (1987) found that analysis of structure was oriented most frequently towards some other goal and examples of comparative analysis are rarely found. Accordingly, there has been very little opportunity to chart the progress of regions over time in terms of the changes in this internal, interdependent structure and the ways in which this structure might be linked to a set of macro-economic indicators.

Of course, the application of the bi-proportional or RAS technique has been widely adopted in regional and interregional analysis to estimate structure under conditions of limited information (see Hewings and Jensen, 1986; Miller and Blair, 1985). In fact, the early interests of Stone, and Leontief (1953), with structure, and the work of Simpson and Tsukui (1965) in developing the notion of the *fundamental structure of production* stimulated Jensen et al. (1988) to conduct a comparative analysis of a set of regional economies within Australia. They generalised Simpson's and Tsukui's terms to *fundamental economic structure* and subsequently linked this notion to a possible evolutionary path through which economies might progress. With the exception of some work by Harrigan et al. (1988a, b), interest in regional and interregional structure has languished. Occasionally, there is renewed interest in the relationship between internal and external structure drawing on some initial explorations of interregional feedback effects by Miller (1966, 1969, 1986); this issue has been adapted by Akita (1992) to examine a growth factor decomposition of external linkages in examining the changing structure of a regional economy in Japan.

The dynamics of change, associated with new production organisations and what Scott (1988) refers to as new production spaces, would seem to call for a much greater investigation of what goes on inside regions and the degree to which the interactions between sectors can be characterised as stable or unstable in the context of growth and development. Notions of switching and re-switching, introduced by Stone's colleague Sraffa (1973), would seem to have a strong spatial analogue; with the exception of Barnes and Sheppard (1984) and Scott (1988), few have accepted the challenge posed by these ideas. The net result is that regional growth and development theory, as currently postulated, seem strangely anaemic in terms of their ability to shed light on contemporary processes of evolution and change. With few exceptions, regional analysis seems to have strayed from the general to the partial and the particular. There have been few attempts to explore Isard's (1960) call for channels of synthesis, in essence the whole complex of interactions within a set of regions nested within a nation, drawing on an underlying set of social accounts.

In this volume, there are two contributions that address several different perspectives within the general concern of economic structure. In particular, the authors share a common concern with the problems that increased model complexity generates in terms of tractability and the ability to explain results obtained from systems with many equations covering one or more sets of economies. Dewhurst and Jensen in chapter 6 explore the problems of structure and structural change with reference to two input–output tables developed for the Scottish economy. The two approaches that they adopt draw first on some earlier comparative analysis by Simpson and Tsukui (1965) and some later derivatives that attempted to identify *fundamental economic structure*. The second approach examines structural change in a comparative static framework in which price effects have been removed. This analysis is very much within the spirit of some recent work by Feldman *et al*. (1987) on the US economy; this latter work suggested that changes in final demand were often the most important elements in explaining changes in gross outputs on a sector by sector basis. Dewhurst and Jensen disaggregate these changes even further and explore the degree to which changes in the composition of final demand might be important; in a sense, economic change can be considered to embrace an allocation component (across various categories of final demand) as well as a distribution component (within any specific vector of final demand). One of their major findings reveals just how important changes in distribution have been in the process of development. Furthermore, they are able to link their work with the notion of fundamental economic structure and raise questions about the possible paths of evolution of regional economies as they become nested within larger economic communities. Over the time period addressed, 1973–9, the Scottish economy became less dependent on the rest of the UK and more dependent on the rest of the world. This finding has been reinforced by some recent work by Sonis *et al*. (1993) that has shown that most EU countries have decreased their internal dependence and increased their linkages with other EU member countries.

In many presentations of economic structure, there has been a tendency to exploit the virtuosity of one method; the Sonis *et al.* chapter in this volume takes a different approach. Here, comparative analysis of several alternative techniques provides the basis for an examination of the structure of a four-region Bangladesh social accounting system. The chapter proceeds on the assumption that it is unlikely that any one technique will illuminate all the features of an economy's structure and thus the ability to view the economy from a variety of perspectives might be valuable. In addition, some alternative perspectives on the problem of hierarchy and hierarchical decomposition are presented. One of the attractive features of a comparative analysis of techniques is the ability to view economic structure at a variety of levels. For example, the insights provided by structural path analysis operate at the micro level; the analyst is able to trace sector by sector impacts along the various paths that can be unravelled by decomposing the Leontief inverse. As an alternative, the field of influence approach offers a meso-level perspective, creating a view of the economy that traces the impacts of any sectoral change (one coefficient, several or a whole vector) on the rest of the system. Finally, the various hierarchical decompositions provided in this chapter draw attention to the macro-level structure of the economy. With these different perspectives, it is much easier to understand why regional development policies focussing on one region or sector may generate significant activity elsewhere in the system. The analysis complements some earlier work done by Bell *et al.* (1982) in which they showed, for a single region, how development strategies can often yield unintended results.

Demographic–economic relationships

Stone, together with Airov (1967) and Miyazawa (1976), was concerned with the consumption-induced effects of change. In later papers, he addressed the issue of the disaggregation of the household sector (Stone, 1985, 1986). It is along this path that one may point to some important extensions and developments at the regional level. Perhaps, the best known and most widely cited is the set of work pioneered by Batey and Madden (1983). By integrating demographic and economic activities within a consistent set of accounts, they have been able to shed considerable light on the effects of alternative policy and non-policy interventions. In particular, they have been careful to devote attention to the nature of consumer expenditures by differing household types (e.g., employed and unemployed) and to account for transfers between employment status in a way that ensures application of *marginal* rather than *average* effects on consumption. Their work and extensions (see Batey and Madden, 1983; Batey, 1985; Madden and Batey, 1980, 1983; Batey, Madden and Weeks, 1987; Sonis and Hewings, 1991) reinforces the need for regional accounts that are more extensive than those considered in the development of closed-model input–output systems. Yet, as has been noted on several occasions (Hewings and Jensen, 1988), attention to consumption expenditures and income generation within regional models has been accorded far fewer resources than the collection of data on interindustry transactions.

Extensions of the Batey–Madden framework to include interregional components (Madden, 1985) and duration of unemployment effects (Batey, Madden and Weeks, 1987) provide examples of the richness of the system and its potential for addressing a broader range of issues than can be accomplished with simple demographic or input–output accounts alone. A parallel development by van Dijk and Oosterhaven (1986) provides ways in which a set of interregional accounts can be enhanced through linkage with a vacancy chain model. In their formulation, one is able to trace the impacts of job creation along two paths. The first path follows the money flows associated with marginal changes in expenditures while the second focusses on consideration of the labour market processes. In this context, one needs to estimate the source of the worker filling a new job – whether from an unemployed pool (within the region or from another region) or from an existing job. In the latter case, one then needs to trace the chaining effect as vacant jobs are filled. In both the Batey–Madden and van Dijk–Oosterhaven models, one can point to considerable progress from the stages where a simple impact analysis was presented as a *before* and *after* comparative static analysis. By tracing out some of the more complex labour market and expenditure processes, the richness and accuracy of the model are enhanced considerably.

In this volume, three extensions to demographic–economic accounts are provided, in chapters 4, 7 and 8, one of which (chapter 8) also makes an important contribution to the problem of the household sector, an issue that is discussed under the heading Linear expenditure systems later in this chapter. However, two of the three contributions (chapters 7 and 8) provide some important perspectives on the incorporation of details about labour force status in accounting systems and are therefore discussed in this section. The third contribution (chapter 4) is discussed in a later section.

Stelder and Oosterhaven (chapter 7) present a detailed analysis of some of the major consistency problems that arise when demographic components are linked within economic systems. The issues become even more critical when more than one economy is considered; the interregional dimension adds a further complication, especially when the problems of adding up are considered. Many data are only available at the national level; how should the apportionment process be administered? When regional data are available, how can one ensure that regional estimates sum to national values? Furthermore, at the regional level, there has been a tendency to view the directions of causality as coming from the nation to the region; explicit region to nation feedbacks are often ignored. When they are incorporated, significant consistency problems may arise. If the adjustment processes employed are too severe, the model might degenerate into a more complex version of shift and share analysis. Hence, some balance and some explicit decision rules have to be developed to maximise use of regional data and, at the same time, ensure consistency. Stelder and Oosterhaven move through the various demand and supply components of their model and find that they are able to provide much more regional specificity on the supply-side of the model. As with their earlier work, the issue of domestic (i.e., interregional migration) creates significant problems; in parallel with some earlier work of Rogers (1990), they note the need for age- and sex-specific migration information given the significant degrees of selectivity in migration streams.

Trigg and Madden in chapter 8, using a different demographic–economic model, address a variety of issues that have been the subject of Stone's attentions – linking demographic and economic accounts, the role of the household and the problem of micro and macro data. Drawing on some of the earlier work of Madden and Batey (1980, 1983), they begin with the now familiar Type IV extended input–output framework and explore a number of options for extending it further to accommodate the following problem: expenditure data are usually collected for households as the decision-making unit, while, on the other hand, labour as a factor input is usually considered at the individual level. How can these two units be linked? Obviously, the consistency issue raised by Stelder and Oosterhaven is a prominent problem. The contribution here may be seen to parallel the micro-to-macro modelling of the industrial sector by Eliasson (1985); in his model, several individual, large firms were handled differently from the rest of the economy and a complex linkage/feedback mechanism developed to produce consistency. In Trigg's and Madden's case, the micro-to-macro connection focusses on the individual-to-household linkage. In earlier work, they were able to separate out the positive and negative consumption impacts of workers moving from unemployed to employed status; however, the assumption usually employed was that the worker taking up a job came from an unemployed household. With many households containing several workers, this assumption may be distorting to the overall impact. Here they explore two alternatives, one a limited dependent variable model and the other a productivity-based approach. The latter is preferred and linked with the input–output system in a computable general equilibrium framework. One of the significant advantages of this technique is the ability to create different multipliers from different assumptions about the micro-level behaviour.

Linear expenditure systems

While there is clear evidence of Stone's contributions in consumer expenditure theory in the development and evolution of regional and interregional econometric models, the use of the linear expenditure system in regional and interregional computable general equilibrium models (CGE) represents a new source of influence. Regional CGE models are of relatively recent vintage (see, for example, Ko and Hewings, 1986; Harrigan and McGregor, 1988a; Bröcker, 1988; Roson, 1992; Gazel et al., 1993) since the often daunting data requirements have deflected analysts to alternative formulations (such as Conway, 1979). However, as Robinson and Roland-Holst (1987) have shown, the development of national accounts, social accounts and CGE models may be seen as complementary developments, not isolated, independent ventures. Furthermore, as noted earlier, it is becoming very clear that, at the regional level, variations in the propensity to consume, variations between the average and marginal propensities to consume (or, in the Batey–Madden models, between employed and unemployed households) and variations in the propensity to consume locally as opposed to non-locally produced goods provide major sources in the identification of analytically important components in regional models. Yet, until very recently, household consumption has not been accorded significant priority in the data assembly and data generation tasks in the development of regional models. In developing countries, this problem cannot be avoided but there remain few studies that focus on this issue at the regional level (e.g., the four-region Bangladesh model of Jahan and Hewings, 1993).

Several contributions in this volume deal with the problem of consumption by households of different types (urban and rural in the cases of Bigsten and Kilkenny; households by status in the labour force in the case of Trigg and Madden). Households play a significant role in the demographic contributions that complete the volume. The linear expenditure system has proved to be a popular and important method for handling issues related to income cross- and self-elasticities in consumption; there is increasing evidence that household expenditures are a source of considerable importance in the generation of economic impacts at the regional level. Hence, their correct specification – by commodity type, and by location – plays a critical role; given the absence of detailed regional data, issues of non-survey estimation enter again, creating further concerns about the dependence of results on initial parameter estimations.

Population–economic linkages

The contribution of Clarke in this volume addresses one of the areas in which Stone made some of his most important analytical and policy-oriented contributions. Stone clearly possessed the vision to look beyond the narrow perspectives that tend to become associated with the applications of a particular technique. Reading his published work, it is obvious that he relished the opportunity to move across a broad spectrum of social science and policy applications; in the field of demographic applications, Stone brought some entirely innovative approaches to the problem of population forecasting, migration estimation and the applications of demographic techniques to education and manpower planning.

His translation of the economic input–output system into demographic terms (Stone, 1970) enabled an accounts-based analysis of population change which led to a whole new series of developments in population analysis and forecasting, exemplified by the work of Rees and Wilson (1977) on population accounts methods, or Schinnar (1976) who pioneered attempts to link together population and economic models, offering a comprehensive approach in which the demographic accounting system was extended via cohort-activity analysis in an attempt to develop a migration-mix policy model for multiple activities through the use of goal programming. Stone himself was dubious about linking the two systems, commenting two decades ago:

I do not see very clearly how a general system of demographic accounts can best be linked with a general system of economic accounts. (Stone, 1970)

This challenge has been accepted by a number of regional scientists and represented in this volume by the contributions of Trigg and Madden and Stelder and Oosterhaven.

Clarke's contribution in chapter 11 calls for accounts-based models, using micro-analytical techniques in the same spirit as those employed by Trigg and Madden, basing the information set on the individual decision-making unit. From this basis, Clarke explores the degree to which traditional demographic processes can be modelled; not only is the decision-making unit reduced to the smallest possible scale, but the spatial unit of reference is similarly scaled to more manageable proportions. Rees and Wilson (1977) presented an alternative set of demographic accounts that enables a decision-making unit to take more than one action within any given time period (e.g., to be born and migrate). Clarke now faces the problem of (1) estimating which of the micro-level decision units will take which action and (2) what the timing and sequencing of these actions will be. Further consideration leads him to suggest reducing the time scale to a short period so that it is feasible to consider only one action per time period. Almost all economic models operate within a time frame that is a quarter or a year in length; in addition, disclosure problems make it difficult to present data for individual decision-making units. However, the attraction of these micro-to-macro problems needs to be explored more extensively at the regional level.

Chapter 10 exploits social accounting as a way of illustrating some of the errors that have appeared in demography. In the same spirit in which Rees and Wilson (1977) deconstructed demographic rates using accounting methods, and Rogers (1990) addressed the issue of the existence of the net migrant, the chapter considers various misspecification problems and shows how they might be addressed correctly. Nothing escapes Rogers' scrutiny – births, deaths, migration and labour force participation rates are examined. Given the dramatic changes that have occurred in these latter rates in a number of countries over the last two decades, Rogers' work provides some pause for reflection on the veracity of some of the commentary that has appeared in print. In particular, the distribution of initial allocations turns out to be of crucial importance. Rogers' chapter illustrates one of the advantages of an accounting framework, namely the attraction of having some internal consistency checks; this characteristic applies not only to demographic models but also to many economic models (for example, many CGE models that were not calibrated from social accounting matrices were shown to be inconsistent with underlying national income and product accounts). The lessons to be drawn from this chapter apply to many regional models.

Social accounting matrices (SAM) and CGE models

Perhaps, more than any other area, the development of social accounts must rank as Stone's premier contribution to economic analysis. What has been the impact at the regional level? Here, one would have to acknowledge that the receipt of these ideas by regional analysts has diffused very slowly. There was some considerable interest in the early 1960s in the development of regional accounts (see Leven, 1958; Hochwald, 1961; Hirsch, 1964, 1966). Sourrouille, (1976) and Czamanski (1973) took up the challenge in the next decade, but, for the most part, progress towards a system of regional accounts has been minimal. Polenske (1970) noted the problem of adding up inconsistently developed regional gross state product estimates to arrive at gross national product – a problem recently confronted in Indonesia where independent estimates of regional value added had some industries purchasing negative amounts of intermediate inputs! (see Hulu and Hewings, 1993).

Stone's early work in the development of regional social accounts forms the basis for the contribution by Round that is chapter 2 of this volume. Round provides two important additions: the first distinguishes functional and geographical transactions while the second introduces the notion of a supra-regional account. The accounts build on Stone (1961a) and several contributions that Round has made to the evolving literature on regional accounting (see Round, 1986, 1988). By making a distinction between geographical and functional transactions, Round is able to distinguish a flow of factor income from abroad to a domestic institution as one comprising two transactions – (1) the external to domestic factor accounting flow (the geographical transaction) and (2) the transfer from domestic factors to institutions (the functional transaction). Thus, trade between regions might be considered as emanating from supply/demand pools with the local/interregional contributions calculated separately. This distinction, of course, is one made most familiar by the Leontief and Strout (1966) gravity model of interregional trade, and an echo is also found in the CGE literature. Here, the choice of inputs is determined via a competitive process and then the choice of origin of the purchases is made as a separate competitive process. The second contribution that he introduces provides an important distinction to the nature of transactions. While the notion of distinguishing between tradeable and non-tradeable explicitly details the geographic space over which goods flow, in a multi-economy system there are additional transactions that do not fit into such a categorisation. These are transactions costs and they may be associated with a supra-regional organisation (e.g., the European Union as an institution or, as Kilkenny and Rose propose in chapter 3, multi-establishment, multi-regional firms). Many of these transactions costs may be significant and have often been arbitraged within other current accounts (often erroneously as to the location of the costs) or ignored altogether. Round illustrates his ideas with reference to a SAM for Europe and clearly demonstrates the enormous potential that these accounts possess for insights into the nature and extent of intercountry/interregional linkages.

Bigsten, too, in chapter 4, presents a SAM that is directly derived from the work of Stone on regional social accounts, and also incorporates household disaggregation of the type discussed in the section above. Bigsten concentrates his attention, in a SAM for Kenya, on income distribution analysis. He disaggregates into seven factor accounts and ten household accounts, the latter being divided into urban and rural, with the rural subdivisions related to landholding as well as income differences. The model that he develops is essentially a highly disaggregated Type II closed input–output model, with a submatrix in the inverse that enables the author to identify the effects of changes in incomes in factors upon other factors. This submatrix is analogous to the interrelational income multiplier matrix of Miyazawa (1976) and to the various income multiplier matrices identified by Madden and Batey (1983), and in using it Bigsten is able to model redistribution between urban and rural households in response to different injections into the Kenyan economy and to identify which sectors of the economy should be expanded for particular domestic policy targets.

As we mentioned in the previous section, partly as a response to the demands made on analysts from policy makers, there has been a burgeoning interest in the development of regional and interregional computable general equilibrium models. Two contributions included in this volume illustrate two important aspects of interregional connectivity. The first, by Kilkenny in chapter 9, follows a similar urban/rural disaggregation to that adopted by Bigsten, except that here the emphasis is on dividing the US into two regions, one metropolitan and the other non-metropolitan. A bi-regional SAM is set up and used to operationalise a bi-regional CGE model, which is used, in the tradition of Harris and Todaro (1970) and Becker and Mills (1986), to examine the degree to which changes in one region generate responses in another. In this case, the aim is to develop a model that can be used to concentrate on the effects of changes in rural government farm subsidies. Some very useful observations are made on problems of balancing the SAM within the context of the CGE model.

The second contribution on this topic, by Kilkenny and Rose in chapter 3, examines capital flows within a SAM framework as a precursor for the development of a fully fledged CGE model. Capital flows between regions have not received a great deal of attention, in part because of the scattered data sources, inconsistencies in the data and the problem of measuring flows that are often not recorded. However, beginning with Airov (1967) with his focus on interregional income flows and the work of Romans (1965) on capital flows, regional scientists have been aware of the importance of accounting for non-commodity flows in the economy. The capital-related income flows (interest, dividends, savings and investment) can be considered the current-account counterparts to interindustry flows. In their chapter, Kilkenny and Rose make a strong case for consideration of what Round has referred to as the supraregional flows; in their case, multi-regional firms, with many establishments in different states/regions, present a difficult problem of allocation. Enterprise-based accounts offer one solution to this problem.

One of the great attractions of interregional SAMs and CGE models resides in their ability to explore implications beyond those associated with the direct consequences. In many cases, unintended effects may arise that create doubts about the efficacy of any policy; with a SAM or CGE, it is possible to trace impacts through various sectors of the economy and across space.

The organisation of the chapters

While many of the chapters in this volume draw on several of the areas in which Stone has made significant contributions, the organisation of the book is rooted in the social accounting system. The first two chapters, by Round and Kilkenny and Rose, exploit the analytical framework for the set of regional and interregional social accounts developed by Stone (1961a) with applications to the advanced economies of Europe and the US. Chapter 4 by Bigsten and chapter 5 by Sonis et al. address applications in developing countries. In addition, the Sonis et al. chapter and the chapter by Dewhurst and Jensen examine structure and structural decomposition of economies represented in social accounting and input–output terms. These chapters provide a sampling of some of the current issues involved in the development and applications of regional accounting.

The next three chapters take on more specific tasks; Stelder and Oosterhaven focus on the role of labour in demographic–economic accounts while the Trigg and Madden chapter is organised around a procedure for linking micro and macro accounts within the household sector. The Trigg and Madden chapter also offers a first glimpse at increasingly popular applications of social accounting systems to form the basis for the development of computable general equilibrium models. A more fully specified CGE model is presented by Kilkenny but the link with the social accounting base remains essential.

The final two chapters address demographic issues, not in isolation, but with the recognition that a great deal of important work remains to be done in the creation of more fully specified models. Rogers uses the social accounting system to offer guidance in checking the consistency of estimating procedures while Clarke's perspective returns to the micro-to-macro theme of Trigg and Madden.

Summary comments

No single volume can hope to provide more than a flavour of the contributions and impact that a person of Stone's stature has made to the field of regional analysis. However, the chapters provide a sampling of a broad range of inquiry that spans economic modelling, linked demographic–economic modelling and finally demographic modelling itself. For colleagues who attended the British Section of the Regional Science Association International in Canterbury in September, 1984, during which Stone delivered the keynote address, there was a keen sense of delight that one of our number had received the Nobel Prize in Economic Science when the announcement was made later that fall. While Richard Stone may not have characterised himself as a regional scientist, those associated with the field were delighted that he took the time throughout his long career to devote some of his creative energies to problems in regional analysis. The field is certainly richer for his involvement.

Now it would be appropriate to conclude with some of Stone's own comments; the first appeared in the *Foreword* to a book published over thirty years ago:

Theorising is a visionary activity whose aim should be to propose a mathematical order which will fit reality. Both parts of this statement must be stressed, because if one wishes to analyse the real world it is necessary not only to set up a model but also to test it empirically. The failure to realise this has led to an immense amount of wasted effort in economics. (Stone and Croft-Murray, 1959)

The other comment appeared in 1962; in writing about alternative approaches to the study of economic systems in connection with the Programme for Growth project Stone directed at Cambridge, he comments:

By exaggerating differences in political and social objectives, (one) observes the fact that the main reason why we do not have a more successful economic policy is that we do not understand the economic system sufficiently well, and that what we should be doing is to study its anatomy and physiology instead of endlessly debating quack prescriptions either of inaction or of apocalyptic changes. (Stone and Brown, 1962)

While Johansen (1985) quibbles that an understanding of the mechanism (of the economic system) will not result in obtaining satisfactory results from the applications of policy, it is clear that the need to observe, classify and interpret has not been eliminated. The contributions in this volume illustrate the need for explanation and the essential unity in the scientific method.

2　A SAM for Europe: social accounts at the regional level revisited

JEFFERY I. ROUND

1 Introduction

This purpose of this chapter is to examine the appropriate structure, and the prospects for constructing, a SAM for Europe. The chapter is essentially an exercise in regional accounting and is intended to readdress the issues raised in the seminal paper on the subject by Stone (1961a) which was aimed primarily at regions defined at the subnational level. Supra-national regional systems such as Europe are rather different. Furthermore, in addition to the regional accounting issues, it also provides an opportunity to incorporate some of the features of the SAM approach more directly.

A 'SAM for Europe' is an intriguing concept in a number of respects. In a most obvious sense Europe cannot be considered as a fixed geographical region; its boundaries are continually changing. Even so there may be several ways in which a European SAM might be viewed. One way might be to consider the European region as a whole and investigate the possibilities of assembling a data framework better to reflect, say, Europe's position *vis-à-vis* the rest of the world. A second approach might be to focus on the existence of the European single market and hence ascertain ways in which the economies of the member states interact one with another. A third way might be to take an even more parochial stance and consider the design and application of SAMs for particular member states, perhaps recognising some commonality in both the conventions and the framework, in much the same way as is implicit in the European System of Integrated Accounts (ESA) (Eurostat, 1979). Clearly these three approaches are not mutually exclusive. In the limit they may simply reflect different emphases and aggregations, although it is nevertheless important to consider the consequences in each case.

The main focus here is towards the first and second of these approaches. It constitutes a first look at what might be possible if we were to try to integrate EU member countries' accounts given the data currently available. More especially, it is to reconsider some of the conceptual problems

15

that might arise in constructing a SAM for Europe. In some real sense all of this represents the ultimate challenge in regional accounting. However, it should be stressed that this chapter is merely an initial attempt to reach a satisfactory solution to a wide range of problems in this regard.

Following this introduction the chapter is organised into five sections. In section 2 the salient features of the SAM approach are presented. Section 3 briefly reviews the present state of the art in regional accounting within the context of the system of regional accounts first proposed by Stone thirty years ago. In section 4 some modifications and improvements are incorporated into the basic system in the light of recent work on SAMs. Section 5 then focusses on some further extensions appropriate to designing a SAM for Europe. Finally, section 6 reviews the available data and examines the feasibility of compiling a European SAM.

2 Features of a SAM

Social accounting matrices (SAMs) have now been applied in a wide variety of country contexts. It is well known that SAMs, a concept attributable to Richard Stone, are a detailed representation of the complete economic accounts of society in matrix accounting format. However, the matrix accounting principles on which SAMs are based are far from new, and even predate the input–output tables and linear programming tableaux to which these principles had been previously applied. The main feature of a SAM, which distinguishes it from an input–output transactions matrix, for example, is that it represents a 'complete' economic system. In essence, this means that the SAM describes the full circular flow of income, establishing separate accounts for the activities of production, consumption and accumulation and transactions with the rest of the world (Stone and Croft-Murray, 1959).

Most recent interest in SAMs has stemmed from their application in a developing country context (Pyatt and Thorbecke, 1976; Pyatt and Round, 1985) where income distribution, poverty and structural issues are of paramount concern and where the need for these kinds of data is most acute, in order to sustain serious policy analysis. There is now considerable evidence on what has been achieved in circumstances ranging from the data scarce to the data rich and even instances where purpose-built surveys have been undertaken to complete a desired framework. But the SAM approach is not confined to use in developing countries. For example, apart from the United Kingdom, SAMs have been constructed and used in the United States, the Netherlands and Italy, and there has also been a notable interest in SAMs for the transition economies of former Eastern Europe.

Formally, a SAM is a square matrix $T = [t_{ij}]$ whose elements t_{ij} represent transactions in an economic system, usually in money terms, and where T has the following properties:

each row and corresponding column represents an account of the system;
rows represent incomings (receipts) and columns represent outgoings (expenditures);
each element t_{ij} represents a transaction (or set of transactions) between account i and account j; an element may be negative if expenditures are recorded as negative receipts;
since it is an accounting system, row and column sums must balance, so

$$Ti = T'i = q \qquad (2.1)$$

The above are necessary, but not sufficient, conditions for a transactions matrix to be a SAM.

So what are the particular distinguishing features of a SAM? The generic form of a SAM as many would now know it has derived mainly from the contributions of Pyatt and Thorbecke (1976) in a developing-country context, although this closely follows the early lead from Stone's own work. As indicated already, a SAM represents the transactions in a 'complete' economic system: it shows more detail and places relatively more emphasis on the social dimension than one would find in a standard input–output table. This has usually meant integrating within the macro-economic framework some detailed accounts for factors of production and institutions (especially households) so as to focus on the living standards of different groups in society.

There now exist many studies which serve to demonstrate just how useful a SAM can be as an organising framework for data and as an information base for policy analysis. Some examples and an overview are provided in Pyatt and Round (1985). However, amongst the earliest examples of a SAM is the one produced by Stone and his associates for the United Kingdom economy (Cambridge, 1962). In that study, Stone referred to the SAM as a representation of the 'anatomy' of the economic system, the 'physiology' being represented by a separately specified multi-sectoral model. This underlines the point that a SAM is simply an empirical description of an economy and is not, of itself, either an economic model or a formal specification of economic behaviour. Nevertheless, a SAM is not entirely neutral to the design of economic models either and many authors, including Dervis, de Melo and Robinson (1982) and Pyatt (1988) have examined those features of a SAM which may be advantageous from a modelling standpoint.

3 Regional accounts in a matrix format

The problems involved in establishing accounts for linked economic systems have been considered on many occasions in the past. Some of these problems are beyond easy resolution but others have been more satisfactorily resolved for application. The interest in regional accounts which first began in the early 1960s focussed almost exclusively on regional economies defined in the subnational sense. The macro-economic accounting problems that were then identified were broadly twofold. First, such regions are invariably open economies for which there is incomplete data on the macro-economic transactions both within and across their often ill-defined boundaries. Secondly, regional analysis at that level exposed a significant amount of activity which was supra-regional in nature (e.g., central government activity such as the provision of defence and other public goods) and it is not always appropriate to apportion it to specific regions. Nevertheless, counterbalancing these problems, there are compensations in that the integration and consolidation of subnational regional economic systems does take place in a situation where transactions are valued in a common currency, and where there is perfect harmonisation between institutional and other sectoral classifications.

The paper on regional accounting by Stone (1961a) still stands as a most significant contribution and not least for our purposes because he approached the subject in the context of a matrix accounting framework. However, much of the subsequent work in this field has focussed more on the production accounts and on input–output transactions in particular and rather less on the economy-wide structure and income flows which would be exhibited by a SAM. Therefore, it is useful to begin by reviewing the main ingredients of the framework proposed by Stone. The key features of the 'building blocks' of his system are reproduced as three panels in table 2.1. He distinguished between three types of account, these being the production, consumption and accumulation accounts for a domestic (that is, a regional) economy. He also recorded the transactions between the accounts of a closed system of three interdependent regions. The difference between panels (a) and (b) is simply the result of juxtaposing the order between regions and types of accounts in the hierarchy of accounts. In most other respects the panels are self explanatory, although a few other observations should be made for our purposes.

First, for simplicity, the accounts are consolidated, so there are no own-account transfers in Stone's regional system; hence all the diagonal entries are zero in both panel (a) and panel (b). Secondly, panel (a) shows the intra-regional transactions in the diagonal blocks, while the off-diagonal blocks depict interregional (that is, between region) flows. The block structure of the alternative format for the whole system in panel (b) is similar to that of the individual regions except that the diagonal blocks now contain elements showing interregional flows. It would be especially desirable to be able to note that all the off-diagonal blocks in panels (a) and (b) are diagonal but it is clear that this is not so and that it is the set of income flows recorded by the elements Y which destroys the symmetry. However, as indicated shortly, this can easily be rectified with a slightly revised format and adherence to more rigorous regional accounting conventions.

Stone noted that the accounting system presupposes knowledge of a relatively large amount of information about transactions between regions. If the regions are countries, then there is a possibility that X_{jk}, that is the commodity trade between pairs of countries, will be known. But, if the regions are subnational, that is where they represent geographical subdivisions of a country, then it is unlikely that there will be information even about commodity trade. Beyond the commodity transactions and in respect of income or capital transfers, such as factor income payments or the current and capital transfers of institutions, then it is unlikely that such information will be available for countries and even less likely for smaller geographical regions. This led Stone to seek more feasible alternative systems of regional accounts and to establish panel (c) of table 2.1.

Panel (c) is the same as panel (a) but with a block of three further rows and columns augmenting the blocks of accounts for the three regions. The intra-regional transactions, shown in panel (a), are also shown in panel (c), but the off-diagonal interregional transactions in panel (a) are now removed and accumulated row-wise and column-wise, and then entered in the corresponding positions in the final row and column block. The additional block of accounts is not region specific but is what may be termed a system-level account. This serves to preserve the overall accounting balance for each region without showing the region-to-region detail of panel (a). Formally, the entries in the columns of this system account show the gross receipts paid into each regional account from all other regions of the system, while the rows of the system account record the gross outlays. As already mentioned, were it not for the elements relating to interregional factor income payments the matrices contained in the system account would be diagonal. As it is, they have the same structure as the interregional flow matrices shown in panel (a).

The system of regional accounts described above has underpinned a number of studies at the subnational level. Barnard (1969) compiled a SAM for the state of Iowa in the United States, while Czamanski (1973) and Sourrouille (1976) also discussed applications to regional economies. Barnard's work shows that if only a single region is involved, whether it is part of a country (subnational) or a group of countries (supra-national), the

Table 2.1 *Stone's system of regional accounts*

(a) Accounts for three regions ordered by region and type of account

	Region 1			Region 2			Region 3		
Region 1	0	C_{11}	I_{11}	X_{12}	0	0	X_{13}	0	0
	Y_{11}	0	0	Y_{12}	G_{12}	0	Y_{13}	G_{13}	0
	D_{11}	S_{11}	0	0	0	B_{12}	0	0	B_{13}
Region 2	X_{21}	0	0	0	C_{22}	I_{22}	X_{23}	0	0
	Y_{21}	G_{21}	0	Y_{22}	0	0	Y_{23}	G_{23}	0
	0	0	B_{21}	D_{22}	S_{22}	0	0	0	B_{23}
Region 3	X_{31}	0	0	X_{32}	0	0	0	C_{33}	I_{33}
	Y_{31}	G_{31}	0	Y_{32}	G_{32}	0	Y_{33}	0	0
	0	0	B_{31}	0	0	B_{32}	D_{33}	S_{33}	0

(b) Accounts for three regions ordered by type of account and region

		Production			Consumption			Capital		
	{1	0	X_{12}	X_{13}	C_{11}	0	0	I_{11}	0	0
Production	{2	X_{21}	0	X_{23}	0	C_{22}	0	0	I_{22}	0
	{3	X_{31}	X_{33}	0	0	0	C_{33}	0	0	I_{33}
	{1	Y_{11}	Y_{12}	Y_{13}	0	G_{12}	G_{13}	0	0	0
Consumption	{2	Y_{21}	Y_{22}	Y_{23}	G_{21}	0	G_{23}	0	0	0
	{3	Y_{31}	Y_{32}	Y_{33}	G_{31}	G_{32}	0	0	0	0
	{1	D_{11}	0	0	S_{11}	0	0	0	B_{12}	B_{13}
Capital	{2	0	D_{22}	0	0	S_{22}	0	B_{21}	0	B_{23}
	{3	0	0	D_{33}	0	0	S_{33}	B_{31}	B_{32}	0

(c) Accounts for three regions ordered by region and type of account with no pairwise transactions

Region 1			Region 2			Region 3			Combined		
0	C_{11}	I_{11}	0	0	0	0	0	0	$X_{12}+X_{13}$	0	0
Y_{11}	0	0	0	0	0	0	0	0	$Y_{12}+Y_{13}$	$G_{12}+G_{13}$	0
D_{11}	S_{11}	0	0	0	0	0	0	0	0	0	$B_{12}+B_{13}$
0	0	0	0	C_{22}	I_{22}	0	0	0	$X_{21}+X_{23}$	0	0
0	0	0	Y_{22}	0	0	0	0	0	$Y_{21}+Y_{23}$	$G_{21}+G_{23}$	0
0	0	0	D_{22}	S_{22}	0	0	0	0	0	0	$B_{21}+B_{23}$
0	0	0	0	0	0	0	C_{33}	I_{33}	$X_{31}+X_{32}$	0	0
0	0	0	0	0	0	Y_{33}	0	0	$Y_{31}+Y_{32}$	$G_{31}+G_{32}$	0
0	0	0	0	0	0	D_{33}	S_{33}	0	0	0	$B_{31}+B_{32}$
$X_{21}+X_{31}$	0	0	$X_{12}+X_{32}$	0	0	$X_{13}+X_{23}$	0	0	0	0	0
$Y_{21}+Y_{31}$	$G_{21}+G_{31}$	0	$Y_{12}+Y_{32}$	$G_{12}+G_{32}$	0	$Y_{13}+Y_{23}$	$G_{13}+G_{23}$	0	$\sum_k \sum_{j\neq k} Y_{jk}$	0	0
0	0	$B_{21}+B_{31}$	0	0	$B_{12}+B_{32}$	0	0	$B_{13}+B_{23}$	0	0	0

Key

Intra-regional	Interregional
C Consumption	X exports
Y Income	G gifts and grants (current transfers)
I Investment	B borrowing (capital transfers)
D Depreciation	
S Savings	

Source: Stone (1961a)

conceptual problems are not really very different from these encountered for a single country. However, as Czamanski (1973) discusses at length, the practical accounting problems are often severe, especially at the subnational level, because there are usually higher proportions of economic activities and institutions that do not have a clearly defined location in relation to the boundaries of a region. For example, although the existence of multinational enterprises creates accounting problems at the national level such problems are far more acute at the subnational level. This is because multiplant firms may straddle regional boundaries and have spatially diffuse ownership patterns. Also, the activities of government, and of central government in particular, create regional accounting problems that are not insignificant. Stone's solution was to take parts of central government out of the regional accounts altogether and to show them separately. This solution can be extended and utilised further.

Perhaps because of these difficulties, apart from specific studies such as those by Barnard and Czamanski referred to earlier, the overwhelming majority of empirical studies to do with regional and interregional intersectoral flows at the subnational level have been confined to input–output accounts. There are many studies and it is not the purpose of this chapter to review all of them or even the implementation of regional accounts in general. Many surveys already exist such as Czamanski (1973), and Hewings and Jensen (1989). However, it is pertinent to note that the European context is prominent in the early development of ideas. Chenery, Clark and Cao-Pinna (1953) used an input–output framework for a regional analysis of Italy, while Courbis (1979) constructed economic accounts to build the REGINA model for France.

The system of regional accounts set up by Stone is consistent with some earlier work at the supra-national level, where regions consist of groups of countries rather than geographical subdivisions of them. The United Nations World model devised and implemented by Leontief, Carter and Petri (1977), though also intrinsically an input–output model, can be viewed in the context of the Stone framework shown in table 2.1(c). The lack of sufficiently detailed information on commodity trade between regional blocs led to the adoption of the concept of a 'single international trading pool'. Exports from a particular country or region are delivered to the pool, while imports are drawn from it. This approach to arranging trade data and modelling trade flows is generally favoured by Leontief and is entirely consistent with the more pragmatic accounting schema of table 2.1(c), where there is a system-level account – in this case a commodity pool account – whose purpose is to receive payments for commodities from the regions and to make disbursements from it back to the regions.

Finally, it can be noted that as part of the compilation of a SAM for

Malaysia (Pyatt and Round, 1984), a number of issues to do with regional accounts and linked economies were considered in the context of the two regions of Peninsular and East Malaysia. The particular solution to the accounting problems in the Malaysia SAM has been considered further in Round (1986, 1988). There are two principal conceptual and methodological developments which have stemmed from this work. One is to do with establishing a more precise arrangement of Stone's regional accounts while the other is an examination of ways of accommodating the transaction costs associated with various kinds of geographical flows within the overall framework.

4 Regional accounts in a SAM framework

A useful starting point for further analysis is to introduce a basic SAM framework for a domestic economy. This could be a country, a geographical subdivision of a country, or a political grouping or trading bloc of countries. Hence 'region' and 'domestic economy' can be used interchangeably according to the circumstances. Table 2.2 shows an elementary schema distinguishing the current and capital accounts of domestic institutions and the factor and product accounts. A fifth account encompasses all transactions and transfers between the domestic economy and agents external to it. Clearly, further disaggregations of the accounts are implicit in table 2.2. For example, the institutional subdivisions could include the socio-legal institutional structure for the economy, while the product accounts could distinguish production activities from the commodities which they produce. The basic SAM in table 2.2 is therefore generic and, in that case, is not merely a simplified structure.

The first modification we shall consider in relation to Stone's regional accounting system is the distinction that can be drawn between 'functional' and 'geographical' elements of any transaction between the domestic and external economies (Round, 1986). This is not the only way of accommodating regional transactions within a SAM but it has some useful features. The distinction is most easily seen by means of an example. Consider the remittance of factor income from abroad to a domestic institution. This can be recorded in two stages: first as a remittance from the external to the domestic factor accounts (a geographical transaction) and secondly as a payment from the domestic factor account to the domestic institution (a functional transaction). A second example is also illustrative. Consider two linked regional economies engaging in trade. Commodity flows can be shown first as a transfer from the ith account in one region to the ith account in the other region. The subsequent (functional) use of this commodity is then recorded in the domestic accounts of the recipient region. This

Table 2.2 A basic SAM

			Domestic economy				External economy	Total
			Institutions		Production			
			Current	Capital	Factors	Products		
Domestic economy	Institutions	Current	Current transfers (T_{11})		Factor income (T_{13})	Taxes on products (T_{14})	Current transfers from abroad	Receipt of income
		Capital	Savings (T_{21})	Capital transfers (T_{22})			Capital transfers from abroad	Receipt of funds
	Production	Factors				Domestic product (T_{34})	Factor income from abroad	Factor income receipts
		Products	Consumption (T_{41})	Investment (T_{42})		Intermediate product (T_{44})	Exports	Demand for products
External economy			Current transfers paid abroad	Capital transfers paid abroad	Factor income paid abroad	Imports		Balance of external payments
Total			Use of income	Use of funds	Factor income outlay	Supply of products	Balance of external payments	

Source: Pyatt (1988).

Table 2.3 *A basic SAM for a closed two-region system*

				Region 1				Region 2				
				1	2	3	4	5	6	7	8	Totals
Region 1	Institutions	Current	1	T_{11}		T_{13}	T_{14}	T_{15}				q_1
		Capital	2	T_{21}	T_{22}				T_{26}			q_2
	Production	Factors	3				T_{34}			T_{37}		q_3
		Products	4	T_{41}	T_{42}		T_{44}				T_{48}	q_4
Region 2	Institutions	Current	5	T_{51}				T_{55}		T_{57}	T_{58}	q_5
		Capital	6		T_{62}			T_{65}	T_{66}			q_6
	Production	Factors	7			T_{73}					T_{78}	q_7
		Products	8				T_{84}	T_{85}	T_{86}		T_{88}	q_8
Totals				q_1'	q_2'	q_3'	q_4'	q_5'	q_6'	q_7'	q_8'	

accounting procedure for interregional transactions, together with the identification of separate factor accounts, leads to an improvement of Stone's regional accounting system. Table 2.3 shows the revised SAM for a closed two-region system, but an m-region system would be entirely analogous to it. The main observation from table 2.3 is to note that the intra-regional structure (the diagonal blocks) is exactly as is defined in table 2.2 for domestic transactions, while the interregional structure (the off-diagonal blocks) is diagonal because these cells simply represent the geographical transfers between otherwise similar accounts.

The second modification stems from the need to accommodate transaction costs in the accounting system, especially as the transport costs of traded \goods are not usually negligible. This is a point of considerable importance when the regions are countries and when export data (f.o.b.) are matched against import data (c.i.f.) for individual commodities. But transaction costs can arise in the movement of all kinds of goods and assets (financial and non-financial), especially if the regions (countries) use different currencies and currency exchange is involved. They may also arise from certain kinds of market imperfections. Of course some of the observed discrepancies between, say, imports and exports of goods, could be due to timing differences between their despatch and receipt, or invoice and shipment, but they are also due to the incidence of freight, insurance and distribution charges. Therefore, it is clear that transaction costs do arise, and are often significant, and ought not simply to be buried in the residual column of the accounts or treated as a statistical discrepancy to be smoothed out subsequently. Indeed, they represent the 'flux' in a regional system of linked economies and therefore need to be represented properly in the accounts.

The way to treat distribution services associated with commodity trade in a SAM framework has already been considered in some detail (Pyatt and Round, 1984). For present purposes, it is sufficient to note the broad conclusions of that study. Clearly, since transport and distribution are part of produced services then at the aggregate level (that is, aggregating over all goods and services) the c.i.f. and f.o.b. valuations should differ only if a country other than that which exports the good supplies the freight services. But even if the importing country provides freight the statistical conventions underlying the balance of payments accounts treat such services as re-imports, so the overall balance should still be maintained. Hence distribution costs in commodity trade are wholly internal to the commodity account and will not affect the basic accounting principles just set out regarding geographical transfers. However, the situation is different at the individual-commodity level and it could also cause a problem for all other non-commodity geographical transfers on which transactions costs are levied if they cannot be treated internally to the account in question.

Finally, it should be noted that Stone's creation of a separate central government account, positioned outside the individual regional accounts, has been temporarily suppressed in table 2.3 for the sake of simplicity. However, a more general version of this will be reintroduced in the next section in relation to a European SAM. Also, it is worth noting that the arrangement of accounts described in this section is not unique. Stone and Weale (1986) have developed a stylised two-region demographic–economic accounting matrix which departs significantly from the system developed here. They make no distinction between geographic and functional transactions and one consequence is that their system is quite demanding in terms of the information they would require in practice. This is illustrative of the fundamental dilemma that exists in designing and implementing SAMs more generally: a compromise has to be drawn between the ultimate analytical requirements and their statistical feasibility.

5 A European SAM: aggregation, consolidation and apportionment

The representation of transactions for a two-region system, inclusive of transactions with the rest of the world, can be taken as a starting point for further analysis. Each region in the accounting system can be considered either as a member state or as a group of countries within Europe. For most purposes, it is sufficiently general to consider just two regions as this helps to keep notation within manageable proportions. Also, it is useful for the time being to make certain simplifying assumptions, and in particular to assume that the transactions costs associated with geographical transfers are zero, that there are no supra-regional institutions, and that the information necessary to complete table 2.3 (including all region to region transfers) is generally available.

One obvious rearrangement of the accounts in table 2.3 is to order them first by type of account and then by region, in much the same way that table 2.1(b) in this chapter, derived from Stone (1961a), is a reordered form of table 2.1(a). This is shown in table 2.4 and displays a number of useful features. First, it can be seen that the block structure is identical with that of table 2.2, except that the 'factor to factor' transfers matrix is no longer null but now contains the factor income payments between regions. Secondly, the off-diagonal cells are block diagonal, so they contain only the domestic (intra-regional) transactions that take place between the different types of account. These are the so-called 'functional' transactions referred to earlier. Thirdly, the diagonal cells contain the transfers which take place within each type of account and these now include both the domestic transfers and the interregional transfers. The assumption that the 'geographic' transactions costs are zero ensures that the interregional transfers matrices are all diagonal, and these are shown accordingly.

Classifications

Any extension of tables 2.3 and 2.4 to represent the accounts for three or more regions would result in accounting matrices with very similar formats. Obviously, the number of off-diagonal blocks would increase more than proportionately and so would the data requirements relating to bilateral interregional transfers. Nevertheless, tables 2.3 and 2.4 do represent a useful basis for our discussion at a more detailed level. We now turn to a brief discussion of classifications and the kind of detail of economic structure and distribution upon which SAMs have tended to focus hitherto. For analytical purposes it might be desirable to seek disaggregations of the production accounts (by branch and commodity), the institution accounts

Table 2.4 *A basic SAM ordered by type of account and region*

		Institutions		Production		External account	Σ
		Current	Capital	Factors	Products		
Institutions	Current	$T_{11}\ \hat{T}_{15}$ $\hat{T}_{51}\ T_{55}$		T_{13} T_{57}	T_{14} T_{58}	$T_{1E}\ T_{5E}$	q_1 q_5
	Capital	T_{21} T_{65}	$T_{22}\ \hat{T}_{26}$ $\hat{T}_{62}\ T_{66}$			$T_{2E}\ T_{6E}$	q_2 q_6
Production	Factors			$\hat{T}_{37}$ $\hat{T}_{73}$	T_{34} T_{78}	$T_{3E}\ T_{7E}$	q_3 q_7
	Products	T_{41} T_{85}	T_{42} T_{86}		$T_{44}\ \hat{T}_{48}$ $\hat{T}_{84}\ T_{88}$	$T_{4E}\ T_{8E}$	q_4 q_8
External Account		T_{E1} T_{E5}	T_{E2} T_{E6}	T_{E3} T_{E7}	T_{E4} T_{E8}		q_E
Σ		q'_1 q'_5	q'_2 q'_6	q'_3 q'_7	q'_4 q'_8	q'_E	

Note: $\hat{T}$ denotes that matrix T is diagonal.

(by sector and subsector, including households) and the factor accounts (which typically include some disaggregation by type of labour), as well as further disaggregations of the capital (financial transactions) and rest of the world accounts. Thus the disaggregations may cut across all of the principal accounts C0 to C7 in the ESA system (Eurostat, 1979). However, it is difficult to prejudge what might constitute useful disaggregations in any general sense. The framework of the SAM has to be flexible enough to accommodate a wide range of possible disaggregations without affecting the accounting rules or being unduly demanding in terms of the amount of information required. In tables 2.3 and 2.4 each of the four basic accounts have been replicated for each of the regions in the system. At a disaggregated level we may not want to be so restrictive and thereby allow different degrees of disaggregation for the different regions. Therefore it is necessary to consider the implications of this for the accounting scheme we have proposed. To do so, we shall consider disaggregations of products, factors and households, since these are illustrative of the key accounts for SAM purposes.

The first (and worst possible) case is where there is no harmonisation at all between the classifications of accounts for the individual regions. For products this would mean that the accounts are chosen independently of any ESA (NACE/CLIO) or other international recommendations on classifications which, for the EU countries, is admittedly unlikely. For factors, and for labour in particular, standard international classifications do exist but here it is more likely that we might want to retain options on a flexible and independent classification scheme in the individual regions. Skill levels may vary, there is considerably less mobility of factors across international boundaries than products, and hence more need to recognise distinct regional factor markets in the accounting scheme. For households, while there may be some circumstances where, say for international comparison purposes, it is desirable to harmonise classifications of households according to certain socio-economic criteria, it is even less likely that there will be perfect harmonisation. The household accounts are therefore likely to retain particular country-specific characteristics, such as location or socio-economic groups.

Consider therefore the general situation where n_i accounts are chosen to describe the ith region, and where these accounts are quite distinct from the n_j accounts for region j. Let us consider what would be the implications for the SAM and the regional accounting structure represented in tables 2.3 and 2.4. For a connected system of R regions there would be $\sum_i^R n_i$ accounts in total, excluding the accounts external to the regional system. But because of the rules for distinguishing functional and geographical transactions the regional SAM would have to be considerably larger than this in order to maintain the block structure we have described. Each region would be represented by all $\sum_i^R n_i$ accounts so as to facilitate the transfers between regions as well as the functional transactions within the regions. A simple example should suffice to illustrate this point. Suppose factors in region j remit income to households in region i and we choose to distinguish both regional households and regional factors in the accounting scheme. An account for the factor of type 'region j' should be included in the sets of accounts for both regions i and j so as to enable income to be transferred between that account in each of the two regions. This is the geographical transfer referred to earlier. Once the income has been remitted to region i then the income payment from factor j can be transferred to households in 'region i' in the usual way. So although this device leads to a multiplicity of accounts for each region (over all regions it would total $R\sum_i^R n_i$) it does preserve the diagonal structure for the off-diagonal blocks which is important for subsequent manipulation. If the objective is to generate a connected system of SAMs for EU member states, with no further regional consolidation or aggregation, then the full system could be considerably reduced so as to achieve a matrix of much more manageable proportions. In practice many of the accounts would become redundant because no interregional transfers take place. Obviously, if detailed information on interregional transfers is not available then there can often be recourse to the use of 'dummy' accounts which utilise whatever aggregate information there is.

The second (and best possible) case is where there is truly a 'single European market' in individual commodities, factors, or assets. Here the accounting structure would be greatly simplified because there needs to be only one account, common to each of the regions of the system, to represent that particular market in the SAM. Note, however, that harmonising the accounts is not enough: the 'law of one price' must also prevail (Pyatt, 1988). If prices differ in the regions or if goods, factors, etc. are not perfect substitutes then region-specific accounts should be retained and the accounts organised as described above.

The outcome of all this is to suggest that a feasible format can be drawn up without constraining the choice of classifications for the member countries unduly. However, it may be desirable to harmonise certain accounts and to utilise our knowledge of the existence of single markets at the outset. But, overall, the regional framework is flexible enough to accommodate a wide range of possibilities and is neither more nor less data-demanding than comparable schemata.

Aggregation and consolidation

Suppose now we consider a further aggregation of table 2.4 to suppress the regional detail in certain accounts. The motivation for doing so has already been touched upon. It may be that, for the purpose of analysis, single markets exist or that the regional (individual country) detail is of no immediate interest. For these accounts, moving up the regional hierarchy towards, say, a European-wide account essentially means that the information in the accounts for the separate regions now has to be aggregated and the transfers between them must be eliminated to avoid double counting.

The formal procedure is simply a special case of the process of aggregation and consolidation, which is well known in both the social accounting and input–output literature. To avoid excessive and unnecessary notation the principles involved can best be explained in a simplified two-region SAM format. Let H be a SAM where

$$H = \begin{bmatrix} H_{11} & \hat{H}_{12} \\ \hat{H}_{21} & H_{22} \end{bmatrix}$$

and where the subscripts now refer to regions (countries). Because H is a SAM it follows that

$$Hi = H'i = q \tag{2.2}$$

The matrix H can be viewed as a representation of table 2.3 where $\hat{H}_{12}$ and $\hat{H}_{21}$ are the diagonal matrices recording interregional (intercountry) transfers. Alternatively it could be viewed as a representation of any of the diagonal blocks of cells in table 2.4 linking the transfers (within and between regions) in each type of account. In that case however row sums do not necessarily equal column sums; also, some or all of the matrices H_{11}, $\hat{H}_{12}$, $\hat{H}_{21}$, and H_{22} may be null.

Now consider the aggregation of the SAM across regional accounts. Formally, the procedure is carried out in two stages: first, a straightforward summation of elements in corresponding rows and columns, achieved by applying an appropriate grouping matrix G to H, viz.

$$GHG' = \bar{H}$$

where in this case

$$\bar{H} = [H_{11} + H_{22} + (\hat{H}_{12} + \hat{H}_{21})]$$

Now if $\hat{H}_{12}i = h_{12}$ etc. then $\bar{H}$ is still a SAM because

$$\bar{H}i = q_1 + q_2 + h_{12} + h_{21} = H'\bar{\imath}$$

Note that interregional transfers have not been netted out from $\bar{H}$. The second stage therefore is to consolidate accounts and, in this case, to eliminate the transfers which are internal to the account. The final SAM, $\bar{H}$, is

$$\bar{H} = [H_{11} + H_{22}]$$

which satisfies the requirement

$$\bar{H}i = \bar{H}'i = q_1 + q_2$$

The aggregation across regions for selected types of account involves a partial application of this same procedure to those particular accounts. It amounts to applying the method to the appropriate diagonal blocks of table 2.4 and also simply adding the (diagonal) elements in the cells of the remainder of the rows and columns to which that diagonal block applies. For example, the application of this procedure to the institutions' current accounts would yield a new cell entry for institutional transfers, $(T_{11} + T_{55})$, and the row and column sums would now become the vector

$$(q_1 + q_5 - (\hat{T}_{15} + \hat{T}_{51})i).$$

The most important point to note from this is the ease with which aggregation across regions (countries) can be achieved with this particular SAM format. This is all because interregional transfers are distinguished from functional transactions and also from all other transfers between domestic accounts. Hence the transfers matrices $\hat{T}_{15}$, $\hat{T}_{51}$, $\hat{T}_{26}$, etc., are strictly diagonal so that their row sums correspond to their column sums and consequently they can simply be netted from both sides of the account by subtraction.

Apportionment

Complete or partial aggregation of connected SAMs for each of the member countries of Europe is not the only means of reducing its size for informational or analytical purposes. An alternative approach would be to apply the method of apportionment (Pyatt, 1989) and there are circumstances in which this might be preferred to aggregation. First, however, the method should be explained in relation to the reduction of the SAM already represented by H.

Pyatt showed that from (2.1) and with account totals defined to be q_1 and q_2 in each of the two regions, then providing $(\hat{q}_2 - H_{22})^{-1}$ exists, there will exist a matrix

$$\overset{*}{H}_{11} = H_{11} + \hat{H}_{12}(\hat{q}_2 - H_{22})^{-1}\hat{H}_{21} \tag{2.3}$$

where $\overset{*}{H}_{11}$ is a SAM with row and column totals equal to q_1. A similar reduction of H to $\overset{*}{H}_{22}$ for the second region would also apply. It is important to emphasise that while $\overset{*}{H}_{11}$ is the same order as H_{11} its row and column totals are the same as the region 1 totals in H. Hence $\overset{*}{H}_{11}$ takes account of region 1's transfers to region 2 (and vice versa) by apportioning them across the domestic accounts for the region.

An alternative form for (2.3) is to express $\hat{H}_{12}$ and H_{22} in coefficient terms. This can be achieved in two ways. First, by defining $H_{ij} = A_{ij} \, q_j$ we can express (2.3) as

$$\overset{*}{H}_{11} = H_{11} + \hat{A}_{12}\hat{q}_2(\hat{q}_2 - H_{22})^{-1}\hat{H}_{21}$$
$$= H_{11} + \hat{A}_{12}(I - A_{22})^{-1}\hat{H}_{21} \tag{2.4}$$

Alternatively, by defining $\hat{H}_{ij} = q_i \, J_{ij}$, we can express (2.3) as

$$\overset{*}{H}_{11} = H_{11} + \hat{H}_{12}(I - J_{22})^{-1}\hat{J}_{21} \tag{2.5}$$

An elementary result is to note that

$$i'A_{12}(I - A_{22})^{-1} = i' \tag{2.6}$$

so that the matrices $\hat{A}_{12}(I - A_{22})^{-1}$ and $(I - J_{22})^{-1}\hat{J}_{21}$ may be considered as 'spreading' or 'apportionment' matrices. Their effect is to apportion the elements of $\hat{H}_{21}$ and $\hat{H}_{12}$ respectively to cells in direct correspondence with those of H_{11}. The results in (2.6) are sufficient to confirm that $\overset{*}{H}_{11}$ is a SAM with row and column totals equal to q_1.

The condition which states that $(\hat{q}_2 - H_{22})^{-1}$ exists is important for the result. It is straightforward to show that this will not hold if $\hat{H}_{12}$ is a null matrix. Also, if $\hat{H}_{12}$ is null then so too is $\hat{H}_{21}$. This means that the two countries are unconnected and there is nothing to apportion to H_{11}. Moreover, as the total of all the elements in each of $\hat{H}_{12}$, $\hat{H}_{21}$ and $(\hat{q}_2 - H_{22})$ are equal, then the matrix $(\hat{q}_2 - H_{22})^{-1}$ can be seen to play the role of a normalising term, rescaling the product of $\hat{H}_{12}$ and $\hat{H}_{21}$.

In the case of a two region system equation (2.3) is an especially simple application of the apportionment method because the interregional transfers matrices $\hat{H}_{12}$ and $\hat{H}_{21}$ are diagonal. For three or more regions the expression is less intuitive, and the pattern of transfers between regions now becomes important in the apportionment process. But one property of the method of apportionment is especially noteworthy in the regional context. It is that the consequence of eliminating any set of accounts is independent of the order in which the accounts are eliminated (Pyatt, 1989). Hence in a system with more than two regions (R, say) this means that the accounts for the whole system can be collapsed to those of a single region, either one region at a time, or in groups of regions, or taking the remaining $R-1$ regions en bloc. The final result would be the same in each case.

Transaction costs, European institutions and the external accounts

The existence of transaction costs directly associated with the transfers between regions does seem to create certain technical problems in relation to both their representation in the accounts and their treatment in economic analysis more generally. One possibility has been touched upon earlier which is to attribute such costs by means of a set of margins within the submatrices that record interregional transfers. There is, however, a possible alternative approach which is preferred. It is to take the transaction costs outside the regional accounts altogether and deal with them via a system-level account, a 'supra-regional' account, which does not therefore have a specific regional label. Although at first sight this might seem contradictory it can be defended on the grounds that the costs of distribution, as well as all the other costs associated with exchange between countries, are really to do with the movement of goods and services between geographical locations rather than being associated themselves with any particular location. They are, as referred to earlier, the 'flux' of the system. For example, in the case of the treatment of the regional distribution of goods, although each distributive activity will have its regional location determined by the location of the component, the services it produces will not. Hence, the accounting implication of this is that there would be region-level distribution 'activity' accounts and system-level distribution 'service' accounts. The production of distribution services would be recorded as a transaction between the former and the latter whereas the use of these services would be shown as an appropriate margin in the column of the relevant region-level commodity accounts.

The attraction of introducing system-level accounts is not confined to their use in handling transaction costs in a more appropriate way. Stone introduced a similar idea in his system of UK regional accounts in order to deal with the consuming and accumulating activities (but not the producing activity) of the central government. In the context of a European SAM, central government activity of all kinds would be properly attributed to the accounts for each of the member states. But in a similar way there also exist a range of institutions at the EU level, the activities of which cannot be apportioned to the individual member states. It therefore seems appropriate to retain a further system-level account for these activities and to show transactions between it and the domestic account accordingly. Finally, to record transactions between the system as a whole and the rest of the world, there will need to be an external account, and this will technically constitute a further system-level account.

Overall, therefore, there would seem to be a need to incorporate three distinct classes of system-level accounts to complete the accounts for a general system of regions: transaction costs, system-level (supra-regional) institutions and the rest of the world. Although valid for any system of regional accounts, this would apply in particular to the design and development of a SAM for Europe. As indicated in section 3, however, this is not to say that all other accounts will be region specific. Indeed, the perception of single markets and their existence in practice may mean that, through harmonisation and subsequent aggregation, certain other specific accounts (for example, goods, factors and capital finance) may also be defined at the European-wide level. But this would be a matter of choice and would not be for the same kinds of reasons that necessitated the specification of system-level accounts discussed above.

6 Availability and sources of data

A cursory look at the data availability for compiling a SAM for Europe is encouraging. There exists a wide range of harmonised data sets, compiled and published by Eurostat, including the national accounts, balance of payments statistics, trade statistics and labour force statistics, as well as some household-level data that have been assembled to support an ongoing analysis of poverty and inequality based on EU countries' household expenditure surveys. Clearly, all of this might seem generous in comparison with the situations usually faced in many developing countries. Nevertheless there are some obvious gaps and some quite severe problems which have to be faced and which, in turn, limit the initial range of options in compiling a SAM.

The main obstacle to constructing a SAM which would show the interaction between member states of Europe is inevitably going to be the availability of information about intercountry trade and other transactions and transfers. There are a number of problems here but two of them are of special importance. First, while there are statistics on bilateral commodity trade between member states, there appears to be little or no information on a bilateral basis to do with current and capital transfers. Secondly, even in the case of commodity trade, it would need to be established to what extent trade through intermediaries (that is, entrepôt trade) has already been eliminated. Indeed, the problem of entrepôts is not confined to commodity flows and it is probably at least as severe in connection with the transfers of funds through intermediary financial markets, even if these data were available on a country by country basis.

In view of these problems it is clear that a compromise has to be sought and that the accounting structure of the SAM needs to be simplified even though some loss of information will result. The obvious solution is to aggregate intra-Community trade and transfers into a single account, and to adopt a schema similar to the one suggested by Stone, reproduced in this chapter as table 2.1(c), which is also similar to the accounting arrangement implicit in Leontief's world model. Fortunately, the data sources do permit us to distinguish for each country the trade and transfers to (i) other member countries of the EU, (ii) institutions of the EU and (iii) other countries and international organisations.

Table 2.5 represents a compromise SAM format which accommodates, in broad terms at least, the data that are currently available. Each diagonal cell shows the domestic transactions and transfers for the member states. The three rows and columns bordering the domestic (intra-Union) block of transactions refer to the combined account for intercountry trade and transfers, plus the two accounts representing the EU institutions and the rest of the world.

Against this background it seemed useful to explore the possibility of compiling very aggregative matrix accounts using only the most readily available data. It is an elementary exercise and the only data source used was the set of harmonised national accounts, assembled according to the European System of Accounts (ESA), which shows detailed tables by sector for each member country (Eurostat, 1992). Also, for illustrative purposes, it was decided to distinguish only the four accounts shown in table 2.2 and to try to fit together the accounts for the UK according to the framework shown in table 2.5.

The published Eurostat accounts for the UK are fairly complete and permit some minimal disaggregation of the factor and institution accounts without too much difficulty. Hence, for illustrative purposes, the factor, or 'income generation', accounts are further disaggregated into employee compensation, operating surplus and net indirect taxes, and the institution current accounts, or 'UK institution' accounts, are disaggregated into households (including private non-profit making institutions), corporate enterprises (comprising financial and non-financial corporate and quasi-corporate enterprises) and general government.

At the time of writing the latest available published data for this exercise relate to the year 1990, and after substantial reorganisation of the estimates the UK accounts can be arranged as shown in table 2.6 (see also Round, 1994). This is essentially a condensed and consolidated version of the ESA system, but expressed in matrix format. The main objective is to highlight the functional and intersectoral (interinstitutional) transactions and transfers, and to suppress details of the types of transactions recorded in the Eurostat accounts. Nevertheless this detail is important in order to assemble the accounts. Clearly the resulting matrix does not really qualify as a SAM because there is no disaggregation of the societal accounts relating to households or factors. Nevertheless there are some points of

Table 2.5 A schematic form of a European SAM

		D	F	I	NL	B	L	UK	IRL	DK	GR	ESP	POR	MemEU	InstEU	Other	Total
Germany	D	H_{11}												H_{1M}	H_{1I}	H_{1O}	q_1
France	F		H_{22}											H_{2M}	H_{2I}	H_{2O}	q_2
Italy	I			H_{33}										H_{3M}	H_{3I}	H_{3O}	q_3
Netherlands	NL				H_{44}									H_{4M}	H_{4I}	H_{4O}	q_4
Belgium	B					H_{55}								H_{5M}	H_{5I}	H_{5O}	q_5
Luxembourg	L						H_{66}							H_{6M}	H_{5I}	H_{6O}	q_6
United Kingdom	UK							H_{77}						H_{7M}	H_{7I}	H_{7O}	q_7
Ireland	IRL								H_{88}					H_{8M}	H_{8I}	H_{8O}	q_8
Denmark	DK									H_{99}				H_{9M}	H_{9I}	H_{9O}	q_9
Greece	GR										$H_{10\,10}$			H_{10M}	H_{10I}	H_{10O}	q_{10}
Spain	ESP											$H_{11\,11}$		H_{11M}	H_{11I}	H_{11O}	q_{11}
Portugal	POR												$H_{12\,12}$	H_{12M}	H_{12I}	H_{12O}	q_{12}
Member Countries	EU	H_{M1}	H_{M2}	H_{M3}	H_{M4}	H_{M5}	H_{M6}	H_{M7}	H_{M8}	H_{M9}	H_{M10}	H_{M11}	H_{M12}				
Institutions	EU	H_{I1}	H_{I2}	H_{I3}	H_{I4}	H_{I5}	H_{I6}	H_{I7}	H_{I8}	H_{I9}	H_{I10}	H_{I11}	H_{I12}				
Other Countries		H_{O1}	H_{O2}	H_{O3}	H_{O4}	H_{O5}	H_{O6}	H_{O7}	H_{O8}	H_{O9}	H_{O10}	H_{O11}	H_{O12}				
Total		q_1	q_2	q_3	q_4	q_5	q_6	q_7	q_8	q_9	q_{10}	q_{11}	q_{12}				

Table 2.6 *UK Accounts 1990 in matrix format* (£ billion)

	Production	Income generation			UK Institutions (current A/C)			Combined capital A/C	Rest of world			Σ
		Employee compensation	Operating surplus	Net indirect taxes	H'holds	Corporate enterprises	General government		Intra EU	EU instit.	Extra EU	
Production					347.5		109.5	104.5	65.5		69.4	696.4
Employee compensation	316.8								0.1			316.9
Operating surplus	160.7											160.7
Net indirect taxes	71.0											71.0
Households		316.4	82.6			59.7	70.5		0.6		0.8	530.6
Corporate enterprises			70.8		37.2	46.2	12.5		1.9		7.1	175.7
General government			7.3	67.9	112.4	23.6	43.0		0.2	0.3	1.3	254.9
Combined capital A/C					31.5	35.9	17.6					85.0
Intra EU	75.4	0.5			0.2	4.8	0.2	−13.0				68.1
EU instit.				3.1			0.3	−2.7				0.7
Extra EU	72.5				1.8	5.5	1.3	−3.8				77.3
Σ	696.4	316.9	160.7	71.0	530.6	175.7	254.9	85.0	68.1	0.7	77.3	

interest in this matrix. The heavily outlined submatrices are similar to the 'N' aggregates in the ESA accounts and show the transfers from one block of accounts to the next in the logical sequence. They are important national accounts aggregates which can be interpreted as follows.

The first box represents the income generated, or GDP at market prices, which totalled £548.5 billion in 1990. The initial allocation of this factor income to UK institutions is shown in the second box, allowing for some factor income transfers from, and to, the rest of the world. The third box shows the domestic savings of UK institutions, while the fourth box shows the current account balance of payments surplus with the rest of the world. In the latter case, the disaggregation of the 'rest of the world' into separate accounts for 'Intra EU', 'EU institutions' and 'Extra EU' highlights the net balance of payments position on each account. So while the overall UK current account balance of payments deficit in 1990 was £19.5 billion, the deficit with EU member states was £13.0 billion, the net transfer to the EU budget was £2.7 billion, and the current account balance with the non-EU rest of the world amounted to a deficit of £3.8 billion.

Table 2.6 is useful in showing some of the effects of distribution and redistribution, at an aggregate level, within both the UK and the EU. The initial distribution of factor income to UK institutions has already been referred to. The redistribution of income between UK institutions is shown by the nine cells bordered by dotted lines, and estimates of these transfers can be identified without too much difficulty from the use and resource tables in Eurostat (1992). For the most part these have been recorded as gross flows except in relation to interest payments and receipts which have been recorded net. So transfers between corporate enterprises or within general government have not been eliminated but are shown instead as diagonal entries in the matrix. Income-augmenting transfers from, and income-depleting transfers to, the rest of the world are also recorded and are further disaggregated according to each of the three separate rest of the world accounts. The result is that the row and column totals for UK institutions essentially represent sectoral gross disposable income, except for the fact that transfers are recorded gross.

In principle it should be possible to replicate table 2.6 for each of the EU member states as the information has been drawn from the standard Eurostat statistics. However, in practice, the published statistics are incomplete for all but three or four member states, and the degree of completeness is also quite variable. For all member states there are a few discrepancies in the accounts, some of which are relatively large, and irreconcilable without recourse to more detailed information. This may be indicative of differences in the conventions which countries adopt, as well as of the quality and availability of data. Nevertheless, and notwithstanding these problems, the matrix is broadly illustrative of what can be achieved at an aggregate level.

Stone (1985) has demonstrated how to disaggregate the household sector accounts further. He utilised Family Expenditure Survey (FES) data, national accounts (UK Blue Book) data and the UK 1968 input–output tables to distinguish seven household categories by income level, plus one separate account for private non-profit institutions. Relatively recent household expenditure surveys exist for all member states, so it seems within the realms of possibility to replicate this exercise for other countries, to compile more detailed modules based on table 2.6, and ultimately to complete a SAM for Europe.

7 Conclusions

The paper by Stone (1961a) established a standard accounting framework for representing social accounts at a regional level. Some of the issues raised by Stone have been readdressed here in the context of developing a SAM for Europe, at the heart of which is a desire to seek the best way of representing interdependence between connected economic systems which is both practicable and useful. Most of the emphasis in Stone's paper, and all of the subsequent published discussion of it, was in the context of commodity flows and input–output modelling. However, the lessons from the work on SAMs have underlined the importance of capturing the societal and distributional dimensions, as well as production detail, within a single, comprehensive and integrated framework. This chapter has demonstrated the feasibility of compiling SAMs of modest dimensions from existing data sources although a full-scale system is still some way from being achieved.

3 Interregional SAMs and capital accounts

MAUREEN KILKENNY AND ADAM ROSE

1 Introduction

All countries keep accounts of national product and income, and many countries keep accounts of flows of funds. Even subnational regions such as states in the USA maintain income and product accounts. But subnational regions do not keep track of the flows of loanable funds within and across their boundaries, even though outflows may drain locally generated income and inflows may be a source of new local investment and, hence, economic growth.

Due to the increasing need for interregional accounts that include financial flows, the US National Science Foundation has sponsored basic research on this topic (Kilkenny and Rose, 1994). Our task is to account for transboundary[1] flows of capital-related income among the fifty states of the US. The point of departure is a set of fifty social accounting matrices (SAMs) that document the generation and distribution of state value added. The state SAMs are to be merged into an interregional SAM of the United States. This requires regionally articulated data on the distribution of current account returns to capital, land and other productive asset accounts.

---

[1] 'Transboundary flows' is a generic term intended to cover the various types of income and consumption flows across regions, as when the source of income generation is located in one region and the recipient of that income is located in another region. The term can refer to income on both current and capital accounts. There are several alternative ways to model these movements, with major differences being in the level of articulation required, i.e., the extent to which regional origins and/or destinations are known (or made explicit). For example, fully articulated data pertains to the case of pinpointing both origins and destinations on a spatial basis, as in a pure interregional model. In some cases, it is sufficient simply to note that these flows originate or are designated for a region outside the region of focus without specifying the secondary region(s), as in the case of the 'pooling' in a multi-regional model framework.

This simple problem statement conceals the complexity of the actual task. Although it is easy to conceptualise the integration of current and capital account transactions in a SAM, it is difficult to construct regionally articulated data on capital-related income flows and may even be prohibitive without the aid of a SAM. The problem must be approached iteratively: define the SAM framework, identify available data, note inadequacies, redefine the SAM to make use of alternative data, and so on.

There are many conceptual and practical problems in implementing such a model. A short list includes: regionally articulating debt and equity transactions between industries with liabilities and households (and firms) holding assets, particularly given the preponderance of co-mingled funds handled by financial intermediaries and custodial banks; tracing intra-firm reallocations of undistributed profits across state boundaries given the large number of multi-division/multi-plant firms; and maintaining stock–flow consistency and balance in financial instrument transactions.

Some of the data can be measured only residually or must be estimated. The SAM framework facilitates this. Its advantages are that one can estimate pair-wise transactions using expenditure or receipt-side observations, and institutional or regional allocations across components in a market, or one can solve for the element residually using increasingly sophisticated matrix balancing techniques. Thus, the SAM framework helps us to marshall all the available data to estimate patterns in capital flows between regions.

This chapter develops the structure of an interregional SAM that tracks both capital account and current account flows of capital-related income. Capital-related income flows (interest and dividends, savings and investment) are current account counterparts of capital account flows (debt and equity transactions, financial assets and liabilities). This suggests that flow of funds type data may be used to proxy or share out national totals in lieu of unavailable direct pair-wise observations of interest and dividend payments between regions. First, we show how flow of funds accounts can be integrated into multi-region SAMs. In so doing, we confront the possible pitfall of proliferating accounts beyond what is necessary for a useful interregional model. We argue for a certain amount of consolidation of the flow of funds accounts to highlight interregional income flows, savings/investment linkages, and regional credit constraints rather than the process of economy-wide money creation. Then we discuss both general and specific empirical considerations in constructing the necessary sets of accounts.

2 Background

We are guided by the seminal literature on regional and interregional social accounts by Richard Stone (1961a). He began with two basic building blocks: one for intra-regional and the other for interregional transactions. Each block contains three sets of accounts: relating to production, consumption and accumulation (the capital accounts). The framework consists of intra-regional blocks on the diagonal with the complementary interregional blocks filling out the off-diagonals. Stone was not satisfied with this fully articulated interregional system because of the unlikely availability of detailed pair-wise interregional information. He simplified the table by introducing a set of accounts that pool all extra-regional transactions together and netted all pair-wise transactions. See table 2.1 in chapter 2 of this volume for a depiction of this system. The rest of Stone's work and all multi-region SAMs thereafter have been based on the resulting multi-regional framework.

The classic literature also guides us in capital-flow accounting. We find that capital and current accounts were given equal attention in early SAMs. Subsequently, production and consumption accounts became more and more detailed and disaggregated, while the capital accounts remained summarised. We know of few economy-wide SAMs with both current accounts and flows of funds accounts. Most recently, Hughes (1991, 1992) presents a SAM for modelling the interdependence between real and financial activity in a single region with respect to an aggregate rest-of-the-world account. There is also the implicit SAM of the computable general equilibrium model of Korea due to Adelman and Robinson (1978), and the SAM for Botswana by Greenfield (1985), replicated for Kenya and Swaziland as discussed in Hayden and Round (1982). The paucity of examples is somewhat surprising, especially to those who believe that information on regional wealth or credit availability would be of more value to regional analysis than income and product accounts.

In a list of suggestions for how his own multi-regional SAMs could be improved, Stone noted among them, 'the introduction of capital and income from capital, and of the destination of investment' (Stone and Weale, 1986). In fact, flow of funds accounts are quite amenable to display in SAMs (see, e.g., Roe, 1985; Hughes and Nagurney, 1990; Hughes, 1991). Even decades ago, square transactions accounts were used alternatively with the rectangular series of T-accounts to illustrate the complete set of sectoral gross saving and investment accounts (Ruggles and Ruggles, 1956; Stone, 1961a).

As an illustration, we have reorganised the summary flow of funds accounts for the United States for the year 1978 and presented it as a SAM in table 3.1. Two basic considerations are required to accomplish this

Table 3.1 Collapsed flow of funds SAM

Account	1	2	3	4	5	6	7	8	9	10	11	12	13	14	15	16	17	18	19	20	21	22	23	24	25	26	27	Total
1 Activity		551.7																										
2 Commodity			298.2	247.9					4.2	1.4	181.0	157.3							2.6	3.2	20.1	104.8		1.4			6.3	504.7
3 Households				3.2					30.3	20.4	172.7	22.9									25.1	43.3	5.2	45.5	−20.8		27.3	355.9
4 Business									33.9			7.6												1.0			−1.6	32.1
5 State/local government																												
6 Rest of the world			18.3						18.3			23.5							−0.5		4.0		6.6	−0.3			14.9	66.5
7 US Government												−34.9	1.7				7.2	5.9				−0.1		2.4		53.8	0.2	28.6
8 Monetary and credit agents												1.7		6.3				5.9								41.4	5.3	60.6
9 Commercial banks											2.7	0.7	0.7	22.0	65.0			9.7	1.1		0.2		6.7			18.8	12.2	139.1
10 Private non-banks						2.8			2.8		3.3	10.0			59.2	6.9	70.6		0.5		7.3	0.9	7.9			2.1	32.8	204.3
11 Capital consumption	359.7																											359.7
12 Net saving	188.8		18.2	2.0	−1.1	−0.2	4.0																					188.8
13 Mineral rights				2.0	−2.0				0.3	2.3																		28.9
14 Demand deposits				2.0	8.1	1.1	0.1			7.7																		
15 Time deposits			105.2																									124.2
16 Money mkt. fund shares			6.9																									6.9
17 Life insurance & pension			77.8			5.4																						77.8
18 Net interbank claims						5.9		3.6	5.9																			14.9

19 Corp. equities	-6.2		2.4			7.5							3.7
20 State/local securities	3.3	0.2	1.0			9.6	14.2						28.3
21 Corp & foreign bonds	-1.4	1.0	1.6			-0.3	31.6						32.5
22 Mortgages	14.5		-0.4	30.6	35.0	68.3							148.0
23 Open market paper	14.6	1.7	7.9	-1.6	-1.3	5.1							26.4
24 Trade credit		54.9	3.4	2.7		1.3							62.3
25 Non-corp equity	-20.8												-20.8
26 Fed. financial instruments	27.0	-0.9	14.6	28.2	7.7	0.5	20.1						106.5
27 Other money & finance	0.6							0.7	0.9	-0.9	12.3	9.6	
Total	-32.6	39.5	32.1	66.5	28.6	60.6	139.1	204.3	359.7	188.8	28.9 124.2 6.9 77.8 14.9	3.7 28.3 32.5 148.0 26.4	62.3 -20.8 106.5

504.7 355.9

transformation. Consider a financial system with n sectors (households, business, federal government, etc.) and m financial instruments or market transaction categories (money, savings accounts, mutual funds, bonds, equities, etc.). The first consideration is the dimension of the SAM. The most straightforward approach is to construct the SAM with $(n+m)$ rows and columns; i.e., an account for each sector and for each instrument (see, e.g., Hughes and Nagurney, 1990). The second consideration is to remember that 'uses' entries in the flow of funds correspond to sector expenditures (column entries) in the SAM, while 'sources' usually correspond to sales of instruments (instrument market row entries) in the SAM. These considerations justify collapsing separately itemised transactions into single accounts. For example, the separate 'savings' and 'investment' rows can be collapsed into a single account, because in a SAM, savings are distinguished from investments as row entries and column entries, respectively.

When the flows of funds are organised as a SAM the accounts suffer from some discrepancies, i.e., there are financial markets that are not likely to balance, e.g., transactions in Federal Funds and trade credit. The reason for the discrepancy in the Federal Funds and security repurchase agreements account is severe data limitations (Federal Reserve, 1980). In contrast, there is a real world explanation of the discrepancy in trade credit: 'The check is in the mail.' The purchasers have recorded the trade credits paid, but there is a lag or 'float' before the payment appears as a receipt on the seller's accounts. To simplify the presentation we have simply collapsed all discrepancies into the 'Other money and finance' account.

It is also important to remember that *instrument transactions* in the flow of funds are presented on a net basis – asset sales are shown as a negative use of funds (column entry for sector) deducted from purchases of the same type of asset. For example, the household sector sold $20.8 million more non-corporate equities than it purchased (see the Non-corp. equity row and Household column). Likewise, debt repayments are deducted from sources of funds (row entries) for sectors. This convention is less than desirable for constructing interregional SAMs to present gross pair-wise data, but it is sufficient for multi-regional SAMs. However, changes in liabilities are not deducted from changes in assets. For example, the household sector used funds to increase mortgage assets by $14.5 million and received funds by creating mortgage liabilities of $104.8 million.

3 Conceptual framework

A flow of funds SAM can be added to the typical current account SAM of a country or a region most simply by adding the $(n+m)$ rows and columns to the current account SAM in place of the single consolidated capital account row and column (e.g., Greenfield, 1985). It is possible to reduce the dimensions by recognising that this introduces some unnecessary redundancies. Typical SAMs already include accounts for institutions: households, businesses, governments and the rest of the world. Furthermore, durable goods and capital are purchased in commodity markets and already exist as commodity accounts. This means that one must only add the m financial market accounts and a few financial intermediary and monetary authority sector accounts.

We have constructed an interregional SAM for capital flows by adding some financial market accounts to the intra-regional and interregional building blocks of the interregional SAM. The new intra-regional and interregional building blocks take the forms exhibited in table 3.2.

Table 3.2 presents four blocks. The upper left block is an intra-regional block. It encompasses within-region real activity, trade, income distribution, fiscal flows, credit, and financial market transactions. The centre left block is an interregional block. It tracks interregional trade, payments to commuting labour or absentee factor owners and interregional credit, and financial flows. The bottom block is the set of pooled interaction accounts. It shows the outflows from a region to the federal government and the rest of the world. The reverse flows from the federal government to the region are shown in the upper right block.

The first superscript indexes the regional location of the row account (sink). The second superscript indicates the column account (source). The subscripts denote the types of accounts engaged in the transaction. For example, Y_{hfi}^{RR} labels receipt of income 'Y' to a household 'h' residing in region R, paid by industry i for services provided by factor 'f'. An example is wages to a farm labourer who lives in the same region as the farm is located.

The entries in the first row of table 3.2 are transactions in region R's commodity market. These are the make/use tables (T), consumption by local households (C), local government (GD), and to meet investment demand (I) by businesses in the region. The second row shows income to factors of production. The first record of a capital-related flow is the distribution of value-added from production to capital ($VA_{f=\text{capital},i}$), in exchange for the input of capital services. The capital factor account pays interest to bondholders and other lenders and distributes dividends to local owners (Y_{hfi}^{RR}), and pays state and local taxes (tax_{Lf}^{RR}). The rest is considered undistributed profit (π), which includes the capital consumption allowance for depreciation and the cost of inventory. This 'residual' is available for internal financing of new investment (physical assets) (I_{iB}^{RR}) and/or (I_{iB}^{QR}), extending credit to consumers (cred_{hB}^{RR}) reallocation to other plants (T_{BB}^{RR}) and (T_{BB}^{QR}), or for acquiring new financial assets (UF_{KB}^{RR}) or (UF_{KB}^{QR}).

The financial instrument account consolidates the off-diagonal blocks of

Table 3.2 *Collapsed interregional SAM framework*

	Region R							National	
	Industry	Factors	Households	Business	Local gov.	Fin. bus.	Instrument	Fed. gov.	RoW
Region R									
Industry	T_{ij}^{RR}		C_{ih}^{RR}	I_{iB}^{RR}	GD_{iL}^{RR}			$GD_{ig}^{R\circ}$	M_i^{RW}
Factors	VA_{fi}^{RR}								
Households		Y_{hfi}^{RR}		$cred_{hB}^{RR}$		$cred_{hF}^{RR}$	SF_{hk}^{RR}		T_h^{RW}
Business		π_{Bi}^{RR}		T_{BB}^{RR}		$cred_{BF}^{RR}$	SF_{Bk}^{RR}		T_B^{RW}
Local gov.	tax_{Li}^{RR}	tax_{Lfj}^{RR}	tax_{Lh}^{RR}				SF_{Lk}^{RR}	$tax_{Lg}^{R\circ}$	
Fin. bus.						$cred_{FF}^{RR}$	SF_{Fk}^{RR}		
Instrument			UF_{kh}^{RR}	UF_{kB}^{RR}	UF_{kL}^{RR}	UF_{kF}^{RR}		$UF_{kg}^{R\circ}$	UF_k^{RW}
Region Q									
Industry	M_{ij}^{QR}		C_{ih}^{QR}	I_{iB}^{QR}	GD_{iL}^{QR}				
Factors	VA_{fi}^{QR}								
Households			T_{hh}^{QR}	$cred_{hB}^{QR}$		$cred_{hF}^{QR}$	SF_{hk}^{QR}		
Business				T_{BB}^{QR}		$cred_{BF}^{QR}$	SF_{Bk}^{QR}		
Local gov.							SF_{Lk}^{QR}		
Fin. bus.						$cred_{FF}^{QR}$	SF_{Fk}^{QR}		
Instrument			UF_{kh}^{QR}	UF_{kB}^{QR}	UF_{kL}^{QR}	UF_{kF}^{QR}			
National									
Fed. Gov.	$tax_{gi}^{\circ R}$		$tax_{gh}^{\circ R}$				$SF_{gk}^{\circ R}$		
RoW	M_i^{WR}		T_h^{WR}			$cred_F^{WR}$	SF_k^{WR}		

Notes:

Indices:

°,W	nation, world		B	business by type
R,Q	region		L	local gov't
i,j	industry sector		F	fin. bus. by type
f	factor by type		k	instrument by type
h	household by type		g	federal gov't

flows

T	make/use		SF, UF	sources, uses
VA	value added		C	consumption
tax	tax (net of transfers)		I	investment
Y	income (functional)		GD	government demand
π	profit (undistributed)		$cred$	credit
M	interregional trade			

a flow of funds SAM. The row entries show the sector uses (UF) of financial funds and the column entries show sources (SF) of funds. For example, demand deposits are a type of financial instrument. Row entries are the incomings into local checking accounts from local residents. The outgoings are sources of funds from banks.

The interregional building block has the same dimensions as the intraregional block. However, the column entries are pair-wise or articulated data on the expenditures of region R directly in the markets (or to the agents) of region Q. By the same token, the row entries are the incomings to region Q from region R. For example, households in state R purchase commodities and services produced in state $Q(C_{ih}^{QR})$. Industries in state R pay wages and salaries to residents who commute from state $Q(VA_{fi}^{QR})$. Some businesses also reallocate undistributed profits among plants across states (T_{BB}^{QR}).

The SAM in table 3.2 is elaborated and deconsolidated for actual data collection and organisation. The principle for distinguishing types of accounts is if there are major differences in objectives among agents, and if there are different prices among transaction categories. In the intraregional blocks of the full-scale SAM we propose: two commodity and activity accounts; three factor accounts for labour, land and plant/ equipment; five agent or sector accounts (households, businesses, local government, commercial banks and non-bank financial institutions). Also, we have eight local financial markets: mineral rights, demand deposits, time deposits, local government securities, mortgages, open market paper, trade credit and non-corporate equity. Then, as in Stone (1961a), there are three nationwide institutions (the federal government, federal money and credit institutions and the rest of the world); and seven nationwide financial markets (a money market, life insurance and pension funds, corporate equities, corporate and foreign bonds, interbank claims, federal financial instruments, and all other financial instruments not elsewhere classified).

Having seen how to construct SAMs with flow of funds, and to construct interregional SAMs from regional SAM building blocks, we now proceed to address some of our solutions to the data problems.

4 General measurement issues

The typical approach taken to quantify capital flows in regional modelling is to determine net capital income residually from all other current account information. In regional input–output models, the sum of personal consumption expenditures on both locally produced and imported goods and services is often taken as a control total for endogenous (intra-regionally generated) income. Subtract employee compensation and income transfers, and the remaining expenditure is assumed to have been financed by a current account inflow of capital-related income. No distinction is made between types of capital contracts, the sectors in which capital is employed, or between gross inflows and outflows of returns to capital.

Some implications of the latter, the 'no cross-payments' assumption, have been discussed by Rose and Stevens (1991). It typically leads to a gross overstatement of the amount of locally generated income that is spent within a region. Rose and Stevens show that the procedure results in overestimation of the induced (input–output) multiplier effects of base perturbations of the order of 75 per cent or more for a typical state. They make a strong case for the need to account correctly for the regional disposition of all types of value-added, and the regional source of all types of income, and suggest ways of using available data to do so.

The root of the problem with the typical approach to capital flow accounting takes two forms. First, the typical approach confounds current and capital account transactions. Secondly, it confounds the supply side with the demand side in capital markets. The only correct way to classify dividend, interest, royalty, rent, and other returns to agents who hold claims on those income streams is as current account expenditures by firms. The firms are paying for the use of the physical capital they have hired. The purchases of stocks, bonds, T-bills, mortgages, and other paper claims on these capital-related income streams cannot be added to those current account transactions without confounding the capital and current accounts. If these accounts are confounded, we cannot determine whether a region's capital outflows are payments for factor services (absentee ownership), which reduce net regional income, or purchases of claims on capital-related income in other regions (diversification), which ultimately expand regional income.

The typical approach in SAM specification has been to distinguish between current and capital accounts, but to consolidate the separate contributions of households, firms, etc., into a pool of domestic savings, out of which all investment is funded (Chander et al., 1980). As the practitioners themselves state, 'The principal loss in information content is therefore in the origin of investment expenditures and the details of the flow of funds which would otherwise be recorded as transfers between the capital accounts. To capture such detail ... a good deal more work needs to be done, and this might deserve a high priority in future developments' (Chander et al., 1980, p. 70). The notable exception in detailing flows of funds in national SAMs (Hayden and Round, 1982; Greenfield, 1985; Hughes, 1991) can, however, be easily extended, as shown above, to the interregional level.

The typical interregional SAM is, in fact, a version of Stone's multi-regional SAM discussed above. Institutional accounts pool current account payments for factor services from all sectors and regions, and then distribute these as earnings to households across regions. This intermediary pooling only serves to confound sector-specific and interregional factor market linkages (Kilkenny, 1990). If data on pair-wise payments to factors across regions can be obtained or constructed, factor income can be mapped directly from the activity in the region in which it is generated to the household in the region in which it is received.

Within the net savings/investment framework there is a further risk that assumptions masquerade as results. Consider the capital-market clearing constraint that saving equals investment. This market is the key link between the financial transactions among savers and borrowers and the real transactions among those borrowers and suppliers of investment goods. The assumed result is that regions are largely self financing because net regional savings often equals regional investment.

Feldstein and Horioka (1980) studied a number of countries and found that increases in regional savings and investment were strongly associated, supporting a hypothesis that capital is immobile. They also reconsider their results in light of the obvious mobility of short-term capital. Others have distinguished gross from net capital flows (which may understate capital market linkages) to identify regional economic integration (Carlino and Lang, 1989).

The various subsets of a nation's financial system take net liability or asset positions in the capital market. If we focus on regions as the subsets, some regions are net borrowers because they are in an expansionary phase or experiencing a short-run shortfall of revenues over expenditures. Other regions must be net lenders. The regional subsets may be further disaggregated according to primary business activities as well. Some businesses in some regions may be borrowers and others lenders.

Current account interregional interdependence, above and beyond interdependence in intermediate and consumer goods, is made possible through interregional capital flows. The net borrowing/expanding regions will demand capital goods from the regions that produce those goods. The existing current account approach to estimating regional investment demand, however, will fall far from the mark. This is because savings are a poor proxy for total regional investment demand since the single largest source of savings is retained earnings by firms (see table 3.1), which are not necessarily reinvested internally (within the plant, firm or region). Firms may be parts of conglomerates headquartered outside the region.

5 Specific empirical considerations

In recent years capital-related income payments have averaged about 20 per cent of total adjusted gross income of households in the US (see, e.g., IRS, 1990). From the production side, they have been about 10 per cent as large as total outlays of firms (see table 3.3), though there is relatively more annual variation here because of the volatility of net income (normal and economic profits).[2]

The data in table 3.3 demonstrate the need for a multi-sector analysis. The large variations across industries indicate that capital returns are strongly influenced by the sectoral composition of an economy. The sectoral mix differs significantly between regions (e.g., agricultural-based versus mining-based versus manufacturing-based regions). These differences in regional economic structure have implications for transboundary flows of capital-related income payments, owing to different patterns of absentee ownership between sectors. They also affect transboundary flows of investment funds, owing to differences in needs for external (to the firm) financing, some of which becomes external to the region.

Recently, the IRS has made data tabulations on transboundary capital-related income flows available to the authors. The tabulations, on the surface, would appear to be fully articulated in that they make use of data on the state of origin and the state of destination. However, there are some serious complications in identifying the appropriate payer and payee that we discuss below.

The hierarchical firm

One major complication in the tabulation of data on capital-related income and its subsequent use to analyse the allocation of loanable funds across regions is the hierarchical firm. The multi-divisional/conglomerate firm structure is defined as a collection of semi-autonomous operating divisions (subsidiaries or 'profit centres') organised along product, brand or geographic lines (Williamson, 1981). While the subunits separately manage operations, decisions about the allocation of retained earnings and/or new investment capital are centralised. Capital is generally allocated among divisions (regions) to favour high profit yielding uses. The conglomerate's headquarter officers act as an administrative interface between stockholders and operating divisions in lieu of a capital-market interface. There is no reason to assume that retained earnings within a division (in a region)

---

[2] Also, bond interest yields, and to a lesser extent, dividends, have some rigidity, while retained earnings are typically of a residual nature.

Table 3.3 *Capital-related payments from selected industries, 1986*

Type of payment	All industries	Agriculture, forestry and fishing	Mining	Manufacturing	Transportation & utilities	Finance related	Services
Capital payments:							
Rent	14.7%	31.5%	31.2%	13.6%	24.2%	3.9%	50.5%
Interest	58.0%	48.1%	133.3%	43.3%	51.8%	74.9%	33.7%
Net income[a]	27.3%	20.4%	−64.6%	43.1%	24.0%	21.2%	15.8%
Total	100.0%	100.0%	100.0%	100.0%	100.0%	100.0%	100.0%
Total Capital Payments[b]	$987.7	$5.4	$4.8	$236.3	$90.9	$470.1	$46.7
Total Outlays[b,c]	$8,394.9	$76.3	$102.1	$2,723.7	$740.7	$1,245.5	$584.3

Notes:
[a] Consists of dividends and retained earnings.
[b] Money amounts are in billions of dollars.
[c] Note that only rent and interest (but not net income) are cost items.
Source: Adapted from IRS (1988).

are reinvested in the division (region). Retained earnings that are reallo-cated externally do not provide a stream of investment funds for the operating unit like other savings.

If a branch plant or separate division operates in region R, how much of its net income is attributable to its own efforts versus headquarters and other supporting units, or, more practically, how much revenue actually remains in R? Accordingly, what proportion of the dividend and retained earnings actually flow to the various locations? The basic data are inadequate because they are reported on a company rather than on a division or establishment basis. With respect to the IRS data base, the address of the payee is that of corporate headquarters or financial officer.[3] On the investment side, do reinvested earnings correspond to local plant retained earnings or company-wide plant profitability in general? Is it conceptually sound to consider a national pool of investment funds for the company, thereby lessening the data requirements? Even a somewhat tenuous assumption on the division of retained earnings on a pooling basis, however, is likely to be superior to current (no cross-payments) practice in empirical model construction.

The multi-plant firm problem cannot be taken too lightly. The 1982 Census of Manufacturers lists 298,429 companies with 358,061 plants. This understates the importance of this organisational form, since it is so heavily weighted among larger companies which account for the majority of capital flows. In addition, multi-plant firms, or, in this case, franchises, are ubiquitous in retail trade and service industries.

In the state of Pennsylvania, for example, 47 per cent of the hierarchical firm subsidiaries operating within the state are owned by a parent corpor-ation not headquartered within the state (see table 3.4). Moreover, although less than 10 per cent of all firms in Pennsylvania are either parents or subsidiaries, they account for over 43 per cent of total employment in the state. Also, 55 per cent of the Pennsylvania conglomerates own operating subsidiaries outside the state. Thus, it is also necessary to consider the regional disposition of retained as well as distributed earnings.

The reallocation of investment and, in fact, the level of economic activity itself, reflects behaviour in the context of the multi-plant firm. A vast literature on the business organisation hierarchy and its implications has arisen (see Erickson, 1980; Watts, 1981; Williamson, 1985; and Malmberg, 1990), including viewing the phenomenon as a way to capitalise on resource availabilities and price differentials at alternative locations, to minimise transactions costs, and to enhance economic imperialism. In general, the theories conclude that there is a decrease in self-determination through

---

[3] In addition, there may be some instances where the address is that of the transfer agent.

Table. 3.4 *Transboundary relationships of multi-plant firms, 1988*

	Subsidiaries located in PA	Subsidiaries not located in PA	Totals
PA parent	a. 899 (2.3%)	b. 1,118 (2.9%)	c. 2,017 (5.2%)
Non-PA parent	d. 819 (2.1%)	e. 35,774 (92.7%)	f. 36,593 (94.8%)
Totals	g. 1,718 (4.4%)	h. 36,892 (95.6%)	i. 38,610 (100.0%)

Notes:
a. Total PA parents (DCA) times PA subsidiaries per parent (DCA sample);
   $212 \times 4.24 = 899$.
b. Total PA parents (DCA) times Non-PA subsidiaries per parent (DCA
   sample); $212 \times 5.27 = 1,118$.
c. $a + b = c$.
d. $g - a = d$.
e. Computed as a residual. Note direct estimation yields a slightly different
   value: Total non-PA parents (DCA) times subsidiaries per parent (DCA
   sample); $3,824 \times 9.5 = 36,595$.
f. $d + e = f$.
g. DCA.
h. $b + e = h$.
i. DCA.
Source: National Registry Publishing Co. (1988).

external control or the spatial interdependence of the firm. Some analysts have found higher closure rates among branch plants, while others note the gains, even if not permanent, stemming from an infusion of investment capital and new technology.

The upshot is that the full cycle of the income–investment–growth process is subject to more spatial leakages and injections, and is therefore less self-determined, than the conventional modelling approach implicitly assumes. Rose and Stevens (1991) have characterised the process of generating income, distributing it to factor owners, and their subsequent spending of it in terms of a three-part cycle. Each dollar must meet an endogeneity test at all three stages to be incorporated into a single regional multiplier. When investment is taken into account the counterpart of the income generated–received–spent cycle is the income generated–retained–reinvested cycle, where each dollar would have to meet the endogeneity test at all three stages.

In this case, however, further analysis may warrant a less strict requirement or a less mechanical allocation of investment funds. For example, if a branch plant can be sure of a return from its contribution to pooled net income within the corporation, this flow should be included in the intra-region cycle. Other variables explaining investment might also be included in models more sophisticated than the fixed coefficient version of the SAM. The prevalence of the multi-plant firm suggests that this would not just include the simplistic theory of interest rate differentials, but would also include institutional constraints, resource immobilities and depletion, and market imperfections.

Financial activities of firms

The original formulation of production accounts in input–output tables in terms of industries has given way to more sophisticated formulations that reflect the importance of joint-product outputs. Industry by commodity classifications have now become the norm in input–output tables, as they have long been in SAMs.

Still, the present convention focusses on goods and services and thereby ignores financial activities of business enterprises. Through their diversification efforts, investment of idle cash, escrow accounts, etc., firms are able to generate revenues quite apart from their production process. As indicated in table 3.5, the extent of this is somewhat surprising, as, in 1986, 13.2 per cent[4] of overall firm revenues were attributable to their receipts of capital-related income from other firms. While this percentage varies across all industries, there are very few sectors for which these flows are not a significant source of total revenues. Moreover, for every major sector grouping, these capital-related receipts exceed net income (see table 3.3).

The extent to which these receipts are transboundary flows cannot be determined at this time, but there are reasons to presume that it is significant, especially for large firms. The sizable percentage of interest payments emanates mainly from national bond markets. Capital gains are also likely to be transboundary, as are, by definition, dividends from foreign firms.

In the conventional input–output table, these receipts are likely to be omitted since they are not part of revenue from commodity production and because standard input–output tables do not contain any control variables related to financial operations such as this. At least at the national level, SAMs are more likely to include them, though typically capital flows are pooled and not linked between individual sectors (see, e.g., Hanson and Robinson, 1989). The typical input–output modelling approach would involve an additional joint-product financial 'commodity' for all firms reflected in a 'make' table. The alternative approach consistent with the real

---

[4] This figure is strongly affected by finance-related industries, but still amounts to 5.3 per cent if these industries are excluded.

Table 3.5 *Capital-related revenues to selected industries, 1986*

Type of receipt	All industries	Agriculture, forestry and fishing	Mining	Manufacturing	Transportation & utilities	Finance related	Services
Capital Revenues:							
Interest	58.4%	12.6%	27.0%	25.9%	27.2%	75.2%	16.6%
Rents	8.3%	7.5%	4.8%	16.3%	18.7%	4.1 %	24.6%
Royalties	1.4%	2.0%	5.3%	5.8%	0.7%	0.1%	5.2%
Domestic Dividends	1.3%	1.0%	3.5%	2.2%	2.5%	1.0%	7.2%
Foreign Dividends	2.0%	0.8%	5.0%	9.6%	0.7%	0.2%	1.0%
Capital Gains	13.2%	20.2%	22.1%	17.7%	26.5%	10.9%	13.4%
Other Capital Receipts	15.4%	55.9%	32.3%	22.6%	23.6%	8.5%	37.9%
Total	100.0%	100.0%	100.0%	100.0%	100.0%	100.0%	100.0%
Total Capital Revenues[a]	$1,133.9	$5.7	$11.7	$196.2	$44.3	$746.4	$41.3
Total Revenues[a]	$8,669.4	$77.5	$98.6	$2,810.7	$762.2	$1,365.1	$591.8

Note:
[a] Money amounts are in billions of dollars.
Source: Adapted from **IRS** (1988).

and financial flow distinction typically made in SAMs is illustrated in table 3.2. The cell UF_{kB}^{RR} or UF_{kB}^{QR} represents the purchase of assets and the cell VA_{fi}^{RR} represents the earnings from those assets. If the earnings are undistributed profits, they show up as π_{Bi}^{RR}. Moreover, models based on SAMs, such as computable general equilibrium models, are likely to be more satisfactory than the fixed coefficient model of an input–output transactions table from an analytical standpoint. For example, a CGE model can readily incorporate the non-linearities and price responsiveness of the side-line financial activities of firms.

Financial intermediaries

Financial transactions are facilitated by financial intermediaries and markets. They offer channels of indirect financing between surplus-spending units (savers) and deficit-spending units (investors). The banking industry is the major financial intermediary, and its existence facilitates the allocation of savings and investment. This allocation differs spatially according to type of investment and type of institution. In the case of real estate (especially home mortgages), local institutions such as savings and loan associations are likely to dominate. Thus, there is a minimum of transboundary flows, though there are some exceptions such as federally funded programmes, exemplified by the Veterans Administration or the Federal Housing Administration.

Secondary financial markets, such as stock exchanges, might also be considered. They provide for trading of existing financial issues rather than the creation of new ones. They can, however, be said to increase the flow of investable funds by enhancing the liquidity of assets such as corporate securities.

Short-term borrowing by major corporations, however, is often handled by large commercial banks, which draw from a large regional or national pool of savers. In this case, transboundary flows may be significant, but interregional articulation may not be necessary. In a model, funds can readily be apportioned to individual regions in a manner analogous to apportioning import flows from a national pool in multi-regional input–output models (see, e.g., Polenske, 1980). In the absence of primary data to gauge the actual situation, utilisation of the 'national pool' approach, in either of its variants, would be superior to a 'no cross-funding' approach.

Financial intermediaries also have an important bearing on the usefulness of IRS data on transboundary flows. The vast majority of household stock and bond transactions are done by brokerage houses and related enterprises. For tax reporting purposes, the brokerage is considered the 'owner'[5] of the financial instruments and is the recipient of the capital-related income payment. This breaks the reporting linkage between firms and households, because the latter receive their IRS Form 1099 reports from the holders of their portfolios.[6] There is no obvious indication that this implies a national pooling of household assets, or the loanable funds they earn. However, further investigation is warranted.

5 Conclusion

In this chapter we have stressed the importance that capital-related income has in regional economic development. Flows of capital-related income are not normally considered adequately in input–output analyses nor in SAM analyses. We have developed a SAM for the US which is highly disaggregated in terms of capital flows and transfers, and have outlined a further development of this, in conceptual terms only, to an interregional economic system. The inter-regional SAM framework that we present is able to track capital and current account flows of capital-related income between different accounts and within and across regional boundaries. The framework takes its inspiration from the work of Richard Stone. As with Stone's own experience, and as indicated by our initial exploration of major empirical considerations, the actual construction of the SAM is the major challenge.

[5] The terminology is that the debt or equity is held in (Wall) 'street name'.
[6] The authors are exploring several ways to overcome this data problem. For example, brokers are only licensed to sell stock in states in which they and their customers reside.

4 Social accounting matrices and income distribution analysis in Kenya

ARNE BIGSTEN

1 Introduction

A large number of studies of income distribution and development have shown that it is difficult to improve living standards of the poorest groups in LDCs, even in cases where aggregate growth has been rapid (see Bigsten, 1983; Sundrum, 1990; World Bank, 1990). To improve our understanding of the relationship between economic change and the incomes of the poor, analyses of poverty issues must be undertaken at a disaggregated level. In response to this need, new analytical tools have been developed while old ones have been refined. One of the most useful of the new tools is the Social Accounting Matrix (SAM), developed by Richard Stone and others in the Cambridge Growth Project. The SAM has increasingly been used for income distribution analyses in LDCs (see, e.g., Pyatt and Round, 1977). It can be applied in many ways from simple sectoral descriptions to incorporation in full-blown CGE models. The type of SAM analysis provided here represents a half-way house between partial analyses and a full-scale model.

In this chapter we use the Kenyan SAM of 1976 for income distribution analysis. Another SAM has been constructed for 1986, but unfortunately it is not a proper update of the SAM of 1976. In particular, it is lacking in detail with regard to information on household receipts and outlays. The household sector is in fact not disaggregated at all in the 1986 SAM. It is therefore not possible to repeat the analysis for 1976 for the latter year.

2 The SAM

The aggregated treatment of the household sector makes the System of National Accounts system poorly suited for income distribution analysis. The SAM framework, on the other hand, simultaneously allows for a disaggregated treatment of the household sector and for consistency. It provides the 'best possible' quantitative description of the economy, by socio-economic groups, on the basis of existing data. Factor incomes and their distribution over spending units are also brought into focus.

The SAM is expressed in the form of a set of linear, fixed-coefficient, behavioural and technical equations expressed at constant prices. The SAM applied here relies on changes in the distribution of production among sectors to determine changes in income distribution. If the distribution of assets is assumed to be given, this seems to be a justifiable first approximation. Although within-sector inequality is large in Kenya (Vandemoortele, 1982; Bigsten, 1980), the emphasis on sectoral differences is, from the perspective of policy makers, still highly relevant.

The Kenyan SAM, used in the analysis, is a 77 × 77 matrix. Since this fully disaggregated version is not presented in this chapter (see Kenya, 1981) we instead present an aggregated (12 × 12) version of the matrix (see table 4.1).

There is only one factor account and one household account here, while there are seven and ten respectively in the full matrix. In the latter, the production account is disaggregated into twenty-eight sectors. The rows show receipts by account, while the columns show expenditures by account. Current and capital accounts have been distinguished.

We can see in the table that total factor incomes in 1976 were 1,310.4 (K£ million) and that 1,296.1 of this came from domestic production activities, while 14.3 were factor incomes from abroad. In the factor column we see how much of the factor income goes to labour and unincorporated enterprises – mainly smallholdings (905.1), to enterprises in the form of profits (320.9), to the government (2.0) and to the rest of the world (82.4). We can also identify the transfers between different types of institutions, savings, incomes to producers from sales and external transactions. The capital accounts show how funds are acquired and allocated.

The sum of the first row is equal to total factor incomes and that of the second row to total household income before tax. These two figures are of particular interest here, since we focus on income distribution. It is the further disaggregation and explanation of these entries that we shall dwell on in what follows.

3 Factorial income distribution

The SAM shows the distribution of value added among the seven factors in the twenty-eight production sectors. The distribution of total income among these seven categories is given in table 4.2.[1]

---

[1] The choice of factor categories used is a compromise between what is desirable from an analytical point of view and what is statistically feasible. The first two categories, that is

Table 4.1 *Aggregated SAM for Kenya, 1976 (K£ million)*

EXPENDITURES

		Current					Gross fixed cap. form.	Capital				Fin. claims liab.	Total
			Institutions			Production			Institutions		RoW		
Receipt		Factors	House-holds	Enter-prises	Govern-ment	Prod	RoW		House-holds	Enter-prises	Govern-ment	RoW		
		1	2	3	4	5	6	7	8	9	10	11	12	Total
Current														
Factors	1					1296.1	14.3							1310.4
Institutions:														
Households	2	905.1	16.5	163.9	8.9		5.3							1099.7
Enterprises	3	320.9	6.8	16.4	12.3		8.0							364.4
Government	4	2.0	82.2	79.5	7.3	109.0	83.0							363.0
Production	5		816.7		253.8	932.1	471.7	198.7						2673.0
Rest of world	6	82.4	110.0	7.3	3.2	335.8		95.5						634.2
Capital														
Gross fixed capital form.	7								96.1	117.8	80.3			294.2
Institutions:														
Households	8		67.5										45.6	113.1
Enterprises	9			97.3									213.8	311.1
Government	10				77.5							9.0	40.4	126.9
Rest of world	11						51.9						30.6	82.5
Financial claims assets	12								17.0	193.3	46.6	73.5		330.4
TOTAL		1310.4	1099.7	364.4	363.0	2673.0	634.2	294.2	113.1	311.1	126.9	82.5	330.4	

Table 4.2 *Distribution of Value Added by Factors*

	Percentage share of Value Added
1. Unskilled and semi-skilled workers	12.9
2. Skilled workers	7.1
3. Office workers and semi-professionals	9.1
4. Professionals	11.4
5. Self-employed and family workers	29.1
6. Operating surplus	23.7
7. Consumption of fixed capital	6.7

We see in table 4.2 that the last three categories taken together receive almost 60 per cent of total value added, while the first four only get about 40 per cent.[2] This is a typical LDC pattern with employees getting less than half of total incomes. However, a large part of the incomes in category 5 are in reality returns to labour in agriculture. In the full SAM one can see how much of the income generated in different sectors goes to the poorer strata, that is mainly category 1, but also to some extent categories 2, 3 and 5. The sectors where unskilled labour receives a large share of incomes are forestry and fishing, mining, textiles, wood, water, building, hotels and restaurants, and the public sector. Naturally, agriculture is also important for unskilled labour, but most people working in this sector are either self employed or family workers. This reduces the percentages for unskilled wage labour.

Note 1 (*cont.*)
unskilled and skilled workers, are straightforward. The third category, office workers and semi-professionals, is problematic. It is a group which has a very large intra-group variance. This reduces its analytical usefulness. There is also a problem of keeping the classification consistent across sectors. This problem is particularly difficult with regard to the fourth category. It is pointed out (Kenya, 1981) that all teachers had to be classified as professionals in the education sector, despite the fact that many of them had qualifications which in other sectors were taken to indicate a 'non-professional'. This problem has meant that in the SAM as many as 48 per cent of all professionals in Kenya are considered to be employed in education, and it also implies that as much as 87 per cent of labour costs in the educational sector go to professionals. On both counts the figures are exaggerated. With regard to the fifth category, 'self-employed ad family workers', there are also problems. In this category are also included small unincorporated firms, that is firms employing less than twenty people. Of course, agriculture is the dominating activity here, but also trade is of considerable importance. Ideally, we should like to classify part of the incomes of the fifth category as labour incomes, and part as operating surplus.

[2] In the SAM for 1986 the breakdown has been changed. We can only distinguish the shares of aggregate labour and surplus. Returns to farming have been aggregated with the surplus category. Still, over the period the share of labour seems to have increased by two percentage points.

One may tentatively conclude that unskilled labourers are concentrated in sectors where Kenya has a comparative advantage in international trade and in some non-tradable sectors, such as the building industry and the public sector. In the trade sector there is a lot of self employment and family labour, but their income levels vary a lot. Skilled labour is particularly important in manufacturing sectors, water, building and parts of the public sector.

4 Household income distribution

In the SAM, income is distributed among ten household categories. The first distinction being that between urban and rural households. Analytically, the urban–rural distinction is somewhat problematic for a country like Kenya, where the urban rural links still are very strong. Many families have members in both the urban and the rural economy (see, e.g., Bigsten, 1984, Bevan et al., 1989), but the importance of this problem for the choice of household definition is not discussed in the SAM report (Kenya, 1981).[3]

It has not been possible to create an urban classification based on distinct socio-economic groupings. Instead, income criteria with class boundaries at 6,000/- and 20,000/- per year have had to be used. However, as explained in the notes to table 4.3, the incomes in the three urban categories must be higher than what is stated in the SAM. The average income of the poorest group of urban households should be 10,700/- a year, while the average incomes for the two other groups should be 28,300 and 60,200 respectively.

In the rural areas, there are seven income categories. Six of these relate to smallholder households, grouped according to the size of their land holding and whether they have substantial non-farm incomes (e.g., as teachers) or not. The seventh rural class 'other rural' is a very broad and problematic one, since it includes poor households without land and landless households with large earnings, as well as wealthy landowners. Policy conclusions for this group are therefore not particularly useful. Obviously, nomadic households have little in common with wealthy plantation owners or professionals working in rural areas. There is also the case that some urban employees really should be included in a rural household. This is because either the urban employees are only temporarily resident in town or commute from rural areas near town.

In table 4.4, we take a look at the importance of the different income

---

[3] Since there are large differences between different geographical areas we could also consider a regional breakdown of the accounts, but this has been avoided to keep the size of the matrix small. See Bigsten (1980) for an analysis of regional inequality.

sources for the ten household categories.[4] The poorest urban households get most of their incomes from unskilled labour, the intermediate urban category gets its incomes from all types of employment, while the top category derives its wage incomes mainly from professional employment.

For the six rural smallholder categories, most of the income is from self employment, but categories 13 and 15 also get substantial unskilled labour incomes. The disparate character of the residual rural category (18) is reflected in the diversity of its income sources.

According to the SAM, 42 per cent of the income accrues to urban households, while 58 per cent accrues to rural households. Since the urban share of the population was below 15 per cent, this implies a very large gap between average urban and rural incomes. Using our estimate of the number of households in each category we can derive per household incomes. These are given in table 4.5. The poorest groups were in the rural areas and consist of families with little land and little additional income from other sources. All urban groups seem to be better off, but this conclusion should be qualified on at least two points. First, no adjustment has been made for differences in urban–rural price levels. The cost of living may be 30–50 per cent higher in town. Second, there are large intra-group variations, and many households in the bottom urban group are obviously very poor. Still, even after allowing for this, the conclusion that poverty is mainly a rural problem is certainly valid (see, e.g., Collier and Lal, 1980, Bigsten, 1983). When it comes to disposable incomes, that is income adjusted for direct tax payments, there is a slight shift in favour of the rural areas. This is because most smallholders do not pay direct taxes. The after tax rural share is 60 per cent.

We have computed the coefficient of variation for the three distributions in table 4.5, assuming away intra-group inequality. A clear pattern emerges from a comparison of the three. The distribution of earnings is more even than the one we obtained after allowing for transfers, since most of these, especially from the enterprise sector, go to the better-off households. According to our estimates, however, the system of taxation manages to reduce the inequality to the level it was at before the transfers. Still, since we neglect the within group distribution issue here, we need to exercise some caution with regard to the distributional impact of the taxation system.

---

[4] The constructors of the SAM were unable to go from individual incomes to incomes by socio-economic household categories. Instead, they went from total income to household groups. They first split total income into urban and rural and then split urban households between the three categories using information from the labour force survey. The numbers of households in the first six rural categories were taken from the Integrated Rural Survey 1974/73 (Kenya, 1977). No information is available on the tenth socio-economic category, so its size has to be estimated residually.

Table 4.3 *An Estimate of the Number of Households by Socio-Economic Categories ('000)*

Urban households[a]	
9. Poor urban	183.1
10. Middle urban	116.4
11. Rich urban	43.8
Rural Households[b]	
12. Holding <0.5 ha and with little additional income	133.3
13. Holding <0.5 ha with substantial additional income	73.1
14. Holding ≥0.5 ha but ≤1.0 ha with little additional income	173.8
15. Holding ≥0.5 ha but ≤1.0 ha with substantial additional income	92.0
16. Holding ≥1.0 ha but ≤8.0 ha	959.8
17. Holding ≥8.0 ha (small farms only)	51.5
18. Other rural[c]	501.3

Notes:

[a] The SAM constructors at the ODA derived their population estimates from the urban labour force survey carried out by the CBS in 1977/8 (Allen, 1991). The number of households in the three categories specified according to the ODA were 270,259, 513,272 and 186,337 respectively. This gives an estimate of the total number of urban households of 970,000. Given that the urban population, at the time, has been estimated (from interpolation between the 1969 and 1979 population censuses) at about 1,885,000, the ODA estimate implies a completely unrealistic household size.

It is not quite clear how the SAM constructors managed to derive these figures, but since the table is based on their breakdown we have tried to use the same source to derive a sensible estimate of the number of households in each category. We have had access to one of the urban cycles of the survey, and on the basis of this we have estimated household incomes. We then allocated the households to the three categories suggested in the SAM. With this method, we got 54.34 per cent in the lowest category, 33.89 per cent in the middle category and 12.76 per cent in the top category. The average household size in the urban areas, according to the labour force survey, was 5.49, which gives a total number of households of 343,324 for 1976. We thus estimate that there were 183,129, 116,353 and 43,808 households in the respective income brackets.

Now, obviously, the total urban incomes implied by these figures (multiplying realistic group means by the total number of households in the respective groups) is too low. The income figures from the Labour Force Survey must therefore also be too low on average. The number of households estimated by us should be relatively close to the true number. The question is therefore whether or not incomes have been underestimated to varying extents for the different groups. The SAM constructors do not discuss this point, but have still allocated total urban incomes among the three categories. Without further information about the method used, it is very difficult to determine the reliability of their income

5 Analytical framework

In this section we set out the framework for a multiplier analysis within a fixed price SAM framework (see Pyatt and Round, 1979, Stone, 1985). We must first distinguish between endogenous and exogenous accounts in the SAM. Given our interest in income distribution, a reasonable breakdown is to treat the accounts for factors (rows 1–7), households and enterprises (9–20), and production (23–50) as endogenous. Remaining as exogenous accounts are indirect taxes (8), the government (21–2), the current 'rest of the world' accounts (51–2), and all the capital accounts (53–77). In table 4.6 the accounts are ordered so that the endogenous ones are at the top left-hand corner.

Note *a* (*cont.*)
breakdown, though we accept it in this context. We therefore proceeded to divide the total income figures for the respective category by the number of households in each category using own estimates. The average household incomes then become 10,670, 28,310 and 60,127 Kshillings per year. These estimates are very uncertain, but represent an attempt at reasonable revisions without contradicting SAM estimates of total group incomes.

Vandemoortele (1982) has pointed out that in the Nairobi Household Budget Survey of 1974 the income distribution between the three groups was estimated to be 12.5 per cent to the poorest, 39.2 per cent to the middle group, and 48.3 per cent to the top category, while in the SAM the percentages are 24.8, 41.8 and 33.4 per cent, respectively. He argues therefore that the SAM underestimates the degree of income concentration in the urban areas. Since we do not know how the SAM constructors derived their estimates, it is not possible to say whether Vandemoortele's argument that the results of the Nairobi Household Budget Survey are more reliable is valid or not.

It may be noted for example that the average household size in the Nairobi Household Budget Survey was 4.35, while it was 5.49 in the *Urban Labour Force Survey 1977/8* (Kenya (CBS) (1980)). The inclusion of urban areas other than Nairobi may in part explain this and possibly also some of the discrepancy in the income distribution patterns. Still, in this context, we have to remain within the SAM framework and therefore accept the estimates given there but with this note of caution.

[b] IRS (1974/5), p. 53. Information from Allen (1991) about the splits between 12 and 13 and 14 and 15 respectively.

[c] From interpolation between the censuses of 1969 and 1979 the total population in 1976 was 13,853,472. The estimate of the urban population was 1,884,851. This gives a rural population of 11,968,621. According to the labour force survey of 1977/8 the average household size in the rural areas was 6.03. This gives 1,984,846 rural households, and after deducting categories 12–17 we are left with a residual of 501,300 in category 18.

Table 4.4 *Percentage contribution of factors to total household incomes by socio-economic categories*

		Unskilled and semi-skilled workers	Skilled workers	Office workers and semi-professionals	Professionals	Self-employed and family workers	Consumption of fixed capital	
Urban	9 Poor urban	54.1	22.9	16.1	4.9	2.0		100
	10 Middle urban	19.7	23.0	32.2	21.5	3.7		100
	11 Rich urban	2.3	6.8	20.8	39.5	30.5		100
Rural	12 Holding <0.5 ha and with little additional income	5.3	1.1	1.1	1.6	87.8	3.2	100
	13 Holding <0.5 ha with substantial additional income	25.6	3.8	3.8	6.2	58.3	2.4	100
	14 Holding ≥0.5 ha but <1.0 ha with little additional income	1.8	0.3	0.3	0.6	93.3	3.8	100
	15 Holding ≥0.5 ha but <1.0 ha with substantial additional income	23.2	3.4	3.4	5.6	61.8	2.6	100
	16 Holding ≥1.0 ha but <8.0 ha	11.8	1.8	1.9	2.7	78.7	3.2	100
	17 Holding ≥8.0 ha (small farms only)	7.0	1.3	1.3	1.3	85.4	3.8	100
	18 Other rural	23.4	11.3	13.0	28.5	22.0	1.7	100

Table 4.5 *Incomes per household (K£ p.a.)*

			Earnings per household	Earnings plus current transfers per household	Disposable inc. per household
Urban	9	Poor urban	529.8	556.5	533.6
	10	Middle urban	1477.7	1664.9	1414.9
	11	Rich urban	2552.5	3858.4	3009.1
Rural	12	Holding <0.5 ha and with little additional income	141.0	155.3	153.8
	13	Holding <0.5 ha and with substantial additional income	288.6	359.8	354.3
	14	Holding ≥0.5 ha but <1.0 ha with a little additional income	196.2	219.2	218.1
	15	Holding ≥0.5 ha but <1.0 ha with a substantial additional income	253.3	313.0	309.8
	16	Holding ≥1.0 ha but <8.0 ha	285.3	316.3	311.5
	17	Holding ≥8 ha (small farms only)	304.9	407.8	400.0
	18	Other rural	274.3	392.0	308.0
		Coefficient of variation	1.040	1.182	1.040

The figures in the transactions matrix show the absolute values of the various flows. However, to be able to use the matrix for analysis the endogenous columns must be normalised, that is changed to coefficient form by dividing each column entry in the endogenous accounts by the overall column sum. In table 4.7 we show this and the relationships among the different accounts.

Since table 4.7 is more or less self explanatory we shall make only brief comments. Formulae (4.1) and (4.2) show the relationships between the flows of the transactions matrix and the corresponding coefficients. Formulae (4.3)–(4.6) are accounting relationships showing how the row entries are summed to make the row total. Formulae (4.7)–(4.10) do the same for columns. Formula (4.11), finally, just indicates that the sum of injections must equal the sum of leakages.

The system described in table 4.7 can be regarded as a partitioned,

Table 4.6 *Endogenous and Exogenous Account in the SAM*

		Endogenous					Exogenous			
		Factors	Households	Enterprises	Production	Indirect taxes	Government	RoW current	Capital	Total
Endogenous	Factors				1296.1			14.3		1310.4
	Households	905.1	16.5	163.9			8.9	5.3		1099.7
	Enterprises	320.9	6.8	16.4			12.3	8.0		364.4
	Production		816.7		932.1		253.8	471.7	198.7	2673.0
	Indirect taxes				109.0			66.5		175.5
Exogenous	Government	2.0	82.2	79.5		175.5	7.3	16.5		363.0
	RoW current	82.4	110.0	7.3	335.8		3.2		95.5	634.2
	Capital		67.5	97.3			77.5	51.9	964.0	1258.2
	Total	1310.4	1099.7	364.4	2673.0	175.5	363.0	634.2	1258.2	

Table 4.7 *Notation used in the analysis*

		Expenditures		
		Endogenous	Exogenous	Totals
Receipt	Endogenous	$T_n = A_n \cdot \hat{X}_n$ (4.1)	F	$X_n = T_n \cdot i + f$ (4.3) $= A_n \cdot X_n + f$ (4.4)
	Exogenous	$\Lambda = A_l \cdot \hat{X}_n$ (4.2)	T_x	$X_x = l + T_x \cdot i$ (4.5) $= A_l X_n + T_x \cdot i$ (4.6)
	Totals	$X''_n = (i' \cdot A_n + i' \cdot A_l)\, \hat{X}_n$ (4.7) $i' = i' \cdot A_n + i' \cdot A_l$ (4.8)	$X''_x = i' \cdot F + i' \cdot T_x$ (4.9) $A_l \cdot X_n - F \cdot i = (T_x - T_x')\cdot i$ (4.10)	$\lambda'_a \cdot X_n = f' \cdot i$ (4.11)

Source: Pyatt and Round (1979)

Explanations to Table 4.7:

T_n = matrix of transactions between endogenous accounts
F = matrix of injections
Λ = matrix of leakages
T_x = matrix of transactions between exogenous accounts
$A_n = T_n \cdot \hat{X}_n^{-1}$ = matrix of average endogenous expenditure propensities
$A_l = \Lambda \cdot \hat{X}_n^{-1}$ = matrix of average propensities to leak

$T_n \cdot i$ = vector of row sums of $T_n = A_n \cdot X_n$
$F \cdot i = f$ = vector of row sums of F
$\Lambda \cdot i$ = vector of row sums of $\Lambda = A_l \cdot X_n$
$\lambda'_a = i' \cdot A_l$ = vector of column sums of A_l, i.e., the vector of average propensities to leak
X_n = vector of endogenous incomes
X_x = vector of exegenous incomes

generalised Leontief matrix. As in traditional input–output analysis the values of the endogenous variables x_n can be solved for a given set of exogenous variables according to

$$x_n = (I - A_n)^{-1} f = E.f \qquad (4.12)$$

where f are the exogenous injections and E is the multiplier matrix. Once the endogenous variables x_n have been solved, the exogenous variables x_x can be derived directly from the accounting identities given in table 4.7.

Injections into the system are current transfers to the endogenous institutions, that is households and enterprises, government demand, investments and exports. Leakages are direct and indirect taxes, savings. imports, and income transfers to the rest of the world. With this system it is possible to trace the effects of exogenous injections via outputs to factor demands and household incomes. The income distributional consequences of each experiment can thus be determined.

By looking at the multipliers we can unravel the structure of the economy and how the different variables are interrelated. One can, by comparing multipliers, also determine the sectors where expanded production has the most beneficial effects on income distribution. Even where there are many poor people in a sector, its direct expansion may not necessarily have a beneficial effect on their incomes, especially when all secondary effects have been taken into account. It is also possible to ascertain the extent to which the effects of an expansion, intended to benefit certain target groups, leak to other groups in society. This may help in devising strategies which are most cost efficient in improving the lot of the poor.

The model is closed in much the same way as an input–output model, but with a wider range of endogenous variables. The approach thus constitutes a generalisation of input–output analysis. Pyatt and Round (1979) regard analyses using fixed-price multipliers in a SAM framework as the missing link between the simpler traditional input–output analysis and the more sophisticated CGE models where prices are determined endogenously (see for example the model discussed by Kilkenny in Chapter 9 of this volume).

6 Multiplier Analysis

The assumption of a constant A matrix here is stronger than the traditional assumption of constant input–output coefficients, since it also encompasses other types of coefficients such as those determining the distribution of factor incomes by activity and by household, transfers among institutions, and institutional demand by sector. The difference, relative to standard input–output analysis, is that here the output structure and income distribution are determined simultaneously. The multiplier matrix $(I - A)^{-1} = E$ shows how an increase in any element of the exogenous vector f

Table 4.8 *Multiplier matrix E_{11}*

	1	2	3	4	5	6	7
1 Unskilled and semi-skilled workers	1.1206	0.1118	0.1066	0.0947	0.1327	0.0413	0.0616
2 Skilled workers	0.0499	1.0493	0.0473	0.0408	0.0471	0.0170	0.0240
3 Office workers and semi-professionals	0.0704	0.0685	1.0658	0.0581	0.0687	0.0245	0.0347
4 Professionals	0.0543	0.0542	0.0530	1.0474	0.0522	0.0199	0.0276
5 Self-employed and family workers	0.3806	0.2958	0.2720	0.2543	1.5592	0.1252	0.2158
6 Operating surplus	0.3648	0.3386	0.3081	0.2483	0.3442	1.1033	0.1558
7 Consumption of fixed capital	0.0744	0.0673	0.0634	0.0559	0.0845	0.0247	1.0378

will change the corresponding element of the endogenous vector x_n and also has indirect effects on other elements of x_n.

We first look at the submatrices which form the diagonal of the multiplier matrix. E_{11} in table 4.8 shows the full multiplier effects of an exogenous increase in the income of a particular factor on that factor and all other factors. These multipliers include both direct and indirect effects. The result of a unit exogenous increase in the income of unskilled and semi-skilled labour is an ultimate increase of 1.12 in the income of that factor. Other factors receive increased incomes through indirect repercussions. The largest increases occur for the self employed (0.38) and for operating surplus (0.36). As a matter of fact, the multiplier effects are generally high for these two factors (rows 5 and 6). The indirect effects for these categories are substantially larger than those for the rest taken together. The indirect effects of an increase in operating surplus (column 6) on other factors, however, is low compared to an increase in other types of income. Thus increased profits do not benefit the poor directly. According to the estimates presented here there are definite constraints on the 'trickle-down' process in the short run. What the long-term impact of high profits is depends, of course, on investment behaviour, but this issue is beyond the scope of this chapter.

The multipliers in the E_{22} matrix (not shown) measure the effects of an exogenous increase in income for twelve different types of institutions. Before we draw conclusions about the net effects of redistribution, we must divide the multipliers for all categories by the total income of the respective categories. This allows us to compare proportionate changes. These adjusted figures are given in table 4.9. Redistribution from private enterprises (column 19) gives a large proportionate increase to the wealthiest

Table 4.9 *Adjusted E_{22}-matrix*

	9	10	11	12	13	14	15	16	17	18	19	20
Urban Households												
9 Poor urban	0.0110	0.0006	0.0004	0.0008	0.0006	0.0007	0.0007	0.0007	0.0007	0.0006	0.0003	0.0001
10 Middle urban	0.0007	0.0065	0.0005	0.0008	0.0006	0.0007	0.0007	0.0008	0.0007	0.0007	0.0007	0.0002
11 Rich urban	0.0012	0.0010	0.0096	0.0016	0.0011	0.0014	0.0013	0.0014	0.0013	0.0011	0.0022	0.0003
Rural households												
12 Holding <0.5 ha and with little additional income	0.0008	0.0008	0.0006	0.0551	0.0013	0.0017	0.0015	0.0017	0.0015	0.0011	0.0006	0.0001
13 Holding <0.5 ha with substantial additional income	0.0010	0.0009	0.0007	0.0018	0.0486	0.0016	0.0014	0.0015	0.0014	0.0011	0.0012	0.0002
14 Holding ≥ 0.5 ha but <1.0 ha with little additional income	0.0009	0.0009	0.0007	0.0020	0.0013	0.0312	0.0016	0.0017	0.0015	0.0012	0.0006	0.0001
15 Holding ≥ 0.5 ha but <1.0 ha with substantial additional income	0.0010	0.0009	0.0006	0.0018	0.0012	0.0016	0.0444	0.0016	0.0014	0.0011	0.0012	0.0002
16 Holding ≥ 1.0 ha but <8.0 ha	0.0009	0.0008	0.0005	0.0018	0.0012	0.0017	0.0015	0.0053	0.0014	0.0010	0.0007	0.0001
17 Holding ≥ 8.0 ha (small farms only)	0.0012	0.0010	0.0006	0.0022	0.0015	0.0020	0.0018	0.0019	0.0654	0.0012	0.0016	0.0002
18 Other rural	0.0011	0.0009	0.0006	0.0014	0.0010	0.0013	0.0012	0.0013	0.0011	0.0082	0.0018	0.0003
Companies												
19 Private enterprises & non-private inst.	0.0014	0.0010	0.0006	0.0013	0.0009	0.0012	0.0011	0.0012	0.0011	0.0009	0.0040	0.0004
20 Parastatal bodies & public companies	0.0017	0.0012	0.0008	0.0016	0.0011	0.0014	0.0014	0.0015	0.0013	0.0012	0.0015	0.0250

urban class as well as the richer rural classes. That recipients of profits are relatively richer hardly comes as a surprise.

Redistribution from urban households seems to be fairly equally spread among the different categories according to the Kenyan SAM. The same goes for the redistributions from rural to urban classes. With regard to redistribution between the two poorer urban classes and the rural classes, there seems to be a certain net advantage for the rural classes. However, when one considers the wealthiest urban class, the opposite seems, strangely enough, to be the case. This may be due to strong indirect effects in the system or to data deficiencies, but could also reflect a difference in behaviour which is due to the fact that the richer urban households are more permanently assimilated into the urban economy. There is, however, considerable evidence to suggest that urban–rural links have remained strong for all urban groups (e.g., Elkan, 1976).

We can also show the effects of increased demand for the output of producing sectors on factor incomes (E_{13}) (table 4.10) and institutional incomes (E_{23}). The relative increases in incomes of different household categories can best be compared if the latter multipliers are divided by total incomes for each category. This is done in the adjusted matrix shown in table 4.11.

We can see in table 4.10 that the most beneficial effects on the incomes of the unskilled and semi-skilled workers come from expansion of agriculture (23, 24), forestry (25), the wood industry (29), water (37), building (38), hotels and restaurants (40), domestic services (45), public administration (46), and various types of public services (48, 49, 50). The category of skilled labour has therefore benefitted from the import-substitution policy pursued, which has mainly protected the manufacturing sector. The liberalisation reforms undertaken during the 1980s, however, have tended to increase domestic relative prices of exportables, such as agricultural goods and tourist related services, relative to those of importables, such as manufacturing goods, while the impact on non-tradables has been more diffuse (Bigsten and Ndungu, 1992). Relative to a continuation of existing policies, the policy changes would thus have tended to reduce inequality since they have favoured sectors where a large share of the poorly paid employees are found.

It was shown in table 4.5 that the poorest households were categories 12 and 14, that is smallholders with little additional income. Also part of category 18, other rural, should be included but it is not possible to separate the poor nomads included here from the wealthy landowners. The most beneficial effects on the urban poor (see table 4.11) are obtained by expanding production in the public sectors (46–50), domestic services (45), forestry and fishing (25), water (37), building (38), trade (39), and finance

Table 4.10 *Multiplier matrix* E_{13}

	23	24	25	26	27	28	29	30	31	32	33	34	35	36
1 Unskilled and semi-skilled workers	0.1525	0.1875	0.6085	0.1476	0.1266	0.1120	0.1808	0.0999	0.0025	0.0883	0.0904	0.0753	0.1115	0.0718
2 Skilled workers	0.0507	0.0416	0.0915	0.1034	0.0570	0.0705	0.0851	0.1057	0.0028	0.0563	0.0950	0.0671	0.1065	0.0743
3 Office workers and semi-professionals	0.0712	0.0616	0.0972	0.0958	0.0766	0.0751	0.0982	0.1123	0.0031	0.0826	0.0786	0.0645	0.0642	0.0786
4 Professionals	0.0538	0.0469	0.0647	0.0960	0.0562	0.0582	0.0725	0.0889	0.0044	0.0597	0.0562	0.0590	0.0784	0.0548
5 Self-employed and family workers	1.3992	0.8748	0.2787	0.1917	0.4239	0.2034	0.2325	0.1858	0.0071	0.2262	0.1546	0.1337	0.1385	0.1485
6 Operating surplus	0.3393	0.5155	0.4604	0.2841	0.3749	0.2094	0.2395	0.2922	0.3336	0.3179	0.3649	0.1827	0.2294	0.4192
7 Consumption of fixed capital	0.0847	0.1160	0.1088	0.1274	0.0952	0.0806	0.0849	0.1031	0.0086	0.0862	0.1103	0.0561	0.0727	0.1507

Table 4.10 (*cont.*) *Multiplier matrix* E_{13}

	37	38	39	40	41	42	43	44	45	46	47	48	49	50
1 Unskilled and semi-skilled workers	0.2640	0.1802	0.1434	0.1790	0.1383	0.1086	0.1324	0.0482	0.4090	0.3201	0.1417	0.2676	0.3124	0.3417
2 Skilled workers	0.2344	0.1559	0.0898	0.0846	0.1105	0.1083	0.0837	0.0265	0.0894	0.1780	0.0736	0.2513	0.2232	0.1842
3 Office workers and semi-professionals	0.1067	0.1038	0.2191	0.1055	0.1536	0.2168	0.2937	0.0283	0.1596	0.2806	0.1061	0.1316	0.1398	0.3071
4 Professionals	0.0808	0.0967	0.1494	0.0836	0.1009	0.0620	0.2432	0.1288	0.0240	0.1144	0.7766	0.2943	0.1318	0.1171
5 Self-employed and family workers	0.2239	0.2107	0.4581	0.3967	0.2350	0.1728	0.2298	0.1187	0.2569	0.2843	0.2647	0.2912	0.2728	0.2929
6 Operating surplus	0.5117	0.2495	0.4050	0.4040	0.2749	0.2929	0.3748	0.9152	0.3351	0.3023	0.2659	0.2993	0.2822	0.3083
7 Consumption of fixed capital	0.0885	0.1074	0.1087	0.1119	0.1259	0.0990	0.0800	0.0287	0.1168	0.0865	0.0642	0.0775	0.0973	0.0831

Table 4.11 *Adjusted E_{23} matrix*

	23	24	25	26	27	28	29	30	31	32	33	34	35	36
Urban households														
9 Household income <6000/- p.a.	0.0008	0.0008	0.0023	0.0009	0.0007	0.0006	0.0009	0.0007	0.0000	0.0005	0.0006	0.0006	0.0007	0.0005
10 Household income between 6000 and 20000/-p.a.	0.0007	0.0007	0.0013	0.0009	0.0007	0.0006	0.0008	0.0008	0.0000	0.0006	0.0007	0.0005	0.0007	0.0007
11 Household income ≥20000/- p.a.	0.0013	0.0012	0.0009	0.0008	0.0008	0.0006	0.0007	0.0008	0.0001	0.0007	0.0007	0.0005	0.0006	0.0008
Rural households														
12 Holding <0.5 ha and with little additional income	0.0031	0.0021	0.0009	0.0006	0.0011	0.0006	0.0007	0.0006	0.0000	0.0006	0.0005	0.0004	0.0004	0.0005
13 Holding <0.5 ha with substantial additional income	0.0022	0.0017	0.0015	0.0007	0.0010	0.0006	0.0008	0.0006	0.0000	0.0006	0.0006	0.0004	0.0005	0.0006
14 Holding ≥0.5 ha but <1.0 with little additional income	0.0033	0.0021	0.0008	0.0006	0.0011	0.0006	0.0006	0.0006	0.0000	0.0006	0.0005	0.0004	0.0004	0.0005
15 Holding ≥0.5 ha but <1.0 ha with substantial additional income	0.0023	0.0017	0.0014	0.0007	0.0010	0.0006	0.0007	0.0006	0.0000	0.0006	0.0006	0.0004	0.0005	0.0006
16 Holding ≥1.0 ha but <8.0 ha	0.0029	0.0020	0.0011	0.0006	0.0010	0.0006	0.0007	0.0006	0.0000	0.0006	0.0005	0.0004	0.0005	0.0005
17 Holding ≥8.0 ha (small farms only)	0.0027	0.0020	0.0010	0.0007	0.0011	0.0006	0.0007	0.0006	0.0000	0.0007	0.0006	0.0004	0.0005	0.0007
18 Other rural	0.0012	0.0011	0.0013	0.0008	0.0008	0.0006	0.0007	0.0007	0.0000	0.0006	0.0007	0.0005	0.0006	0.0007

Table 4.11 (*cont.*) *Adjusted E_{23} matrix*

	37	38	39	40	41	42	43	44	45	46	47	48	49	50
Urban households														
9 Household income <6000/- p.a.	0.0015	0.0011	0.0010	0.0009	0.0009	0.0009	0.0011	0.0003	0.0017	0.0018	0.0010	0.0017	0.0017	0.0019
10 Household income between 6000 and 20000/- p.a.	0.0013	0.0010	0.0012	0.0009	0.0010	0.0011	0.0015	0.0005	0.0013	0.0017	0.0017	0.0017	0.0014	0.0018
11 Household income ≥20000/- p.a.	0.0010	0.0008	0.0012	0.0009	0.0009	0.0008	0.0013	0.0009	0.0010	0.0011	0.0020	0.0013	0.0010	0.0012
Rural households														
12 Holding <0.5 ha and with little additional income	0.0007	0.0006	0.0012	0.0010	0.0007	0.0005	0.0007	0.0004	0.0008	0.0009	0.0008	0.0009	0.0008	0.0009
13 Holding <0.5 ha with substantial additional income	0.0010	0.0008	0.0011	0.0010	0.0008	0.0007	0.0009	0.0006	0.0012	0.0011	0.0010	0.0011	0.0011	0.0012
14 Holding ≥0.5 ha but <1.0 with little additional income	0.0007	0.0006	0.0012	0.0010	0.0007	0.0005	0.0007	0.0004	0.0008	0.0008	0.0008	0.0009	0.0008	0.0009
15 Holding ≥0.5 ha but <1.0 ha with substantial additional income	0.0010	0.0008	0.0011	0.0010	0.0008	0.0006	0.0008	0.0006	0.0011	0.0011	0.0010	0.0011	0.0011	0.0011
16 Holding ≥1.0 ha but <8.0 ha	0.0008	0.0007	0.0012	0.0010	0.0007	0.0006	0.0007	0.0004	0.0009	0.0010	0.0009	0.0010	0.0009	0.0010
17 Holding ≥8.0 ha (small farms only)	0.0009	0.0007	0.0012	0.0011	0.0007	0.0006	0.0008	0.0008	0.0009	0.0009	0.0008	0.0009	0.0009	0.0009
18 Other rural	0.0011	0.0009	0.0011	0.0009	0.0009	0.0008	0.0012	0.0008	0.0012	0.0012	0.0017	0.0014	0.0012	0.0013

(43). The most beneficial effects on the rural poor are obtained by expanding production in agriculture (23, 24), and also to some extent forestry and fishing (25), food and beverages (27), trade (39) and hotels and restaurants (40). As expected, the expansion of agriculture benefits primarily the rural population, even though urban dwellers also benefit due to the indirect effects. Increased production of government services, on the other hand, has the greatest proportionate effect on the urban dwellers, while the effects of an expansion of manufacturing production are very widespread. Here, the proportionate effect is approximately the same for both urban and rural dwellers in all classes. The interlinkages between this sector and other sectors are thus unusually high. Expansion of manufacturing activities to rural areas would thus probably have widespread beneficial effects on the whole of the rural economy. It would help absorb the surplus labour of smallholder households.[5] In the other sectors, the proportionate effects are not that different, even if there is a certain urban bias in transport, communications and finance.

7 Changes in income distribution since 1976

It is difficult to say what has happened to inequality since 1976.. The most comprehensive recent attempt is reported in World Bank (1988). From this it seems as if both the urban–rural gap and the formal–informal-sector gap declined somewhat from the mid 1970s to the mid 1980s. This suggests that the distribution of income among workers and smallholders has become more even. What can we then say about income differences between those and profit receivers? There have been some fluctuations in the wage share, but there is really no clear trend. It seems as if the factorial income distribution has been stable. However, the number of people has increased so that real wages have fallen. Smallholder agricultural incomes have been increasing at a slower rate than the rural population, which means that also smallholder agricultural income levels have been decreasing. However, smallholder families derive incomes from a whole range of other activities, and non-farm rural activities as well as urban informal activities have expanded at a very rapid rate. This may have compensated for the falling agricultural income. At present it is not possible to say in what direction inequality may have changed. Most probably the change has been small.

To come up with more definite conclusions, we would need a fully worked out SAM for a recent year. The need for a SAM in the analysis of income distribution is particularly acute in situations where most households have a whole range of income sources. In rural Kenya, multi-activity

---

[5] For a further discussion, see Bigsten and Collier (forthcoming).

households are the norm, but even in the urban centres multiple sources of income are common.

8 Concluding remarks

The multipliers derived here may be called *ex post* multipliers, since the coefficients measure average propensities. However, to get better predictions of the effects of changes in injections on the level of endogenous variables in that year, we would need to know the marginal expenditure propensities (or the *ex ante* multipliers). It is reasonable to assume they are different from the average propensities, but this issue is not pursued further here.[6]

In this chapter we have focussed on the income distribution in Kenya by factors and socio-economic groups and shown which patterns of change have the most beneficial effects on the incomes of the poorest categories. The next step in the analysis would be to discuss what policy changes are required to bring about the beneficial structural changes identified. This issue is only touched upon here.

One important conclusion from our discussion of income distribution in Kenya is that to be able to understand the dynamics of income distribution and policy impacts in a situation characterised by a diverse pattern of income sources, we need an appropriate social accounting framework. Starting from incomes by sector we must proceed with appropriate mappings first to factors and then to households. Such mappings require extensive empirical work, but given the relative abundance of household data in Kenya it would be possible to continue this work beyond what is reported in this chapter.

[6] The multiplier analysis of this paper can be extended further. Pyatt and Round (1979) have shown how the multipliers can be decomposed to show the relative magnitudes of different types of effects.

5 Structure of the Bangladesh interregional social accounting system: a comparison of alternative decompositions

GEOFFREY J. D. HEWINGS, MICHAEL SONIS, JONG-KUN LEE
AND SARWAR JAHAN

1 Introduction

While the economic base model has been the object of continuing, almost relentless criticism, it possesses one major characteristic of considerable importance, namely, the ability to trace the direction of causality without resort to complex mathematical manipulation. Of course, such transparency of action-through-to-reaction is bought at a very high price – the litany of problems and limitations is well known and will not be repeated here. However, in recent years, tractability in model development has been lost in the rush to produce more complex systems; while our current stable of regional and interregional models is far more elegant than two decades ago, the inability to provide insights into the finer structure of some of these systems has reduced them, for all intents and purposes, to black boxes. The objective of this chapter is not to provide a call for a return to the parsimony of the past, but rather to incorporate, in the present models that favour system-wide visions of economic structure, some of the flavour of transparency that accompanied the simpler expressions of structural interrelationships in earlier, regional models.

This chapter draws on a four-region interregional social accounting system (BIRSAM) developed for Bangladesh (see Jahan and Hewings, 1990) and proceeds to examine several alternative decompositions of this system to provide insights into the way changes move between sectors and across regions. The ultimate hope is to harness the benefits of economy-wide vision with an ability to explore the finer structure of change without too much compromise. At the same time, the chapter will afford an opportunity to compare several decomposition techniques and examine the ways in which the views of the economic structure so revealed are consistent, conflicting or merely presented from a different vantage point. With the exception of some work by Sonis *et al.* (1993), this form of comparative analysis has not been undertaken. The important conclusions of our analysis suggest that the micro-, meso- and macro-level visions of the social accounting system provide different but complementary decomposition procedures.

In the next section, a presentation of the alternative techniques used in the analysis will be provided. The third section begins with a brief description of the BIRSAM prior to the empirical interpretations while the fourth section attempts to compare and evaluate the alternative perspectives provided. Some concluding remarks on the state of the art round out the chapter.

2 The decomposition methods[1]

The methods that will be used to describe and interpret structure are referred to as (1) multiplicative decomposition, (2) additive decomposition, (3) structural path analysis, (4) field of influence, (5) Matrioshka principle and (6) superposition principle. All the methods attempt to extract, from the social accounting matrix, insights into the way in which the fine structure might be identified and analysed.

Multiplicative decompositions

In the literature we can find three major approaches to the decomposition of single-region SAMs. Let A^* be a matrix of input coefficients for the SAM shown below

$$\begin{bmatrix} 0 & 0 & A_{13}^* \\ A_{21}^* & A_{22}^* & 0 \\ 0 & A_{32}^* & A_{33}^* \end{bmatrix} \tag{5.1}$$

A generalised inverse solution would be

$$X^* = (I - A^*)^{-1} f = E^* . f \tag{5.2}$$

where f is a vector of final demands. Instead of E^*, Pyatt and Round (1979) suggested

$$X^* = N_3 . N_2 . N_1 . f \tag{5.3}$$

[1] This section draws on Sonis and Hewings (1988) and Sonis, Hewings and Lee (1993).

where

N_1 are the own direct effects,
N_2 are the own transfer effects and
N_3 are the cross multiplicative effects.

Sonis and Hewings (1988) proposed a modification of the Pyatt and Round (1979) scheme; with some rearrangement in the manner in which the decomposition proceeded, they provided the following definitions of the N_i''s

N_1' showed the influence of all divisions on production;
N_2' was a triangular matrix revealing increasing structural complexity as analysis moved from factors to institutions and
N_3' showed the own direct effects as in the original Pyatt and Round (1979) system.

In diagrammatic form, the two multiplicative decompositions may be compared as follows:

Pyatt and Round:

$$(I-A)^{-1}=N_3.N_2.N_1=\begin{bmatrix} I & * & * \\ * & I & * \\ 0 & 0 & I \end{bmatrix}.\begin{bmatrix} * & 0 & 0 \\ 0 & * & 0 \\ 0 & 0 & * \end{bmatrix}.\begin{bmatrix} I & 0 & 0 \\ 0 & * & 0 \\ 0 & 0 & * \end{bmatrix} \qquad (5.4)$$

Sonis and Hewings:

$$(I-A)^{-1}=N_3'.N_2'.N_1'=\begin{bmatrix} I & 0 & * \\ 0 & I & * \\ 0 & 0 & * \end{bmatrix}.\begin{bmatrix} I & 0 & 0 \\ * & I & 0 \\ * & * & I \end{bmatrix}.\begin{bmatrix} I & 0 & 0 \\ 0 & * & 0 \\ 0 & 0 & * \end{bmatrix} \qquad (5.5)$$

The non-uniqueness of the decomposition procedures creates attractive opportunities for revealing characteristics of the structure of an economy when attention is confined to just one economy; however, when the economy is composed of a set of regions, the number of alternative decompositions increases at an alarming rate. The analyst is thus faced with the need to provide a system that will reveal some fine details of the structure without burdensome complexity.

In this chapter, we restrict ourselves to the problems of decomposition of interregional social accounting systems, extensions of the system that have been associated with the work of Round (1985). The major problem identified by Round has been the often difficult task of manipulating these systems when the number of regions exceeds three.

Additive decompositions

Defourny and Thorbecke (1984) suggested an additive decomposition of the following form

$$N_3.N_2.N_1 = f + [N_1 - I] + [N_2 - I].N_1 + [N_3 - I].N_2.N_1$$
$$= I + T + O + C \tag{5.6}$$

where

f is the initial injection,
T is the net contribution of the transfer multiplier effect,
O is the net contribution of the open loop or cross-multiplier effects and
C is the net contribution of the circular closed loop effects

This formulation provides for a more formal movement of impacts through the system in terms of a set of paths; this perspective led naturally to the use of structural path analysis described later in this section. The next two methodologies we discuss here, structural path analysis and the field of influence, view the complexity of interactions within a social accounting system as comprising a set containing a relatively small number of elements. However, the two methods differ in the way in which this set is identified and, hence, it is more than likely that two different decompositions will result.

Structural path analysis

Structural path analysis operates on the basis of identification of an influence graph whose elements are the vertices that comprise the set of sectors in the social accounting system. Interpretation of the associated coefficients in this system is different from that usually associated with interindustry and social accounting matrices. The coefficient a_{ij}^* is considered in a different light, in the following fashion. The influence in a graph is the strength of the connection; the magnitude of the direct influence $J^D(j,i)$ transmitted from vertex (i.e., sector) j to vertex i through the arc $(j \rightarrow i)$ is equal to a_{ij}^*. In analogous fashion to the ripple effects associated with a multiplier, the 'flow-on' effects of individual transactions may be identified by defining an appropriate path (a sequence of arcs). An elementary path $tr(j,i)$ from vertex j to vertex i might appear as

$$(j,k_1), (k_1,k_2), \ldots, (k_r,i), \quad k_r \neq k_s$$

from which the total influence, $J^T tr(j,i)$ of vertex j on vertex i along the elementary path $tr(j,i)$ is given by

$$J^T tr(j,i) = a^*_{klj}a^*_{k2kl}\ldots a^*_{irk} \frac{\min[tr(j,i)]}{\det(I - A^*)} \tag{5.7}$$

where $\det(I - A^*)$ is a determinant, and $\min[tr(j,i)]$ denotes the minor of the matrix $(I - A^*)$, obtained by removing the rows and columns $j, k_1 k_2, \ldots, k_r, i$ and is a path multiplier. The global influence of the vertex j on the vertex i, $J^G(j,i)$, is the component e^*_{ij} of the associated inverse $E^* = (I - A^*)^{-1}$. Thus, the Leontief Inverse of an interindustry system can be considered as a matrix of global influences.

Since, for most interindustry and social accounting systems, the flows exhibit complex patterns, the global influence of vertex j on vertex i can be considered equal to the sum of the total influences of vertex j on vertex i along all elementary paths, $tr(j,i)$, joining j to i

$$e^*_{ij} = J^G(j,i) = \sum_{tr(ji)} J^T tr(ji) \tag{5.8}$$

Thus, unlike the usual inverse matrix, which only summarises the 'paths' from j to i in terms of a scalar, e^*_{ij}, structural path analysis provides the analyst with the opportunity to view the myriad patterns of linkages or ripple effects at the micro level – essentially 'unravelling' the inverse matrix and decomposing it into a set of elementary paths.

The next decomposition approach attempts to trace the most important collection of paths at the meso level, through the identification of the set of most important parameters. The set is defined in a more general way but has strong analytical and conceptual links to the notion of 'global influence' introduced by Lantner (1974).

The field of influence

The concept of a 'field of influence' was developed by Sonis and Hewings (1989) to provide a formal, general tool for the measurement of the analytical impact of changes in the direct coefficients matrix of an input–output table, or social accounting matrix, on the associated Leontief inverse, or for measuring the impact of changes within the direct coefficients matrix on the associated decomposed inverse matrices. Interest in the problem of coefficient change is not a recent phenomenon (see Sohn, 1986 and Sonis and Hewings, 1989 for a review of some earlier work); however, the major theoretical developments that provided the basis for the present initiatives were those of Sherman and Morrison (1949, 1950), Bullard and Sebald, (1977, 1988), West (1981), Hewings and Romanos (1981), Crema, Defourny and Gazon (1984) and Defourny and Thorbecke (1984). The condensed form of the solution of the coefficient change problem can be presented in the following manner:

let $A = (a_{ij})$ be an $n \times n$ matrix of direct input coefficients;

let $\Delta = \|\delta_{ij}\|$ be a matrix of incremental changes in the direct input coefficients;

let $E = (I - A)^{-1} = \|e_{ij}\|$ and $E(\Delta) = (I - A - \Delta)^{-1}$ be the Leontief inverses before and after changes and let $\det(E)$ and $\det(E(\Delta))$ be the determinants of the corresponding inverses. Then the following propositions hold:

Proposition 1

The ratio of determinants of the Leontief inverses before and after changes is the polynomial of the incremental changes δ_{ij} expressed in the following form

$$Y(\Delta) = \frac{\det E}{\det E(\Delta)} = 1 - \sum_{j_1 i_1} e_{j_1 i_1} \delta_{i_1 j_1}$$

$$+ \sum_{k=2}^{n} (1)^k \sum_{\substack{i_r \neq i_s \\ j_r \neq j_s}}' E_{or} \begin{pmatrix} j_1 j_2 \cdots j_k \\ i_1 i_2 \cdots i_k \end{pmatrix} \delta_{i_1 j_1} \delta_{i_2 j_2} \cdots \delta_{i_k j_k} \qquad (5.9)$$

where

$$E_{or} \begin{pmatrix} j_1 j_2 \cdots j_k \\ i_1 i_2 \cdots i_k \end{pmatrix}$$

is a determinant of order k that includes the components of the Leontief inverse E from the ordered set of columns $i_1, i_2, \ldots, i_k$ and rows $j_1, j_2, \ldots j_k$. Further, in the sum, the products of the changes $\delta_{i_1 j_1} \delta_{i_2 j_2} \cdots \delta_{i_k j_k}$ that differ only by the order of multiplication, are counted only once.

Proposition 2

This provides a fundamental formula between the Leontief matrices in matrix form

$$E(\Delta) = E + \frac{1}{Y(\Delta)} \left[\sum_{k=1}^{n} \sum_{\substack{i_r \neq i_s \\ j_r \neq j_s}}' FI \begin{pmatrix} i_1 i_2 \cdots i_k \\ j_1 j_2 \cdots j_k \end{pmatrix} \delta_{j_1 i_1} \delta_{j_2 i_2} \cdots \delta_{j_k i_k} \right] \qquad (5.10)$$

where the matrix field of influence

$$FI \begin{pmatrix} i_1 i_2 \cdots i_k \\ j_1 j_2 \cdots j_k \end{pmatrix}$$

of the incremental changes $\delta_{j_1 i_1} \delta_{j_2 i_2} \cdots \delta_{j_k i_k}$ includes the components

$$fl_{ij}\begin{pmatrix} i_1 \dots i_k \\ j_1 \dots j_k \end{pmatrix} = (-1)^k \left[E_{or}\begin{pmatrix} i_1 \dots i_k \\ j_1 \dots j_k \end{pmatrix} - e_{ij}E_{or}\begin{pmatrix} i_1 \dots i_k \\ j_1 \dots j_k \end{pmatrix} \right] i,j = 1,n$$

$$(5.11)$$

Proposition 3

This proposition provides the fine structure of the fields of influence. Initially, two types may be identified, the first order being confined to changes in only one element in the matrix while the second order examines the field of influence associated with changes in two elements. While higher-order fields can be defined, they are not presented here.

The first-order field of influence

$$FI\begin{pmatrix} i \\ j \end{pmatrix}$$

of the increment δ_{ij} is the matrix generated by a multiplication of the jth column of the Leontief inverse E with its ith row

$$FI\begin{pmatrix} i \\ j \end{pmatrix} = \begin{matrix} e_{1j} \\ e_{2j} \\ \cdot \\ \cdot \\ \cdot \\ e_{nj} \end{matrix} . (e_{i_1} e_{i_2} \dots e_{in})$$

$$(5.12)$$

The second-order synergic interaction between two incremental changes may be reduced to the following linear combination of four first-order fields of influence

$$FI\begin{pmatrix} i_1 & i_2 \\ j_1 & j_2 \end{pmatrix} = -e_{i_1 j_1}.FI\begin{pmatrix} i_2 \\ j_2 \end{pmatrix} + e_{i_1 j_2}.FI\begin{pmatrix} i_2 \\ j_1 \end{pmatrix} + e_{i_2 j_1}.FI\begin{pmatrix} i_1 \\ j_2 \end{pmatrix}$$

$$-e_{i_2 j_2}.FI\begin{pmatrix} i_1 \\ j_1 \end{pmatrix}$$

$$(5.13)$$

These developments will now be related to the notions of inverse importance. As generalised by Bullard and Sebald (1977, 1988), if change occurs only in one place, (i_1, j_1), i.e.

$$\delta_{ij} = \begin{cases} \delta & i = i_1, j = j_1 \\ 0 & otherwise \end{cases}$$

then the Leontief inverse $E(\Delta)$ has the form

$$E(\Delta) = E + \frac{\delta}{1 - e_{j_1 i_1}} \cdot FI\begin{pmatrix} i_1 \\ j_1 \end{pmatrix} \tag{5.14}$$

or, in the original Sherman–Morrison (1950) coordinate form

$$e_{ji}(\delta) = e_{ij} + \frac{e_{ij_1} e_{i_1 j} \delta}{1 - e_{j_1 i_1} \delta} \tag{5.15}$$

This formula provides the analytical basis for the notion of inverse important coefficients, namely, the direct input coefficients whose change will create the greatest impact on the rest of the economy (Hewings and Romanos, 1981). If the changes occur in the ith row of the matrix A, i.e.

$$\delta_{rs} = \begin{cases} \delta_s & r = i_1, s = 1, 2, \ldots, n \\ 0 & r \neq i_1 \end{cases}$$

then

$$E(\Delta) = E + \frac{\sum\limits_{s=1}^{n} \delta_s \cdot FI\begin{pmatrix} s \\ i_1 \end{pmatrix}}{1 - \sum\limits_{s=1}^{n} e_{s i_1} \cdot \delta_s} \tag{5.16}$$

or in the coordinate form

$$e_{ij}(\Delta) = e_{ij} + \frac{e_{ii_1} \sum\limits_{s=1}^{n} e_{sj} \cdot \delta_s}{1 - \sum\limits_{s=1}^{n} e_{s i_1} \cdot \delta_s} \tag{5.17}$$

Analogous formulae can be derived for changes in one column.

The procedure can be extended to include changes in whole columns or rows or even in all elements of the matrix. In Sonis and Hewings (1991, 1992), the formulations were used for the construction of a link between error and sensitivity analysis and extended demo-economic input–output analysis. A link was also provided between these formulae and the bi-proportional or RAS adjustment technique.

When developing a decomposition technique, essentially we are trying to uncover sets of coefficients that may be regarded as differentiated from the rest on the basis of their analytical importance. The 'cutting rule' chosen will require judgement by the investigator, but previous work suggests that somewhere between 10 per cent and 20 per cent of the coefficients in a socio-economic matrix may be identified as analytically important; the level of aggregation, level of development and the nature of the matrix itself will all play a role in the identification process.

The Matrioshka principle[2]

The pioneering work of Pyatt and Round (1979), in developing methods for decomposing the structure of complex social accounting systems, has provided possibilities for uncovering the fine structure of these systems to enable policy analysis and economic interpretation to operate at a detailed level within a broader-based accounting system, albeit for a single economy. Sonis and Hewings (1988) have shown that there are a number of alternative decompositions, those based on the multiplicative form proposed by Pyatt and Round (1979), as well as additive forms, those relating to structural path analysis (see Defourny and Thorbecke, 1984) and some more novel approaches based on superposition principles. The 'Matrioshka Principle' has been proposed as a further alternative to those noted above (Sonis and Hewings, 1990). In essence, the Matrioshka Principle examines the nature of intra- and interregional transactions in terms of the hierarchical structure of feedback effects.

Essentially, the matrix of transactions T is decomposed into a set of flows

$$T = T_1 + T_2 + \ldots + T_n \tag{5.18}$$

The entries in the first matrix are found by identifying the largest flow in an $n \times n$ matrix, T, say T_{ij}, removing the ith row and jth column, and moving to the next largest coefficient, t_{rs}, removing the rth row and sth column and so on until n entries are identified. The first n entries become the elements of T_1, a block permutation matrix providing the principal feedback components for the additive decomposition of T. The first n entries in T are now replaced by zeros and the process repeated to extract the second largest n flows. These become the elements of T_2; the process continues until all elements have been extracted. Since the largest transactions flows will be concentrated within the same region, matrix T_1 will probably be a block-diagonal matrix.[3]

One of the characteristics of block-permutation matrices is the property of diagonality at some power z of the matrix T_j; for block-diagonal matrices, the power will be 1. This feature is now exploited in the development of multi-regional multiplicative decompositions, based on a hierarchical additive principle of the kind shown in (5.18).

For any arbitrary matrix T and integer r

$$(I - T)(I + T + T^2 + T^3 + \ldots + T^r - 1) = I - T^r \tag{5.19}$$

Thus, if the flows of T are converted to the familiar input coefficients A

[2] The principle is named after the nested Russian dolls, each one identical to its larger cousin; the principle suggests that the structure can be 'peeled' away, rather like an onion, but with a similar set of procedures applied at each level.

[3] Further details of the methodology may be found in Sonis and Hewings, 1990.

and the decomposed flows T_j are similarly converted to coefficients A_j, then

$$I - A = 1 - A_1 - A_2 - \ldots - A_n$$
$$= (I - A_1^{m'}) \cdot \left[(I + A_1 + A_1^2 + \ldots + A_1^{m'} - 1)^{-1} \cdot \sum_{k=2}^{n} A_k \right] \qquad (5.20)$$

where

$$(I - A_1^{m'}) \cdot [(I + A_1 + A_1^2 + \ldots + A_1^{m'} - 1)^{-1}] = I - A_1$$

Since m' will be chosen such that $I - A_1^{m'}$ will be block diagonal, it implies that its inverse is also block diagonal. Thus, the products $(I - A_1^{m'})^{-1} \cdot A_k$ are block-permutation matrices of the same structure as A_k.

Defining

$$(I - A_1^{m'})^{-1} = \vartheta_1$$

we can then write

$$\vartheta_1 \cdot (I - A_1) - I = N_1,$$
$$I - A_1^{m'} = \vartheta_1^{-1} \qquad (5.21)$$

and

$$I - A = \vartheta_1^{-1} \cdot (I - \overline{A_{22}} - \overline{A_{23}} - \ldots \overline{A_{2n}} + N_1) \qquad (5.22)$$

where

$$\overline{A_{2s}} = \vartheta_1^{-1} \cdot A_s, \qquad s = 2, 3, \ldots, n$$

The procedure continues such that at step $n - 1$, the solution is

$$I - A = \vartheta_1^{-1} \cdot \vartheta_2^{-1} \ldots \vartheta_{n-1}^{-1} \cdot (I - \overline{A_{nn}} + N_{n-1}) \qquad (5.23)$$

and the final step, n, yields

$$I - A = \vartheta_1^{-1} \cdot \vartheta_2^{-1} \ldots \vartheta_{n-1}^{-1} \cdot \vartheta_n^{-1} \cdot N_n \qquad (5.24)$$

This provides the multiplicative multiplier decomposition

$$(I - A)^{-1} = \Omega \cdot \vartheta_n \cdot \vartheta_{n-1} \ldots \vartheta_1 \qquad (5.25)$$

where Ω is equal to N_n^{-1}. Here the matrices $\vartheta_1, \vartheta_2, \ldots, \vartheta_n$ are the block-diagonal matrices providing the 'own indirect multiplier effects' corresponding to the hierarchical structure of closed feedback transactions loops; the block-diagonal matrix Ω provides the results of the cross effects.

The procedure described above has been applied at one level in the system; the process would now move to the next level and continue as before, producing a finer and finer decomposition of the system. Further, the multiplicative decomposition (5.25) of the Leontief inverse $(I - A)^{-1}$ can be converted into an additive decomposition which is, in essence, a generalisation of (5.6)

$$(I-A)^{-1} = \underbrace{\underbrace{\underbrace{\underbrace{\underbrace{I+(\vartheta_1-I)}_{\vartheta_1} +(\vartheta_2-I)\vartheta_1}_{\vartheta_2\vartheta_1} +(\vartheta_3-I)\vartheta_2\vartheta_1}_{\vartheta_3\vartheta_2\vartheta_1} +\ldots+ (\vartheta_n-I)\vartheta_{n-1}\ldots\vartheta_1}_{\vartheta_n\vartheta_{n-1}\ldots\vartheta_1} +(N-I)\vartheta_n\vartheta_{n-1}\ldots\vartheta_1}_{\Omega\vartheta_n\vartheta_{n-1}\ldots\vartheta_1}$$

$$(5.26)$$

Therefore, it is possible for the analyst to evaluate the joint economic actions of the 'own indirect multiplier effects' with the assistance of the following decomposition

$$(I-A)^{-1}-I \qquad = \vartheta_1+(\vartheta_2-I).\vartheta_1+(\vartheta_3-I).\vartheta_2.\vartheta_1+\ldots+(\vartheta_n-I).\vartheta_{n-1}\ldots\vartheta_1+(\Omega-I).\vartheta_n\ldots\vartheta_1$$

$$(I-A)^{-1}-\vartheta_1 \qquad = \qquad (\vartheta_2-I).\vartheta_1+(\vartheta_3-I).\vartheta_2.\vartheta_1+\ldots+(\vartheta_n-I).\vartheta_{n-1}\ldots\vartheta_1+(\Omega-I).\vartheta_n\ldots\vartheta_1$$

$$(I-A)^{-1}-\vartheta_2\vartheta_1 \qquad = \qquad (\vartheta_3-I).\vartheta_2.\vartheta_1+\ldots+(\vartheta_n-I).\vartheta_{n-1}\ldots\vartheta_1+(\Omega-I).\vartheta_n\ldots\vartheta_1$$

$$(I-A)^{-1}-\vartheta_n\vartheta_{n-1}\ldots\vartheta_1 = \qquad (\Omega-I).\vartheta_n\ldots\vartheta_1$$

$$(5.27)$$

These formulae represent, in an explicit form, the accumulation of the 'own indirect multiplier effects' within an economy. Furthermore, the matrix $(\Omega - I)$ represents the accumulation of all synergic cross interactions created by the self-influence effects.

Superposition principle

While the first two methods operate on the coefficients and associated inverse matrices, the superposition principle draws attention to the nature and strength of the transactions flows; these flows are interpreted hierarchically in an analogous fashion to the Matrioshka principle. The superposition principle (see Sonis, 1980, 1982, 1985, 1986; Sonis and Hewings, 1988) examines the degree to which the structure of flows might be decomposed into a set of subflows, each acting according to some extreme tendencies. In very simple systems of flows, a few of these extreme tendencies will account for a large percentage of the flows; as systems become more complex, the extreme tendencies will only be able to account for a portion of the flows. These portions or weights may be considered as analogous to weights in a multi-objective programming context; the decomposition proceeds hierarchically, with the most important flows extracted first. This method differs from the Matrioshka principle in that the slicing takes place at one level in the system, whereas the Matrioshka principle slices at one level, moves to the next (usually more disaggregated) level and proceeds to invoke the same slicing rules. However, both methods revolve around the identification of dominant flows in the system.

Essentially, the system of flows appears in the following form

$$T = p_1 T_1 + p_2 T_2 + \ldots + p_k T_k \qquad (5.28)$$

where

$$0 \leq p_i \leq 1; p_1 + p_2 + \ldots + p_k = 1$$

In this decomposition, only one non-zero element appears in each column; the largest flow is identified in each column and a coefficient calculated by taking this flow and dividing it by its column sum (intermediate transactions only). In a simple flow matrix with only one transaction per column, all the coefficients would be one and the value of p_1 would be 1. The hierarchy would be a simple structure with only one slice needed to reveal the complete set of connections. Since this is rarely the case, the identification of only one flow per column generally provides only a partial picture of the total flows; the minimum value of the coefficients just calculated becomes the value of p_1. For at least one column (i, j), this accounts for all the flows between i and j; for the other columns, it presents only a portion of the flows. The entries in matrix T_1 are the largest flows for each column; the product $p_1 T_1$ provides an indication of the degree to which these n flows (in an $n \times n$ matrix) can be considered as the 'most important' or dominant in the system. Note that importance here has a very different connotation from the one used in the development of analytically important coefficients in the field of influence approach. The partial set of flows derived from $p_1 T_1$ is now removed from T and the procedure continues to extract the second level in the hierarchy of flows.

In many cases, k^* levels $(k^* < k)$ will account for a large percentage of the flows; thus, the procedure may also be used as an approximation for the complete set of transactions (see Hewings et al., 1989).

3 Empirical interpretation

The Bangladesh interregional social accounting matrix (BIRSAM)

The Bangladesh Interregional Social Accounting Matrix (BIRSAM) was developed by Jahan and Hewings (1990); it is a partial survey-based system, relying on the 1976–7 national social accounts augmented with regional data. Four regions, Dhaka, Chittagong, Rajshahi and Khulna, are identified; these are shown in figure 5.1. For each region, a familiar three-fold division of the economy was made into factors, institutions and activities. Initially, in the complete 62×62 BIRSAM public capital was included in

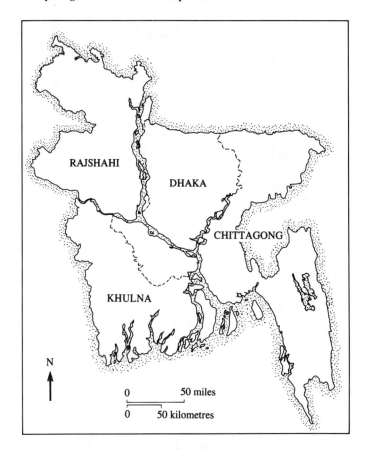

Figure 5.1 The four regions of Bangladesh

the endogenous part of the matrix. However, because it was associated with the exogenous accounts of government, it was excluded since its presence resulted in a null column vector. Two factors and three types of households[4] (institutions) are identified and there are nine activities in the full presentation of the model; the aggregated version is shown in table 5.1. Government and external accounts comprise the rest of the system; for the purposes of this analysis, these were regarded as exogenous to the system.

The fields of influence

Essentially, the field of influence decomposition attempts to extract the set of analytically important coefficients, coefficients whose change or

---

[4] Households were categorised on the basis of income as lower, middle and upper.

Table 5.1 *The aggregated Bangladesh interregional social accounting matrix (BIRSAM)*

		DHAKA			CHITT			RAJSH			KHULNA			Govmt	Other	TOTAL
		Activ	Factors	Hholds	Activ	Factors	Hholds	Activ	Factors	Hholds	Activ	Factors	Hholds			
DHAKA	Activities	7134	0	6944	6132	0	7436	2693	0	6242	2282	0	4937	2780	5798	52378
	Factors	14632	0	66	5315	0	0	3735	0	0	3186	0	0	0	0	26934
	Households	0	24903	0	0	0	0	0	0	0	0	0	0	600	195	25698
CHITT	Activities	6221	0	7699	8845	0	8175	3073	0	6960	2601	0	5495	2415	6409	57892
	Factors	5332	0	0	16216	0	57	3845	0	0	3293	0	0	0	0	28743
	Households	0	0	0	0	26678	0	0	0	0	0	0	0	370	103	27151
RAJSH	Activities	3129	0	5766	3590	0	5794	3192	0	5089	1282	0	4099	2222	3874	38037
	Factors	3770	0	0	3863	0	0	13530	0	53	2615	0	0	0	0	23831
	Households	0	0	0	0	0	0	0	22816	0	0	0	0	260	60	23136
KHULNA	Activities	2580	0	4477	2966	0	4689	1282	0	4055	2362	0	3256	1852	3215	30736
	Factors	3133	0	0	3189	0	0	2522	0	0	10225	0	44	0	0	19113
	Households	0	0	0	0	0	0	0	0	0	0	18063	0	272	72	18407
	Government	2526	2031	707	3055	2065	775	912	1015	561	797	1050	439	850	0	16783
	Other	3921	0	40	4721	0	226	3253	0	175	2092	0	137	5162	0	19727
	Total	52378	26934	25698	57892	28743	27151	38037	23831	23136	30736	19113	18407	16783	19727	408566

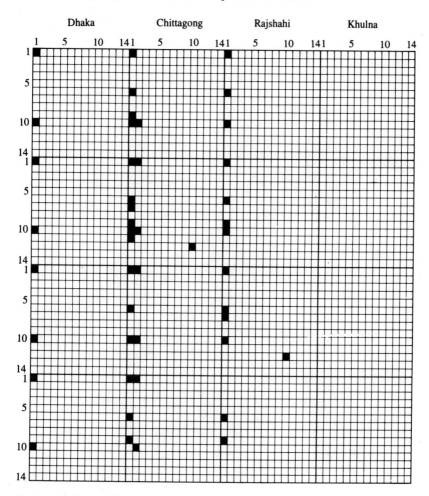

Figure 5.2 The top fifty single-element fields of influence: Bangladesh interregional social accounting matrix

influence can be shown to have more important implications system wide.[5] Figures 5.2 and 5.3 show the location of the fifty most important elements (single fields) or synergic, two-element fields. The number chosen for display is somewhat arbitrary; prior research by Bullard and Sebald (1977, 1988), Hewings *et al.* (1989) and West and Jensen (1980) has suggested that between 5 per cent and 20 per cent of the coefficients in a matrix may be

[5] This does not imply that the field of influence must be spread throughout the system; for some coefficients, the effects of change will be very heavily concentrated while others will have smaller, but more diffused effects. At the present time, the methodology does not provide for a typology of field types.

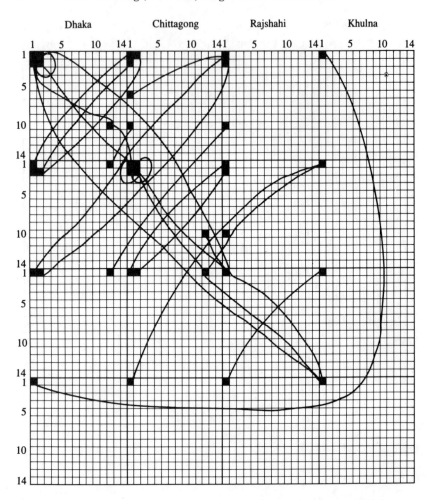

Figure 5.3 The top fifty two-element fields of influence; Bangladesh interregional social accounting matrix

regarded as analytically important. Zero elements in the original matrix were excluded; while a zero element in the input–output table might reflect a non-zero flow that was smaller than the minimum size shown, many of the zero cells in the social accounting system are that way by definition. Hence, to avoid confusion, all zero cells were ignored.

The dominant roles that agriculture, and labour as a factor of production, play in this economy are revealed by these two figures; with only two exceptions in figure 5.2, all the top fifty elements involve purchases and/or sales relationships with one or both of these two sectors. Chittagong's dominant role in the regional system is also revealed; thirty-six of the top fifty cells are located within the region or indicate flows into or out of the region.

A complementary perspective is provided by the synergic fields of influence; while agriculture and labour are once again dominant, note the strong interaction between agriculture and industry within and between Dhaka and Chittagong and between these two regions and agriculture in the other two regions. This result is consistent with the findings in Jahan and Hewings (1990); there it was shown that the interregional effects of change in agriculture are broadly diffused throughout the economy, although the volume of flows still favoured Dhaka and Chittagong.

Structural path analysis

The application of the Pyatt–Round or Sonis–Hewings decompositions requires a choice to be made; in Sonis, Hewings and Lee (1993), the decompositions of this kind were applied to an aggregated BIRSAM in which all sectors were aggregated into one activity, one institution and one factor. In the case of the fifty-six sector BIRSAM, these decompositions can be applied to any one representative regional SAM separately or up to three regional SAMs within the interregional context. An alternative perspective, one that uses the whole system at a disaggregated level, is provided by structural path analysis. Here, we may focus on a decomposition that provides an analytical framework for identifying important interactions that originate in specific sectors in one region and terminate with a specific sector in the same or another region.

The basic difference between the additive and multiplicative decompositions and structural path analysis is that the former are matrix oriented while the latter are vector oriented. One major problem, however, is that there are a very large number of paths that have to be identified; illustrating them in a summary form would be very difficult. Instead, an illustration of a form in which the relationships can be presented will be provided. While the field of influence approach in its synergic form can identify sets of cells whose interaction is deemed analytically important, no information is provided on the paths across which these interactions move. Figures 5.4 and 5.5 and table 5.2 reveal the ways in which consumption by the upper income group in Khulna affects agriculture in Dhaka and vice versa. The structural path analysis reveals a complex of interactions via trade activities in each region; in addition, there is a feedback loop reflecting the purchases of Dhaka agriculture by Khulna upper-income households.

Figure 5.5 reveals the complex set of paths through which the latter influence travels. Consider one path: consumption by upper-income groups in Khulna of Khulna agriculture leads to labour income, part of which accrues to middle-income households who then consume Dhaka agricul-

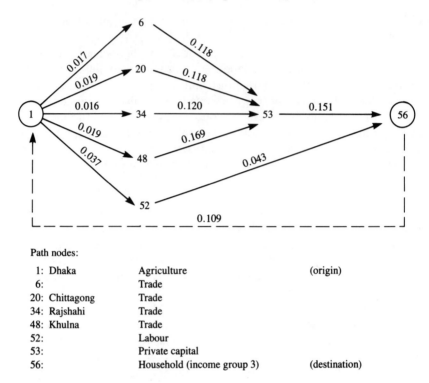

Path nodes:

1: Dhaka	Agriculture	(origin)
6:	Trade	
20: Chittagong	Trade	
34: Rajshahi	Trade	
48: Khulna	Trade	
52:	Labour	
53:	Private capital	
56:	Household (income group 3)	(destination)

Figure 5.4 Structural path analysis from origin 1 to destination 56

ture. Thus, local (intra-Khulna) consumption of agriculture leads to output increasing in Dhaka – not through the normal interindustry linkages, but rather through factors, institutions and then activities. While the direct influence of upper-income consumption on Dhaka accounts for 33.7 per cent of the global influence, the indirect paths through sectors 15 (Chittagong agriculture), 29 (Rajshahi agriculture) and 43 (Khulna agriculture) account for an additional 12 per cent. Note that at each bifurcation, the number of paths increases; however, since the influence is a multiplicative function of the direct coefficients, the number of significant paths (influence greater than 1 per cent) of link-length greater than four is likely to be very small. However, the structural interrelationships that characterise a SAM often result in some paths of length 2 and 3 being insignificant (see table 5.2 and note that the paths $\{i \rightarrow k_1 \rightarrow j\}$ and $\{i \rightarrow k_1 \rightarrow k_2 \rightarrow j\}$ bear this out).

Hierarchical decompositions

The two hierarchical decompositions, the superposition and Matrioshka, will be considered together. The superposition 'slices' the set of flows into a

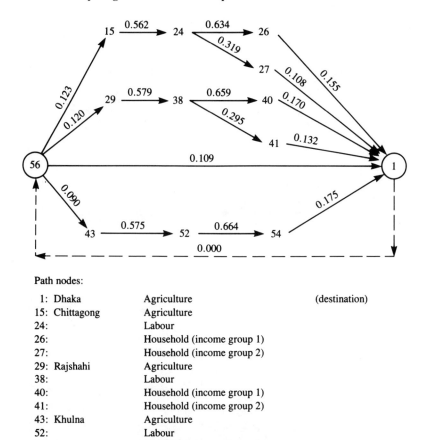

Path nodes:

  1: Dhaka   Agriculture   (destination)
 15: Chittagong   Agriculture
 24:                  Labour
 26:                  Household (income group 1)
 27:                  Household (income group 2)
 29: Rajshahi   Agriculture
 38:                  Labour
 40:                  Household (income group 1)
 41:                  Household (income group 2)
 43: Khulna   Agriculture
 52:                  Labour
 54:                  Household (income group 1)
 56:                  Household (income group 3)   (origin)

Figure 5.5 Structural path analysis from origin 56 to destination 1 (no feedback loop)

set of n (n = size of the matrix) at each level, with each level accounting for a smaller percentage of the total volume of flows than the previous one. Figure 5.6 shows the cumulative volume of flows for successive levels for the disaggregated and aggregated BIRSAM. As Elhance (1992) has noted, the procedure is sensitive to aggregation levels; in addition, it is also sensitive to the complexity of the economy presented. The combination of these two factors makes comparative analysis across economies difficult (unless similar aggregations and sector definitions are used).

The results for the decomposition for the aggregated (14×14) and disaggregated (56×56) social accounting matrices are presented in figure 5.6. For the aggregated SAM, the first tendency accounts for 30.8 per cent

Table 5.2 *Structural path analysis for two selected paths*

Path Node: Origin, 1; Destination, 56	Direct influence (A)	Path multiplier (B)	Total influence (C = B × A)	$D = \dfrac{C}{\text{Global Influence}}$
1 → 56	0.0000		0.0000	9.11%
1 → 52 → 56	0.0016	2.3334	0.0037	1.48%
1 → 6 → 53 → 56	0.0003	1.9827	0.0005	1.68%
1 → 20 → 53 → 56	0.0003	1.9927	0.0007	1.37%
1 → 34 → 53 → 56	0.0003	1.9778	0.0005	1.04%
1 → 48 → 53 → 56	0.0002	1.9628	0.0004	insignificant
$i \rightarrow k_1 \rightarrow k_2 \rightarrow k_3 \rightarrow j$				

Path Node: Origin, 56; Destination, 1	Direct Influence (A)	Path Multiplier (B)	Total Influence (C = B × A)	$D = \dfrac{C}{\text{Global Influence}}$
56 → 1	0.1091	1.8069	0.1971	33.72%
$i \rightarrow k_1 \rightarrow j$				insignificant
$i \rightarrow k_1 \rightarrow k_2 \rightarrow j$				insignificant
56 → 15 → 24 → 26 → 1	0.0068	3.0924	0.0211	3.61%
56 → 15 → 24 → 27 → 1	0.0024	3.1110	0.0074	1.27%
56 → 29 → 38 → 40 → 1	0.0078	3.0064	0.0236	4.04%
56 → 29 → 38 → 41 → 1	0.0027	3.0164	0.0082	1.40%
56 → 43 → 52 → 54 → 1	0.0060	2.7740	0.0168	2.87%

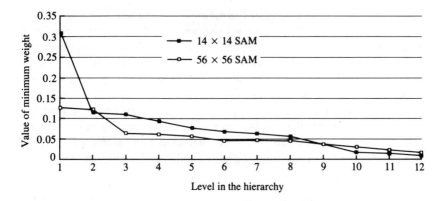

	14 × 14 SAM		56 × 56 SAM	
Level	Value of p	Cumulative	Value of p	Cumulative
		value		value
1	0.308	0.308	0.126	0.126
2	0.113	0.421	0.122	0.248
3	0.110	0.531	0.064	0.312
4	0.093	0.624	0.062	0.374
5	0.077	0.701	0.057	0.431
6	0.068	0.769	0.047	0.478
7	0.063	0.832	0.047	0.525
8	0.056	0.888	0.046	0.571
9	0.037	0.925	0.037	0.608
10	0.018	0.943	0.031	0.639
11	0.015	0.958	0.024	0.663
12	0.010	0.968	0.018	0.681

Figure 5.6 Decomposition of flows according to the decomposition principle for two different levels of aggregation

of the interactions, the top two tendencies cover 42.1 per cent while the top five levels account for 70.1 per cent. Additional levels reveal less and less about the structure of the flows. The effect of disaggregation produces a cumulative weight that increases more slowly; the first five levels now account for only 43 per cent. In both cases, the most important feature of the dominance of the Dhaka region lies in its relationships with other regions.

The Matrioshka principle combines some of the features of the superposition (hierarchical slicing) with the additive and multiplicative decompositions described earlier. One of the major advantages of this approach is that it can be extended to the r-region case and avoids some of the problems noted by Round (1985) in extending the Pyatt-Round decomposition beyond three regions. However, the block-permutation structure properties exploited by Pyatt and Round (1979) are also used here. In the first stage, the Matrioshka uses an additive decomposition $(T = T_1 + T_2 + \ldots + T_n)$ and then solves the non-uniqueness of the multiplier decomposition through a hierarchical stepwise approach in the second stage. In the extreme case, each cell in the 56×56 BIRSAM can be treated as block permutation matrix containing only this cell. In this case, the multiplier could be decomposed into

$$(I - A)^{-1} = \Omega_{56}^{-1} \vartheta_{56} \vartheta_{55} \ldots \vartheta_1 \tag{5.29}$$

The procedure can be illustrated by an application at the four-region level

$$(I - A)^{-1} = \Omega_4^{-1} \vartheta_4 \vartheta_3 \vartheta_2 \vartheta_1 \tag{5.30}$$

where the $\vartheta_r s$ are the block-diagonal matrices representing the own indirect multiplier effects and the matrix $\Omega = \Omega_4^{-1}$ reflects the cross effects. The dimension of A is 56×56 and each block of submatrices $A_{ij} (i,j = 1, \ldots, 4)$ has a dimension of 14×14 (nine activities, two factors and three households). Thus A takes the form

$$\begin{bmatrix} A_{11} & A_{12} & A_{13} & A_{14} \\ A_{21} & A_{22} & A_{23} & A_{24} \\ A_{31} & A_{32} & A_{33} & A_{34} \\ A_{41} & A_{42} & A_{43} & A_{44} \end{bmatrix}$$

Recall that, in the first stage, the additive decomposition provides for a successive ranking of flows with the highest transaction intensities to obtain T_1, T_2, T_3 and T_4 as follows

$$T_1 = \begin{bmatrix} A_{11} & 0 & 0 & 0 \\ 0 & A_{22} & 0 & 0 \\ 0 & 0 & A_{33} & 0 \\ 0 & 0 & 0 & A_{44} \end{bmatrix} \qquad T_2 = \begin{bmatrix} 0 & A_{12} & 0 & 0 \\ A_{21} & 0 & 0 & 0 \\ 0 & 0 & 0 & A_{34} \\ 0 & 0 & A_{43} & 0 \end{bmatrix}$$

Weight (0.4256)   Weight (0.1921)

$$T_3 = \begin{bmatrix} 0 & 0 & A_{13} & 0 \\ 0 & 0 & 0 & A_{24} \\ A_{31} & 0 & 0 & 0 \\ 0 & A_{42} & 0 & 0 \end{bmatrix} \qquad T_4 = \begin{bmatrix} 0 & 0 & 0 & A_{14} \\ 0 & 0 & A_{23} & 0 \\ 0 & A_{32} & 0 & 0 \\ A_{41} & 0 & 0 & 0 \end{bmatrix}$$

Weight (0.1916)   Weight (0.1907)

Tables 5.3, 5.4, 5.5 and 5.6 reveal some of the properties of selected submatrices derived from the Matrioshka decomposition, focussing in on the Dhaka region. Table 5.3 shows the own effects submatrix, derived from the product $(\vartheta_4\vartheta_3\vartheta_2\vartheta_1)_{11}$ while table 5.4 contains the cross effects submatrix, $(\mathbf{\Omega} - \mathbf{I})_{11}$. The most interesting finding here is that the biggest elements of the block $(\mathbf{\Omega} - \mathbf{I})_{11}$, those greater than 0.1, lie in the rows 1, 2, 10 and 12, corresponding to the synergic effects in agriculture and industrial activities, in labour factors and in the lower-income households. Tables 5.5 and 5.6 compare the isolated (no feedback) matrix multiplier for the Dhaka region $(\vartheta_1)_{11}$ with the full interregional multiplier $(\mathbf{\Omega}\vartheta_4\vartheta_3\vartheta_2\vartheta_1)_{11}$. The data provide substantial corroboration of the presence of feedback effects, but, unlike those first articulated by Miller (1966, 1969), these feedback effects include those generated on all accounts, and are not confined to pure interindustry relationships. By inspecting comparable entries in tables 5.3 to 5.6, we can begin to gain an idea of the magnitude of the various contributions made to the 'partial' equilibrium and 'full' equilibrium multiplier. For example, the isolated intra-sectoral multiplier for agriculture is 1.2018; the cross effects provide 1.0840 while including the own-region effects (table 5.3) raises the multiplier to 1.3881 with the interaction between these two effects producing the final result of 1.7743.[6]

Similarly large differences between the isolated and full matrices are found in the rest of the system; note, in particular, the way in which the inter-relational income multipliers within the household submatrix (the bottom right-hand 3×3 submatrix) change. As one would expect, the larger multipliers are associated with the higher-income groups but, in addition, row 12 reveals that income changes in the lower- and middle-income groups contribute substantially to the upper-income group while the reverse is certainly not true for the impact of the upper-income group on the lower one.

Furthermore, the formulae exemplified in (5.29) and (5.30) allow for the analysis of the accumulation of the effects of the economic self influence associated with the block-diagonal matrices $\vartheta_1, \vartheta_2, \ldots, \vartheta_n$ and their superpositions of the type $\vartheta_2\vartheta_1, \vartheta_3\vartheta_2\vartheta_1, \ldots, \vartheta_n\vartheta_{n-1}, \ldots, \vartheta_1$. For example, table 5.7 shows the block.

$$\left[(\mathbf{I} - \mathbf{A})^{-1} - \vartheta_1\right]_{11}$$

This block incorporates the effects of all interregional self-influence effects that remain after the intra-regional self-influence effects have been excluded. One of the most striking results is the appearance of a relatively homogeneous pattern of interregional flows. The columns in this block are

---

[6] Of course, the entry of 1.7743 is obtained from the multiplication of the appropriate two vectors from tables 5.4 and 5.5 and not just the product of 1.0840 and 1.3881.

Table 5.3 *Own effects submatrix from the product* $(\vartheta_4\vartheta_3\vartheta_2\vartheta_1)_{11}$: *Dhaka region*

1.3881	0.1877	0.2270	0.0925	0.1891	0.2725	0.2624	0.1117	0.2641	0.3700	0.3634	0.3882	0.3387	0.3067
0.2203	1.2192	0.4170	0.2815	0.2067	0.1904	0.2501	0.1169	0.2008	0.2445	0.2423	0.2507	0.2372	0.1956
0.0052	0.0025	1.0040	0.0185	0.0057	0.0058	0.0110	0.0086	0.0264	0.0060	0.0064	0.0050	0.0081	0.0064
0.0024	0.0045	0.0031	1.0420	0.0027	0.0033	0.0060	0.0080	0.0026	0.0024	0.0025	0.0022	0.0028	0.0033
0.0342	0.0255	0.0235	0.0288	1.0293	0.0256	0.0464	0.0181	0.0260	0.0323	0.0342	0.0271	0.0419	0.0453
0.0496	0.0549	0.0414	0.0244	0.0248	1.0247	0.0290	0.0151	0.0254	0.0375	0.0369	0.0390	0.0351	0.0304
0.0041	0.0130	0.0049	0.0199	0.0046	0.0097	1.0289	0.0570	0.0032	0.0034	0.0034	0.0034	0.0033	0.0037
0.0032	0.0021	0.0024	0.0066	0.0056	0.0047	0.0081	1.0167	0.0055	0.0036	0.0040	0.0023	0.0043	0.0195
0.0656	0.0303	0.0373	0.0211	0.0445	0.0678	0.0533	0.0230	1.0605	0.0799	0.0842	0.0681	0.1049	0.0795
0.8700	0.1937	0.2616	0.1068	0.2717	0.2747	0.4208	0.1824	0.2594	1.2999	0.2973	0.3071	0.2886	0.2671
0.0700	0.0619	0.0612	0.0297	0.0945	0.2166	0.0504	0.0219	0.2393	0.0714	1.0744	0.0633	0.0888	0.0704
0.6066	0.1596	0.2036	0.0857	0.2279	0.2945	0.3021	0.1310	0.2964	0.8888	0.7634	1.2345	0.2359	0.2121
0.2982	0.0859	0.1066	0.0455	0.1237	0.1762	0.1512	0.0656	0.1810	0.4315	0.5450	0.1215	1.1266	0.1121
0.0353	0.0101	0.0126	0.0054	0.0146	0.0206	0.0179	0.0077	0.0212	0.0511	0.0634	0.0143	0.0149	1.0132

Table 5.4 Cross effects for the submatrix $(\Omega - I)_{11}$: Dhaka region

1.0840	0.1351	0.1682	0.0722	0.1425	0.2261	0.2003	0.0738	0.2110	0.0000	0.0000	0.2228	0.2206	0.1944
0.0637	1.1020	0.1293	0.0576	0.1093	0.1735	0.1539	0.0567	0.1626	0.0000	0.0000	0.1691	0.1672	0.1473
0.0018	0.0028	1.0036	0.0015	0.0031	0.0052	0.0044	0.0016	0.0048	0.0000	0.0000	0.0047	0.0045	0.0040
0.0008	0.0012	0.0016	1.0009	0.0013	0.0021	0.0019	0.0007	0.0020	0.0000	0.0000	0.0020	0.0020	0.0018
0.0090	0.0144	0.0182	0.0078	1.0155	0.0247	0.0218	0.0080	0.0230	0.0000	0.0000	0.0237	0.0234	0.0206
0.0124	0.0194	0.0254	0.0112	0.0217	1.0346	0.0307	0.0113	0.0325	0.0000	0.0000	0.0323	0.0315	0.0278
0.0009	0.0014	0.0018	0.0008	0.0015	0.0024	1.0021	0.0008	0.0023	0.0000	0.0000	0.0024	0.0023	0.0020
0.0009	0.0015	0.0019	0.0008	0.0016	0.0026	0.0022	1.0008	0.0024	0.0000	0.0000	0.0025	0.0025	0.0022
0.0176	0.0283	0.0349	0.0148	0.0295	0.0469	0.0416	0.0153	1.0437	0.0000	0.0000	0.0466	0.0463	0.0407
0.0791	0.1263	0.1606	0.0688	0.1362	0.2171	0.1917	0.0706	0.2025	1.0000	0.0000	0.2095	0.2057	0.1813
0.0249	0.0403	0.0527	0.0227	0.0437	0.0697	0.0611	0.0225	0.0648	0.0000	1.0000	0.0673	0.0649	0.0572
0.0650	0.1040	0.1330	0.0571	0.1123	0.1790	0.1578	0.0581	0.1669	0.0000	0.0000	1.1727	0.1690	0.1490
0.0349	0.0560	0.0718	0.0308	0.0605	0.0964	0.0850	0.0313	0.0899	0.0000	0.0000	0.0931	1.0909	0.0801
0.0041	0.0060	0.0085	0.0036	0.0071	0.0114	0.0100	0.0037	0.0106	0.0000	0.0000	0.0110	0.0107	1.0094

Table 5.5 Single region (no feedbacks) multiplier matrix $(\vartheta_1)_{11}$: Dhaka region

1.2018	0.0669	0.0583	0.0139	0.0355	0.0432	0.0483	0.0197	0.0461	0.1848	0.1793	0.2001	0.1571	0.1459
0.0802	1.1165	0.2655	0.1804	0.0898	0.0361	0.0919	0.0476	0.0406	0.0995	0.0978	0.1045	0.0928	0.0677
0.0010	0.0003	1.0015	0.0164	0.0030	0.0018	0.0076	0.0071	0.0228	0.0011	0.0012	0.0008	0.0017	0.0013
0.0008	0.0028	0.0007	1.0378	0.0012	0.0017	0.0041	0.0071	0.0010	0.0007	0.0008	0.0004	0.0011	0.0017
0.0145	0.0117	0.0042	0.0186	1.0137	0.0033	0.0261	0.0093	0.0045	0.0113	0.0133	0.0057	0.0213	0.0270
0.0226	0.0342	0.0089	0.0056	0.0050	1.0018	0.0036	0.0039	0.0024	0.0061	0.0060	0.0065	0.0055	0.0046
0.0022	0.0116	0.0028	0.0186	0.0030	0.0075	1.0267	0.0560	0.0010	0.0013	0.0013	0.0013	0.0013	0.0019
0.0012	0.0007	0.0006	0.0057	0.0039	0.0019	0.0060	1.0156	0.0028	0.0015	0.0019	0.0003	0.0021	0.0173
0.0270	0.0051	0.0050	0.0068	0.0121	0.0165	0.0094	0.0041	1.0125	0.0422	0.0467	0.0301	0.0675	0.0464
0.6937	0.0744	0.1042	0.0261	0.1390	0.0906	0.2385	0.1036	0.0789	1.1148	0.1127	0.1204	0.1045	0.1006
0.0104	0.0172	0.0173	0.0050	0.0581	0.1698	0.0047	0.0024	0.1945	0.0106	1.0115	0.0081	0.0158	0.0117
0.4596	0.0578	0.0774	0.0197	0.1217	0.1492	0.1586	0.0691	0.1546	0.7353	0.6092	1.0831	0.0768	0.0720
0.2186	0.0302	0.0395	0.0102	0.0674	0.0996	0.0756	0.0330	0.1064	0.3487	0.4614	0.0406	0.0389	0.0360
0.0259	0.0036	0.0047	0.0012	0.0079	0.0116	0.0090	0.0039	0.0124	0.0413	0.0536	0.0048	0.0046	1.0043

Table 5.6 Interregional multiplier matrix $(\Omega\vartheta_4\vartheta_3\vartheta_2\vartheta_1)_{11}$: Dhaka region

1.7743	0.4506	0.5646	0.2653	0.4779	0.6828	0.6558	0.2814	0.6624	0.7693	0.7625	0.7883	0.7418	0.6614
0.5134	1.4183	0.6748	0.4158	0.4271	0.5037	0.5506	0.2465	0.5057	0.5477	0.5453	0.5544	0.5432	0.4648
0.0133	0.0080	1.0111	0.0221	0.0119	0.0148	0.0195	0.0123	0.0351	0.0144	0.0148	0.0135	0.0165	0.0138
0.0059	0.0069	0.0063	1.0438	0.0054	0.0070	0.0096	0.0095	0.0063	0.0061	0.0062	0.0059	0.0065	0.0065
0.0755	0.0535	0.0597	0.0474	1.0604	0.0700	0.0889	0.0364	0.0691	0.0749	0.0768	0.0698	0.0848	0.0831
0.1060	0.0931	0.0915	0.0503	0.0678	1.0861	0.0879	0.0405	0.0853	0.0955	0.0949	0.0973	0.0933	0.0817
0.0082	0.0158	0.0085	0.0218	0.0077	0.0141	1.0330	0.0588	0.0075	0.0076	0.0076	0.0076	0.0076	0.0074
0.0076	0.0051	0.0062	0.0086	0.0088	0.0093	0.0125	1.0186	0.0100	0.0081	0.0085	0.0068	0.0089	0.0235
0.1464	0.0852	0.1076	0.0570	0.1046	0.1533	0.1352	0.0583	1.1433	0.1634	0.1676	0.1517	0.1893	0.1537
1.2332	0.4404	0.5813	0.2705	0.5456	0.6650	0.7941	0.3434	0.6380	1.6750	0.6720	0.6834	0.6662	0.5994
0.1855	0.1406	0.1646	0.0827	0.1821	0.3415	0.1694	0.0732	0.3603	0.1911	1.1938	0.1838	0.2085	0.1757
0.9054	0.3627	0.4677	0.2209	0.4535	0.6161	0.6095	0.2635	0.6083	1.1976	1.0718	1.5446	0.5464	0.4854
0.4590	0.1953	0.2489	0.1184	0.2453	0.3494	0.3167	0.1369	0.3489	0.5978	0.7110	0.2885	1.2936	0.2592
0.0542	0.0230	0.0293	0.0139	0.0289	0.0410	0.0374	0.0161	0.0410	0.0707	0.0829	0.0340	0.0346	1.0305

Table 5.7 *The interregional self-influence matrix*

0.5726	0.3837	0.5063	0.2514	0.4424	0.6396	0.6075	0.2617	0.6163	0.5845	0.5832	0.5882	0.5847	0.5155
0.4332	0.3018	0.4093	0.2354	0.3373	0.4676	0.4587	0.1989	0.4651	0.4482	0.4475	0.4499	0.4504	0.3189
0.0123	0.0770	0.0096	0.0570	0.0890	0.0130	0.0119	0.0052	0.0123	0.0133	0.0136	0.0127	0.0148	0.0125
0.0051	0.0041	0.0056	0.0060	0.0042	0.0053	0.0045	0.0024	0.0053	0.0054	0.0054	0.0055	0.0054	0.0048
0.0610	0.4180	0.0555	0.0288	0.0467	0.0667	0.0628	0.0271	0.0646	0.0636	0.0635	0.0641	0.0635	0.0561
0.0834	0.0589	0.0826	0.0447	0.0628	0.0843	0.0843	0.0366	0.0829	0.0894	0.0889	0.0908	0.0878	0.0771
0.0060	0.0042	0.0057	0.0032	0.0047	0.0066	0.0063	0.0028	0.0065	0.0063	0.0063	0.0063	0.0063	0.0055
0.0064	0.0044	0.0056	0.0029	0.0049	0.0074	0.0065	0.0030	0.0072	0.0066	0.0066	0.0065	0.0068	0.0062
0.1194	0.0801	0.1026	0.0502	0.0925	0.1368	0.1258	0.0542	0.1308	0.1212	0.1209	0.1216	0.1218	0.1073
0.5395	0.3660	0.4771	0.2441	0.4066	0.5744	0.5556	0.2398	0.5591	0.5601	0.5593	0.5630	0.5617	0.4988
0.1751	0.1234	0.1473	0.0777	0.1240	0.1717	0.1647	0.0708	0.1657	0.1805	0.1823	0.1757	0.1927	0.1640
0.4458	0.3049	0.3903	0.2012	0.3378	0.4669	0.4509	0.1944	0.4537	0.4623	0.4626	0.4615	0.4696	0.4134
0.2404	0.1651	0.2094	0.1082	0.1779	0.2498	0.2411	0.1039	0.2425	0.2491	0.2496	0.2479	0.2547	0.2232
0.0283	0.0194	0.0246	0.0127	0.0210	0.0294	0.0284	0.0122	0.0286	0.0294	0.0293	0.0292	0.0300	0.0262

almost proportional to each other; in fact, the ratio of the maximum-to-minimum value is contained within the bound

$$2.35 \leq \max_j b_{ij} / \min_j b_{ij} \leq 2.85$$

with the average ratio of 2.51. Thus, when one abstracts the intra-regional effects, the remaining pattern of interregional self-influence loops reveals a pattern that is relatively unvarying across space.

4 Conclusions

The insights provided by the application of these alternative decompositions to the social accounting systems are not directly comparable, this in part reflecting the differences inherent in the algorithms associated with each decomposition. These differences may be interpreted in the following light: consider that the social accounting system may be viewed at a variety of scales, ranging from micro, to meso and macro levels.

Structural path analysis represents an approach that reveals the micro-level structure of transmission of influence through its articulation of the myriad patterns of linkages and ripple effects associated with the set of elementary paths. The basis for this perspective is provided by analysis of the direct input coefficients; in view of the multiplicity of paths that can be identified, only a small number can be studied and compared. Hence, this perspective is very much a micro-level one and enables detailed interpretation of specific paths of action, reaction and influence within an economy. In the case of changes in the direct input coefficients, all possible combinations of changes move through the same structural path. As a result, it would be difficult to analyse changes within the framework of structural path analysis since the combinations of synergic impacts of different changes, manifested in the paths, would be numerically very small.

The field of influence approach seeks to avoid this difficulty by considering the changes in the multitude of elementary paths considered together. In essence, it may be considered as a meso-level approach, considering the complete set of paths between any two sectors. Direct comparison between the structural path analysis and the field of influence approach is not possible because of the nature of the differences in the algorithms; however, they are close in spirit in conceptual terms, both seeking to uncover the direction and magnitude of influence. The superposition and Matrioshka principles operate at the macro level and reveal the hierarchy of interactions of the different sub-structures. Attention is focussed on dominant transactions flows rather than specific $i \rightarrow j$ paths. The superposition principle seeks to uncover a hierarchical complexity in a sequential fashion as a guide to a determination of the sophistication of the economic system (in the context of some supposed evolutionary process in which economies are assumed to become more complex with increasing development – see Hewings *et al.* 1989, 1990). On the other hand, the Matrioshka principle identifies what may be referred to as the socio-spatial economic structure through the identification of a hierarchical structure of feedback loop effects.

The important part of these principles is the ability to reveal, through the Leontief inverse, in both multiplicative and additive forms, different insights into structure and economic influence. Viewed from this perspective, the alternative decompositions illustrated in this chapter may be considered to represent different complementary perspectives of micro, meso and macro levels of economic analysis. No one method is likely to prove to be sufficient for a complete analysis; each of them reveals a dimension that the others cannot claim to provide.

The essential fragments of the Bangladesh economy can be presented

now. At the micro level, the important interdependencies between agriculture in one region and consumption in another region are revealed, notwithstanding the fact that the direct influence is zero. Here, the analysis reveals a complex path of reaction through trade, labour and private capital. At the meso level, the dominant role of agriculture and labour is underlined by the first-order fields of influence. Synergic fields of influence further reinforce these links to which should be added the strong interactions between agriculture and industry within and between Dhaka and Chittagong. Finally, at the macro level, the Matrioshka principle reveals a hierarchy of pair-wise feedback loops of economic self-influence. Again, the important synergic interaction between agriculture, industry, labour and low-income households in the Dhaka region is revealed. From this perspective, the superposition principle suggests an economy dominated by relatively few large interactions.

The picture that results is consistent; movement across the scales of analysis provides for finer focus or a more aggregate perspective but the resulting patterns appear to be mutually reinforcing. These procedures should prove to be of value in assisting with the formulation and evaluation of policy analysis. Furthermore, they provide the basis for considered attention to the elements that should be updated on a regular basis. Finally, it should be noted that there is scope for more sophisticated decomposition of changes, should a time series of social accounting matrices become available, complementing and extending some of the ideas suggested by Feldman *et al.* (1987).

6 Decompositions of regional input–output tables

JOHN H.LL. DEWHURST AND RODNEY C. JENSEN

1 Introduction

An input–output table is a representation of the production side of an economy; it provides a picture or numerical description of the size and structure of that economy in terms of interactions among producing and consuming components. Probably the most detailed and accessible source of data on economic transactions, it has been a rich source of information for those interested in the study of economic structure.

Transaction flows are central to Richard Stone's pioneering work in national accounting and the development of social accounts. This chapter follows that tradition, as here also the emphasis is on transactions. However the subject of the chapter is changes in transactions rather than the measurement of flows. Of course, Stone was also concerned with changes in input–output tables, the development of the RAS adjustment method being but one piece of evidence for this.

In another way this chapter follows the spirit of Stone's research. It is an implicit assumption of this chapter that an understanding of how economies change and develop over time is enhanced by consideration of the changes in detailed input–output and social accounting matrices, and that this must entail examining actual tables. To the extent that this chapter provides such an example, it follows the tradition of empirical investigation demonstrated so ably in the writings of Richard Stone.

The study of economic structure using input–output tables has followed two paths, which already appear to be related. One path has sought to discover from the table per se some structural attributes of the economy in question. These included initially partial and holistic measures of connectedness, dispersion, ordering of some sectors, pattern analysis and input–output comparisons (see Hewings, Jensen and West, 1987). The triangulation studies in sector ordering (particularly that of Simpson and Tsukui, 1965) sought to identify patterns or block structures within the input–output table, searching for regularities and commonalities in table structure. This work led to the more formal studies of economic structure from the input–output table in the development of the partitioned and tiered concepts of fundamental economic structure (Jensen, Dewhurst, West and Hewings, 1991).

The second path to the study of economic structure, and the one addressed in this chapter, is the structural decomposition approach, which is characteristically associated with the comparative static analysis of the changes in the input–output structure of an economy between two points in time. Developments in this direction have been summarised by Skolka (1989) and include identification of the structural effects of changes in the level and pattern of final demand, changes in productivity, and in column structures as reflected in technology, substitution, value-added shares and import propensities and patterns.

Most studies of structural change have been undertaken at the national level, with relatively few at the regional level. Some regional studies (e.g., Jensen, Dewhurst, West and Bayne, 1990a, 1990b) have chosen to include an approach analogous to shift-share in an attempt to identify additionally the national and industry-mix or proportionality components of regional structural change. This could be considered important in studies of regions that are not expected to reflect closely the change in national industry-mix; however these components are not included in the analysis of this chapter. An interesting further path of research has been the measurement of the effects of structural change on some economic characteristics of the regional economy. For example, Henderson, McGregor and McNicoll (1989) and later Mules (1990) estimated the effect of structural change in a regional economy (respectively Scotland and South Australia) as represented by the change in the Leontief inverse, on the employment generation potential, as represented essentially by the employment multipliers.

In common with the papers cited in the preceding paragraph, this chapter is concerned with the analysis of a regional economy based on the information that is contained in regional input–output tables. In particular it focusses attention on some of the changes that occur in the regional economy over time. The discussion is founded on the premise that at least two input–output tables, constructed for different periods, are available for the same region.

The two sets of economic variables that are considered in detail are the set of industrial gross outputs and the set of intermediate transactions. Both of these are major components of the input–output structure and both may be expected to change over time. In this chapter we seek to use other information contained in the tables to answer two related questions. First, can one identify separate influences that lead to changes in gross outputs or transactions? and, secondly, can one further decompose these changes into effects due to other influences, such as changes in the composition of final demand?

Throughout the chapter the calculations that are done to illustrate the methods are applied to the two input–output tables that have been constructed for the Scottish economy: those for 1973 (Fraser of Allander Institute *et al.*, 1978) and for 1979 (Industry Department for Scotland, 1984). All the empirical work is undertaken using tables that are as consistent as is practicable, relying on work by the Industry Department for Scotland (ibid., vol. 5) and Dewhurst and Haggart (1990). The analysis is conducted at a forty-sector disaggregation of both commodities and industries.

It is, of course, most likely that much of the change exhibited by any entity in an input–output table between two periods will be due to a change in the level of prices. The discussion that follows is based on two tables that have been converted to a common level of prices. In the Scottish case, the 1979 table has been deflated, using various Scottish, UK and import price indices, to 1973 price levels. The mechanism by which this was done is described in Dewhurst (1990), though in that paper both tables were converted to 1979 prices. It is recognised that re-basing input–output tables is a complex and indeed possibly contentious procedure. However, although the decompositions that follow are in a sense partial, in that they do not take any account of the direct effects of the change in the level of prices, it is hoped that the analysis here directs attention to 'real' changes that occurred in the Scottish economy over the period in question.

The following section considers the decomposition of gross output changes in terms of the changing pattern of final demand. The third section of the chapter decomposes the change in individual transactions elements. As mentioned earlier such decompositions are not new (see Skolka, 1989), but they have seldom, if ever, been carried out for a regional economy. In part, this stems from the relative infrequency of survey-based tables at a regional level. The detail available in the Scottish tables allows us to carry the decompositions a little further than has been possible in previous national studies. The link between the two decompositions is elaborated at the beginning of section 4.

As mentioned at the start of this introduction a quite independent line of research into the structure of regional input–output tables is the identification of a Fundamental Economic Structure (FES) in regional tables (Jensen, Dewhurst, West and Hewings, 1991). In the fourth section of this chapter it is shown how changes in input–output tables may be decomposed using the FES classification.

2 The decomposition of gross output changes

The Leontief input–output relationship can be represented simply by

$$x = E.f \qquad (6.1)$$

where

f is a vector of final demands,
x is a vector of gross outputs and
E is an $n \times n$ matrix of disaggregated industry multipliers.

A similar relationship will exist for a second input–output table constructed for a subsequent year, i.e.

$$x^* = E^*.f^*$$

Thus the change in output levels, Δx, may be determined as

$$
\begin{aligned}
\Delta x &= x^* - x \\
&= E^*.f^* - E.f \\
&= (E + \Delta E).(f + \Delta f) - E.f \\
&= E.\Delta f + \Delta E.f + \Delta E.\Delta f \qquad (6.2)
\end{aligned}
$$

As the change in the multipliers matrix may be expressed in terms of the change in the technical coefficients matrix A

$$E = [I - (A + \Delta A)]^{-1} - [I - A]^{-1}$$

it can seen that equation (6.2) decomposes the change in industrial outputs into three components. The first, $E.\Delta f$, is the change in output that arises directly as a result of final demand changes; the second, $\Delta E.f$, is the change in output arising directly from the change in the input–output coefficient matrix A, and the third, $\Delta E.\Delta f$, is an interaction effect, giving the additional change in output that arises because both the final demands and the coefficients matrix have changed. The change in output that arises directly from changes in final demand, $E.\Delta f$, consists of two parts. The first, Δf is the change in final demand itself, and the second, $(E - I).\Delta f$, is the induced effect which arises through the interindustry linkages within the regional economy.

We may apply this decomposition to the changes in output levels that occurred in the Scottish economy between 1973 and 1979, using two consistent forty-sector industry $\times$ industry tables after rebasing the 1979 table. The decomposition is given in table 6.1.

A number of interesting points in table 6.1 should be mentioned. Overall, the change in final demand dominates the other sources of change in gross

Table 6.1 *Basic decomposition of Scottish gross output changes*

Industry	Change in gross output ΔX	Change in final demand Δf	Induced effect $(E-I)\Delta f$	Total change due to final demand change $E.\Delta f$	Change due to change in A matrix $\Delta E.f$	Interaction effect $\Delta E.\Delta f$
Agriculture	68.49	−60.42	−12.08	−72.50	135.92	5.07
Forestry and fishing	7.42	−19.35	−0.40	−19.75	25.48	1.69
Coal, oil products, basic chemicals	−22.17	22.45	45.27	67.72	−106.68	16.79
Oil and gas extraction	32.92	32.90	0.00	32.90	0.01	0.01
Electricity	114.97	82.02	21.88	103.90	12.07	−1.00
Gas	143.65	96.96	4.25	101.21	41.52	0.92
Water	−3.90	−0.54	2.76	2.23	−5.11	−1.02
Building materials and minerals	24.28	26.75	9.58	36.33	−11.35	−0.70
Fertilisers	3.45	4.72	−2.81	1.90	1.12	0.43
Other chemicals	39.51	61.11	−0.48	60.63	−23.14	2.02
Metal manufacture	173.61	173.43	27.40	200.83	−20.58	−6.64
Industrial plant and steelwork	19.50	41.70	5.61	47.31	−23.55	−4.26
Other mechanical engineering and vehicles	−38.20	5.64	7.93	13.58	−46.98	−4.80
Computers and electronics	83.72	94.58	3.82	98.41	−11.41	−3.28
Other electrical engineering	−15.10	−12.48	1.40	−11.08	−3.80	−0.22
Instrument engineering	11.08	14.87	0.42	15.29	−4.21	0.00
Ships and marine engineering	−34.31	−33.09	−1.99	−35.07	1.18	−0.42
Metal goods	−56.05	−26.00	6.12	−19.88	−34.08	−2.09
Food products	67.40	1.71	−9.65	−7.94	61.49	13.85

Table 6.1 *Basic decomposition of Scottish gross output changes (cont.)*

Industry	Change in gross output ΔX	Change in final demand Δf	Induced effect $(E-I)\Delta f$	Total change due to final demand change $E.\Delta f$	Change due to change in A matrix $\Delta E.f$	Interaction effect $\Delta E.\Delta f$
Spirits and whisky	77.46	50.74	3.13	53.86	20.01	3.58
Brewing and soft drinks	44.03	26.83	2.42	29.25	11.99	2.79
Textiles	−67.47	−73.64	−6.09	−79.72	17.47	−5.21
Leather goods	−13.00	−8.27	−1.25	−9.52	−4.86	1.38
Footwear and clothing	2.41	0.47	0.47	0.94	1.51	−0.04
Furniture etc.	−3.56	−4.29	0.48	−3.81	0.82	−0.57
Timber processing	−10.32	6.18	2.64	8.82	−17.97	−1.17
Paper and paper products	−21.67	−19.42	3.43	−15.99	−6.42	0.74
Printing and publishing	21.80	4.21	−0.98	3.23	16.94	1.63
Rubber products	−5.23	−4.49	0.69	−3.80	−1.00	−0.43
Other manufacturing	−6.00	−8.19	0.05	−8.14	1.72	0.42
Construction	−242.88	−15.54	24.10	8.55	−248.38	−3.06
Distribution	157.93	100.82	8.09	108.92	33.81	15.20
Hotels and catering	132.19	141.55	4.99	146.54	−14.61	0.26
Rail transport	10.87	19.92	3.79	23.71	−11.49	−1.35
Road transport	−17.46	3.10	12.55	15.64	−31.77	−1.34
Other transport	160.91	120.94	13.17	134.11	17.07	9.73
Posts and telecommunications	96.20	45.01	8.21	53.22	47.01	−4.04
Finance services	−16.91	−23.56	11.96	−11.60	3.53	−8.84
Other services	261.98	−168.73	25.30	−143.43	368.30	37.11
Public administration and defence	132.26	132.26	0.00	132.26	0.00	0.00
TOTAL	1313.81	832.86	226.19	1059.06	191.59	63.16

Note:
All figures are in £m (1973).

output, a finding consistent with that noted by Feldman *et al.* (1987) in the US. However it is interesting to note that the induced effects of final demand change are, in aggregate, of the same order of magnitude as the changes in gross output due to the change in the A matrix. Inspection of the table indicates that these overall conclusions do not apply at the level of the individual industries. Finally, the interaction effect is always relatively small when compared to either the final demand effect or the A matrix effect or both.

In what follows we concentrate on the first component of industrial output changes, i.e., those that arise directly out of final demand changes. Final demand in an input–output context is the sum of various sectors of final demand. In the case of the tables used here there are seven final demand sectors. These seven sectors are (i) consumers' expenditure, (ii) government current expenditure, (iii) fixed capital formation, (iv) stock changes, (v) tourists' expenditure, (vi) exports to the rest of the UK and (vii) exports to the rest of the world. Thus we may write

$$f = f_1 + f_2 + f_3 + f_4 + f_5 + f_6 + f_7$$

and
$$\Delta f = \Delta f_1 + \Delta f_2 + \Delta f_3 + \Delta f_4 + \Delta f_5 + \Delta f_6 + \Delta f_7$$

$$= \sum_{k=1}^{7} \Delta f_k$$

Let γ_k be the growth rate of final demand sector k and $\gamma_{i,k}$ the growth rate of the final demand sector k for industrial output i. Then

$$[\Delta f_k]_i = \gamma_{i,k} \cdot [f_k]_i$$
$$= \gamma_k \cdot [f_k]_i + (\gamma_{i,k} - \gamma_k) \cdot [f_k]_i$$

Thus Δf may be decomposed into fourteen components, seven components arising through overall changes in the individual sectors of final demand and a further seven within-sector components arising through changes in the distribution of individual elements within each final demand sector.

Table 6.2 gives the implied decompositions of the direct final demand effects in table 6.1. From this table it can be seen that overall the distributional effects are much smaller than the growth effects. However, again, that is not necessarily true for individual industries. It also may be noted that the sum of the overall distributional effects is negative, implying that the change in the pattern of final demand in Scotland over the period reduced the growth of gross output in the economy.

Table 6.2 *Further decomposition of Scottish gross output changes*

Industry	Change due to consumers' expenditure		Change due to government expenditure		Change due to fixed capital formation	
	Growth	Dist.	Growth	Dist.	Growth	Dist.
Agriculture	27.62	−51.64	1.15	3.17	−0.47	−3.30
Forestry and fishing	2.53	−3.25	0.06	1.15	−0.27	−0.95
Coal, oil products, basic chemicals	11.05	20.65	1.31	10.61	−1.28	7.05
Oil and gas extraction	0.00	0.00	0.00	0.00	−0.57	−4.73
Electricity	20.72	35.89	1.58	16.88	−1.34	11.69
Gas	6.20	77.38	0.30	11.28	−0.43	−1.23
Water	3.19	−6.11	0.23	0.94	−0.06	2.57
Building materials and minerals	2.39	7.23	0.62	10.66	−6.90	−8.55
Fertilisers	1.21	−0.61	0.05	0.19	−0.02	−0.09
Other chemicals	1.41	4.80	0.18	4.47	−0.40	2.89
Metal manufacture	1.05	7.41	0.28	6.70	−2.61	3.74
Industrial plant and steelwork	0.62	3.55	0.17	1.13	−2.56	4.24
Other mechanical engineering and vehicles	3.49	4.22	0.71	18.74	−2.68	8.80
Computers and electronics	0.19	8.11	0.09	20.65	−0.25	0.60
Other electrical engineering	0.45	5.98	0.17	4.51	−1.86	−2.39
Instrument engineering	0.24	0.44	0.11	5.67	−0.44	−1.50

Ships and marine engineering	0.28	0.56	0.03	37.26	−1.06	−3.47
Metal goods	1.48	1.15	0.21	2.48	−1.50	−0.26
Food products	40.35	−85.98	0.42	12.38	−0.07	−0.04
Spirits and whisky	7.98	−42.08	0.01	0.28	0.00	0.46
Brewing and soft drinks	9.97	−3.68	0.00	0.57	0.00	0.12
Textiles	4.26	−16.08	0.11	1.78	−0.61	−3.41
Leather goods	0.25	2.19	0.00	0.08	−0.01	−0.06
Footwear and clothing	1.61	−3.61	0.06	0.92	−0.03	0.01
Furniture etc.	1.10	−3.95	0.15	1.55	−0.87	−1.42
Timber processing	1.60	18.59	0.39	3.49	−3.84	−2.89
Paper and paper products	2.43	1.99	0.24	1.60	−0.16	0.40
Printing and publishing	4.93	−5.12	1.23	−2.70	−0.08	0.43
Rubber products	0.25	1.59	0.03	0.19	−0.05	0.46
Other manufacturing	0.84	−2.45	0.05	0.33	−0.06	0.24
Construction	16.88	135.93	9.45	43.86	−116.22	−92.09
Distribution	92.15	−51.89	1.90	18.57	−2.73	30.70
Hotels and catering	27.81	67.34	0.86	12.89	−0.25	0.26
Rail transport	5.32	4.87	0.72	4.77	−0.34	−0.40
Road transport	19.40	−30.49	0.66	18.20	−1.37	5.88
Other transport	4.86	4.89	0.66	2.40	−1.02	−3.12
Posts and telecommunications	7.61	27.51	1.18	15.23	−1.99	4.64
Finance services	6.20	12.81	0.64	−0.21	−0.35	−0.23
Other services	49.68	−97.93	58.83	−284.48	−2.70	21.39
Public administration and defence	41.99	−54.89	127.93	17.22	0.00	0.00
TOTAL	431.58	−4.66	212.81	25.42	−157.43	−24.05

Table 6.2 *Further decomposition of Scottish gross output changes (cont.)*

Industry	Change due to exports to RUK		Change due to exports to ROW	
	Growth	Dist.	Growth	Dist.
Agriculture	20.07	−50.28	10.50	8.55
Forestry and fishing	3.66	−31.50	1.16	0.18
Coal, oil products, basic chemicals	9.45	−2.51	16.55	−7.63
Oil and gas extraction	0.00	20.32	0.00	17.98
Electricity	3.07	10.46	4.19	0.53
Gas	0.50	6.34	0.83	0.02
Water	0.36	0.35	0.57	0.03
Building materials and minerals	3.46	17.45	7.17	3.38
Fertilisers	0.86	−0.73	0.47	0.30
Other chemicals	13.61	17.86	16.99	−1.40
Metal manufacture	21.01	120.69	15.42	37.60
Industrial plant and steelwork	6.77	25.11	6.14	5.91
Other mechanical engineering and vehicles	26.82	−70.96	45.83	−13.86
Computers and electronics	5.18	4.36	18.58	43.37
Other electrical engineering	10.45	−29.86	9.75	−4.01
Instrument engineering	3.28	−0.93	4.95	4.61
Ships and marine engineering	6.09	7.14	23.29	−78.38
Metal goods	7.69	−15.39	10.00	−23.53

Food products	26.98	−4.80	12.34	−2.29
Spirits and whisky	4.75	14.84	65.28	−7.42
Brewing and soft drinks	1.52	17.45	2.64	−2.51
Textiles	17.25	−70.59	20.95	−35.22
Leather goods	1.51	−12.41	1.14	−2.16
Footwear and clothing	6.95	−11.81	2.80	0.17
Furniture etc.	2.07	−4.56	0.15	2.41
Timber processing	4.30	−6.08	2.72	−6.39
Paper and paper products	12.26	−44.42	3.60	7.31
Printing and publishing	4.87	−10.52	1.33	9.03
Rubber products	1.88	−4.41	2.41	−6.14
Other manufacturing	0.79	−5.55	0.98	−2.37
Construction	4.74	5.75	5.59	1.52
Distribution	5.23	7.93	7.96	0.95
Hotels and catering	1.40	7.81	2.95	0.07
Rail transport	0.74	0.39	0.93	0.29
Road transport	6.71	−11.14	5.60	0.74
Other transport	4.35	66.97	9.33	42.58
Posts and telecommunications	4.18	−9.93	1.22	2.29
Finance services	4.41	−33.05	3.82	−6.73
Other services	7.85	76.06	15.17	4.67
Public administration and defence	0.00	0.00	0.00	0.00
TOTAL	267.02	−4.13	361.29	−5.59

Table 6.2 *Further decomposition of Scottish gross output changes (cont.)*

Industry	Change due to tourist expenditure		Change due to stock changes	
	Growth	Dist.	Growth	Dist.
Agriculture	2.79	−5.87	−26.65	−8.13
Forestry and fishing	0.14	−0.26	−0.47	8.07
Coal, oil products, basic chemicals	2.24	−2.12	−2.53	4.87
Oil and gas extraction	0.00	0.00	−0.08	−0.02
Electricity	1.46	−0.18	−1.10	0.06
Gas	0.31	−0.05	−0.21	−0.02
Water	0.36	−0.06	−0.19	0.06
Building materials	0.43	1.11	−1.21	−0.93
Fertilisers	0.11	−0.22	−1.04	1.43
Other chemicals	0.20	0.28	−1.60	1.35
Metal manufacture	0.14	0.02	−5.46	−5.18
Industrial plant and steelwork	0.08	−0.02	−2.23	−1.61
Other mechanical engineering and vehicles	0.42	0.13	−8.88	0.78
Computers and electronics	0.03	0.00	−2.16	−0.33
Other electrical engineering	0.06	0.02	−1.62	−2.72
Instrument engineering	0.02	0.05	−0.93	−0.27
Ships and marine engineering	0.03	0.00	−11.14	−15.70
Metal goods	0.21	0.09	−2.14	−0.38
Food products	3.28	−7.44	−5.39	2.31

Spirits and whisky	0.85	−1.63	−5.80	16.36
Brewing and soft drinks	1.13	−0.10	−0.51	2.65
Textiles	0.71	2.89	−3.08	1.30
Leather goods	0.06	0.09	−0.17	−0.04
Footwear and clothing	0.21	3.23	−0.85	1.29
Furniture etc.	0.10	−0.01	−0.61	0.09
Timber processing	0.19	−0.03	−3.22	0.00
Paper and paper products	0.43	−0.13	−1.08	−0.44
Printing and publishing	0.34	0.46	−1.00	0.04
Rubber products	0.05	−0.05	−0.05	0.04
Other manufacturing	0.04	0.04	−0.47	−0.08
Construction	3.64	−0.60	−4.28	−5.63
Distribution	5.95	−4.45	−3.77	0.42
Hotels and catering	29.41	−4.02	−0.44	0.45
Rail transport	0.81	5.75	−0.20	0.06
Road transport	1.36	0.80	−1.34	0.63
Other transport	1.04	1.21	−0.84	0.79
Posts and telecommunications	1.26	0.37	−0.37	0.03
Finance services	1.30	−0.06	−0.52	0.37
Other services	5.15	3.70	−2.70	1.89
Public administration and defence	0.00	0.00	0.00	0.00
TOTAL	66.35	−7.09	−106.32	3.83

Note:
All figures are in £m (1973).

3 The decomposition of transactions changes

Suppose that there exist two input–output tables constructed for the same region at two different points in time. Let the intermediate transactions for the first table be denoted by the matrix ^0T and for the second table by the matrix ^1T. The elements of the matrices, $^tT_{i,j}$, $(t=0,1)$ represent the purchases made by industry j in the region of the output of industry i in the region at times 0 and 1.

The change in an individual element is

$$^1T_{i,j} - {}^0T_{i,j} = \Delta T_{i,j}$$

This change may be decomposed into five components as follows:

1 The change due to overall regional growth

If ^tX is the total industrial gross output at time $t(t=0,1)$ then we define the regional growth effect, for transaction (i,j), as

$$\Delta^1_{i,j} = {}^0T_{i,j}\cdot({}^1X - {}^0X)/{}^0X$$
$$= {}^0T_{i,j}\cdot\gamma$$

where γ is the overall growth rate of gross output for the regional economy.

This effect is the change in transaction (i,j) that would have occurred if industry j had grown at a similar rate to the regional economy as a whole and if no other changes had taken place. Clearly all the $\Delta^1_{i,j}$ effects will have the same sign, that of γ. In what follows Δ^1 is referred to as the 'regional' effect.

2 The change due to differences in industrial growth rates

The growth rate of gross output for an individual industry may be written as

$$\gamma_j = ({}^1X_j - {}^0X_j)/{}^0X_j$$

where ^tX_j is the gross output of industry j at time $t(t=0,1)$.

The differential industrial growth effect may be defined as

$$\Delta^2_{i,j} = {}^0T_{i,j}\cdot(\gamma_j - \gamma)$$

The sum of Δ^1 and Δ^2 measures the change in transactions that would have taken place if they had grown at the same rate as the output of the particular purchasing industry. All the $\Delta^2_{i,j}$ terms for a given j will be positive if the gross output of industry j grew faster than that of the region as a whole and negative if the gross output of industry j grew slower than that of the region as a whole. In what follows we term Δ^2 the 'industrial' effect.

3 The change due to substitution between intermediate inputs and other value added

Let the total intermediate inputs imported by industry j be $'IM_j$ and the total domestically produced intermediate inputs purchased by industry j be $'T_j$, $(t=0,1)$.

$$'T_j = \sum_{i=1}^{n} 'T_{i,j}$$

Let $\Gamma_j = ('T_j + {}^1IM_j - {}^0T_j - {}^0IM_j)/({}^0T_j + {}^0IM_j)$, i.e., the overall growth rate of intermediate inputs into industry j. Then the effect due to the shift in relative importance between intermediate inputs and other value added may be written as

$$\Delta_{i,j}^3 = {}^0T_{i,j} \cdot (\Gamma_j - \gamma_j)$$

In what follows we refer to Δ^3 as the factor effect as it measures the change that took place due to the fact that the total intermediate inputs used by industry j may not have grown at the same rate as the output of industry j. In part this may be due to the more efficient use of intermediate inputs, although it is recognised that such differences in the growth rates may arise through movements along a production function, in response to changes in relative prices for example, as well as through shifts in the production function.

As with the industrial effects, the factor effects will all be of the same sign for a given producing industry j.

4 The change due to substitution between intermediate inputs

Let $'IM_{i,j}$ be the imports of input i purchased by industry j in the region at time $t(t=0,1)$.

$$'IM_j = \sum_{i=1}^{n} 'IM_{i,j}$$

We may identify the change in transactions that arose due to different rates of growth of individual local and imported inputs as follows

Let $\Gamma_{i,j} = ({}^1T_{i,j} + {}^1IM_{i,j} - {}^0T_{i,j} - {}^0IM_{i,j})/({}^0T_{i,j} + {}^0IM_{i,j})$

then we may define

$$\Delta_{i,j}^4 = {}^0T_{i,j} \cdot (\Gamma_{i,j} - \Gamma_j)$$

In what follows we refer to this as the input effect as it arises due to unequal growth rates of the individual local and imported intermediate inputs.

5 The change in transactions due to changes in the pattern of trade

The final component of the overall change in transactions that we identify is that due to changes in the purchasing patterns of industries. The transactions matrix will change if the purchasing industry imports relatively more (or less) of a particular input.

Letting

$$\zeta_{i,j} = ({}^1T_{i,j} - {}^0T_{i,j})/{}^0T_{i,j}$$

we may define

$$\Delta_{i,j}^5 = {}^0T_{i,j} \cdot (\zeta_{i,j} - \Gamma_{i,j})$$

Δ^5 is referred to hereafter as the 'trade' effect.

Further comments on the decomposition

Two points are important about this decomposition. First the decomposition is exhaustive. This can be shown as follows

$$\begin{aligned}
\Delta_{i,j}^1 + \Delta_{i,j}^2 + \Delta_{i,j}^3 + \Delta_{i,j}^4 + \Delta_{i,j}^5 &= {}^0T_{i,j} \cdot \gamma + {}^0T_{i,j} \cdot (\gamma_j - \gamma) + {}^0T_{i,j} \cdot (\Gamma_j - \gamma_j) \\
&\quad + {}^0T_{i,j} \cdot (\Gamma_{i,j} - \Gamma_j) + {}^0T_{i,j} \cdot (\zeta_{i,j} - \Gamma_{i,j}) \\
&= {}^0T_{i,j} \cdot \zeta_{i,j} \\
&= {}^0T_{i,j} \cdot ({}^1T_{i,j} - {}^0T_{i,j})/{}^0T_{i,j} \\
&= \Delta T_{i,j}
\end{aligned}$$

The second point is that the components Δ^2 and Δ^3 relate to individual producing industries whereas components Δ^4 and Δ^5 or perhaps better their sums over the j producing industries, are best viewed as relating to the input i to which they refer.

The decomposition may be applied to the two input–output tables of the Scottish economy. The published tables are detailed and presented in various forms. However the only disaggregation of imports into Scotland by purchasing industry is a disaggregation by imports in terms of commodities. Thus the decomposition is carried out in a commodity by industry framework. Although commodities are named after the industry responsible for producing most of that commodity the framework should be borne in mind when interpreting the results.

A further consideration is that the set of Scottish tables distinguishes between imports from the rest of the UK and imports from the rest of the world (excluding the rest of the UK). Thus there are available two import matrices rather than the one assumed in section 2. This enables the trade effect to be divided into two components.

Letting $'IM_{i,j}^{\text{UK}}$ and $'IM_{i,j}^{\text{RoW}}$ stand for the imports of commodity i by Scottish industry j from the rest of the UK and the rest of the world respectively in time $t(t=0,1)$ we have

$$'IM_{i,j} = {}'IM_{i,j}^{\text{UK}} + {}'IM_{i,j}^{\text{RoW}}$$

and consequently it is possible to subdivide the trade effect Δ^5 of the previous section into an 'international trade' effect, Δ^{5a}, and a 'regional trade' effect, Δ^{5b}, as follows

$$\Delta_{i,j}^{5a} = {}^0T_{i,j} \cdot (\xi_{i,j} - \Gamma_{i,j})$$

and $\Delta_{i,j}^{5a} = {}^0T_{i,j} \cdot (\zeta_{i,j} - \xi_{i,j})$ where

$$\xi_{i,j} = ({}^1T_{i,j} + {}^1IM_{i,j}^{\text{UK}} - {}^0T_{i,j} - {}^0IM_{i,j}^{\text{UK}})/({}^0T_{i,j} + {}^0IM_{i,j}^{\text{UK}})$$

A full presentation of the results using the forty-sector disaggregation of the Scottish economy is not given here for reasons of space. Only summary results can be presented here; these are given in table 6.3. Although they hide all of the intercommodity and interindustry variation in the results the summary figures do highlight at least two interesting facets of the development of the Scottish economy between 1973 and 1979.

It is clear from the total of the industrial effects that the differences in industrial growth rates in Scotland had a depressing effect on the increase in transactions levels. This suggests that these differences would have had, in the absence of any countervailing influences, the effect of reducing the multiplier effects within the Scottish economy, thus lowering any induced growth effects arising from expansion of final demand.

The totals of the international trade and regional trade effects are also worthy of comment. The negative sign of the first of these means that, overall, industries in Scotland imported relatively more of their intermediate input requirements from the rest of the world (and consequently purchased relatively less from UK sources) in 1979 than they did in 1973. However inputs provided from within Scotland became relatively more important in comparison with imports from the rest of the UK. Given that the period 1973–9 was when the UK was adjusting to entry into the European Community some switch in purchasing patterns seems eminently plausible. The decomposition does not relate directly to this question as it is not possible to disaggregate imports from the rest of the world into those from other European Community countries and those from elsewhere. However the figures are consistent with the view that European sources of inputs were substituted for UK sources and that this substitution was more marked for inputs purchased from the rest of the UK than for locally produced inputs. In a sense this is saying that trade diversion (from the Rest of the UK to the rest of the European Community) was more marked than

Table 6.3 *Summary results of transaction decomposition*

Industry	Sum of effects over commodities by industry				Sum of effects over industries by commodity	
	Region	Industry	Factor	Input	Int. Tr.	Reg. Tr.
Agriculture	33.44	1.58	−25.82	−0.43	30.68	42.10
Forestry and fishing	2.38	−0.42	5.32	24.86	−2.32	2.89
Coal, oil products, basic chemicals	7.43	−11.94	42.74	−49.00	−3.08	−15.29
Oil and gas extraction	0.08	4.40	21.35	0.00	0.00	0.02
Electricity	9.28	29.72	−15.65	34.88	0.00	−2.86
Gas	1.77	33.03	−29.09	43.43	0.00	7.91
Water	1.15	−2.39	−0.57	−3.83	0.00	1.01
Building materials and minerals	6.03	1.30	11.89	−3.91	−9.29	17.90
Fertilisers	1.15	0.08	2.00	1.69	2.51	2.43
Other chemicals	8.60	2.27	−10.78	−12.13	−1.43	1.41
Metal manufacture	14.34	40.32	−29.78	16.52	−34.70	20.00
Industrial plant and steelwork	3.63	0.52	9.81	6.79	−16.79	−4.42
Other mechanical engineering and vehicles	14.76	−22.16	21.95	−13.89	−19.54	−21.99
Computers and electronics	3.81	13.32	8.28	0.89	−1.70	−7.74
Other electrical engineering	4.52	−7.37	−6.13	−3.42	0.83	4.51
Instrument engineering	1.62	0.58	5.14	0.51	−1.43	−0.70
Ships and marine engineering	5.46	−12.91	−1.83	−4.42	−1.73	3.36
Metal goods	4.74	−17.71	2.47	−14.37	−1.51	−8.15
Food products	44.57	−8.95	58.35	41.28	3.68	−4.15

Spirits and whisky	26.93	14.96	−22.52	−6.73	−0.57	0.10
Brewing and soft drinks	5.24	12.95	0.56	4.23	−0.36	−1.62
Textiles	10.98	−28.29	2.27	2.90	0.42	7.05
Leather goods	1.15	−5.76	2.92	−2.49	−0.02	1.01
Footwear and clothing	1.98	−1.60	3.29	3.46	−2.08	1.10
Furniture etc.	1.29	−2.12	0.63	0.62	1.62	−2.40
Timber processing	4.08	−6.91	−2.94	−11.21	0.84	1.89
Paper and paper products	5.36	−10.33	2.84	−10.66	−0.13	−7.02
Printing and publishing	2.87	1.73	6.18	18.26	−0.96	−10.78
Rubber products	1.17	−2.49	5.63	−1.69	−0.02	0.57
Other manufacturing	0.60	−1.96	0.59	−1.58	−0.12	3.62
Construction	61.49	−155.49	−6.97	−121.47	0.00	−4.11
Distribution	16.23	10.28	46.19	−5.93	−0.52	−3.51
Hotels and catering	11.38	29.09	18.19	−18.49	0.00	9.40
Rail transport	1.05	0.55	9.28	−13.28	0.00	0.38
Road transport	5.33	−8.15	−13.10	−23.92	−3.94	−16.94
Other transport	2.68	21.46	75.88	90.45	−50.73	−2.72
Posts and telecommunications	1.00	4.71	7.46	27.20	−1.51	0.10
Finance services	3.54	−7.39	−7.12	−37.87	−0.23	22.92
Other services	19.13	26.75	−14.25	98.22	−4.75	39.84
TOTAL	352.24	−64.75	184.66	55.43	−118.87	77.14

Note:
All figures are in £m (1973 prices).

trade creation, a finding supported by the work of Sonis *et al.* (1993). Even if all of the relative shifts towards the rest of the world shown in table 6.3 were interpreted as reflecting the increased importance of the Community as a provider of inputs to Scottish industries the figures in table 6.2 surely underestimate that effect as no evidence is available on trade diversion to the rest of the European Community from other parts of the rest of the world.

4 The link between the decompositions and fundamental economic structure

The two decompositions given in the preceding sections are linked. It may be noted that the industrial effect in the decomposition of transaction element change is based on individual industrial growth rates of gross output. However it is precisely those gross output changes that are decomposed in section 2. In effect, therefore, one can decompose the change in any one transaction element in the Scottish tables into a large number of separate items.

It will be noted that in the empirical work described in this chapter an open input–output model has been adopted, in that consumers' expenditure is treated exogenously. There is no reason why the same analysis cannot be applied to a closed model. Indeed it would be possible to treat as endogenous as much of final demand as was thought appropriate. Furthermore, an additional perspective may be provided, in which the input–output table is decomposed into transaction effects and primary input effects. Essentially, this decomposition focusses on column properties while the earlier decomposition is oriented to the rows.

An alternative possibility of approaching the decomposition of output changes may be provided by consideration of the Tiered Fundamental Economic Structure (TFES) concept (Jensen *et al.*, 1991). In general terms the concept of TFES suggests that it may be possible to consider an input–output table as being the sum of two subtables.

The first subtable would measure the transactions that took place which had their origins in economic stimuli that took place outside the region. This is the non-FES table. It would include those transactions arising directly from exports, for example, and those transactions that are induced by the level of exports. The second subtable would measure the transactions that took place as a result of exogenous stimuli that affected the region directly, such as exogenous income or population change. Dewhurst and West (1990) present an analysis of such a model which is represented here in a flow diagram (figure 6.1).

The flow diagram indicates three exogenous stimuli to the economy:

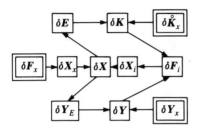

Figure 6.1 Flow diagram of FES model

Notes: F_x is exogenous final demand
X_x is 'externally' generated output
E is employment
X is total gross output
Y_E is income from employment
X_i is 'internally' generated output
K is population
F_i is endogenous final demand
Y is income
$\mathring{K}_x$ is exogenous population change
Y_x is exogenously determined income

exogenous final demand change, exogenous population change and exogenous income changes. It would, in theory, be possible to decompose the change in gross outputs into those changes resulting from the growth and changes in composition of these three external stimuli. Implementation of such a decomposition would rely on two features: identification of the exogenous components and the measurement of the FES and non-FES tables, unless one could assume the A matrices in each case to be identical. In this chapter such a decomposition has not been attempted for the Scottish economy. However it appears to offer another, possibly more instructive, way to look at gross output changes in an input–output context.

With the increasing development of multi-country economic communities (EU, NAFTA, etc.), and the concomitant reduction in tariffs and impediments to trade, it is likely that regional economies will experience significant changes in their structures. The *ex post* methods described in this chapter will provide important contributions to the identification of the sources of these changes, and their particular sectoral manifestations. What is needed is a way of using the methods to make forecasts of changes, especially those changes associated with interregional and international trade flows.

7 Consistency in regional demo-economic models: the case of the northern Netherlands

DIRK STELDER AND JAN OOSTERHAVEN

1 Introduction

The addition of the spatial dimension in regional modelling enlarges the need for data, whereas regional data are usually much less readily available than national data. The econometric time-series approach, which is the common approach in all macro-economic models, cannot be used when regional time series are not available. Hence, it is not surprising that many regional model builders have concentrated their efforts on the cross-section alternative, which aims at getting a detailed description of the regional economic structure at a single moment in time. As a consequence, sectoral disaggregation and input–output analysis have been more popular among regional economists than among their macro-economist colleagues (Rose and Miernyk, 1989).

A second distinctive feature of regional models is the prominence that labour market modelling takes. This is directly related to the greater importance of the labour market in a regional policy setting compared with that in a national policy setting. As far as the labour market itself is concerned, national models concentrate much more on the function of wages as an equilibrating mechanism, whereas regional models concentrate more on quantity adjustments. This reflects the fact that interregional wage differences are smaller as well as more stable than international wage differences, whereas (geographical) mobility is much more important at the regional level. In national models, for example, international migration effects are usually considered to be exogenous (Bodkin, Klein and Marwah, 1991). As a consequence, many regional models contain a strong demo-economic element (Batey and Weeks, 1987; Oosterhaven and Dewhurst, 1990; Madden and Trigg, 1990).

Because of these special interests that regional analysts have, it is not surprising that the pre-eminent work of Richard Stone (1968, 1970, 1971) on sectoral analysis, input–output analysis and demo-economics has been of substantial influence in the field of regional modelling. However, as Stone himself pointed out, the combined use of different techniques such as input–output analysis, econometrics and demographic models can lead to problems of consistency and raises the question of how a consistent integrated approach can be achieved (Stone, 1970; Anselin and Madden, 1990).

Presumably there are today still as many integration methods as there are regional models, each of them having its own, mostly hybrid, combination of different techniques, and our own model of the northern Provinces of the Netherlands is no exception to this rule. In this chapter we use our model as an example and discuss some of the most important consistency problems, paying special attention to the modelling of interregional demo-economic effects (cf. Oosterhaven and Folmer, 1985). In section 2 the general outline of the model is given. In section 3 we give a brief description of the demand side of the model and discuss some of its internal consistency aspects. Section 4 is devoted to a similar analysis of the supply side. Finally, in section 5, we describe the demo-economic and eco-demographic interactions and we discuss the consistency aspects of the model as a whole.

2 A general outline of ISAM

Despite the long macro-econometric tradition in the Netherlands, econometric bottom-up specifications are hardly found in Dutch regional models due to the lack of sufficient regional economic data. It is only in the field of interregional migration that a substantial amount of econometric research has been stimulated by the very detailed registration, by the Central Bureau of Statistics, of migration at the municipal level since 1950. Regional cross-section research and input–output analysis, on the other hand, are well developed, especially for the northern region, an area which has been a major focus for regional policy since 1950.

A recent trend in regional analysis is the development of integrated models, such as those in which input–output is embedded into a larger econometric framework (Anselin and Madden, 1990). However, the absence of price mechanisms and supply effects in input–output models has led to a growing interest in computable general equilibrium (CGE) models as an alternative (Harrigan and McGregor, 1989). The integrated labour market model ISAM[1] for the northern region has been developed along the same lines.

Several studies of the economic structure of the northern Netherlands

---

[1] 'Integraal sectorstructuur- en arbeidsmarkt model' or integrated interindustry labour market model.

were carried out in the 1970s (Oosterhaven, 1981). These resulted in the construction of sets of bi-regional input–output tables of the Isard type for 1975, 1980 and 1986 for each Province at a level of fifty-nine industries. In these tables, the Province concerned is defined as the first region and the rest of the Netherlands defined as the second region. The building of an integrated labour market model based on these tables started in the early 1980s. The first version (FNEI, 1986) consisted of different modules for production, employment, population and migration with little feedback or interaction. The present, second version (Stelder, 1992) is more integrated, with feedback mechanisms between migration, consumption, employment and unemployment, and contains an econometric bottom-up specification of migration (see figure 7.1).

The employment block is driven by national and regional final demand and national labour productivity growth rates. The labour supply block combines bottom-up forecasts of regional population and migration with a top-down forecast of regional labour participation rates. The national exogenous variables are the outcomes of a large national econometric model of the Central Planning Bureau, which publishes a yearly national economic forecast (e.g., CPB, 1991).

ISAM has several feedback mechanisms, most of which are related to migration. The migration model predicts regional net migration for each province. Indicators for the regional labour market and the regional housing market are the independent variables, whereas migration itself co-determines regional labour supply and consumption expenditures.

3 The demand side of the labour market

The structure of the interregional input–output module is shown in more detail in figure 7.2. We have taken the application for the Province of Groningen as an example, in which Groningen is region 1 and the rest of the country is region 2 (the models for Friesland and Drenthe have exactly the same structure).

The input–output model is formulated in growth rate terms for a forecasting period $\sigma \to t$, with the growth rate vectors indicated by the suffix σt

$$F_t = (1 + \mathring{F}_{\sigma t}) \otimes F_\sigma \tag{7.1)^2}$$

$$f_\sigma = F_\sigma \iota \tag{7.2}$$

$$f_t = F_t \iota \tag{7.3}$$

---

[2] The Hadamard cell–to–cell multiplication and division is denoted here as '$\otimes$' and '$/$' respectively. For instance $c = a \otimes b$ is defined as $c_i = a_i b_i \, \forall_i$.

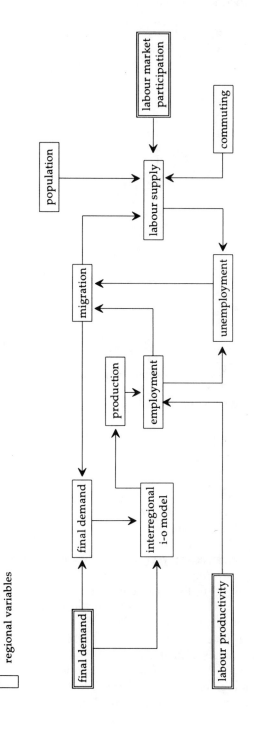

Figure 7.1 General outline of the ISAM model

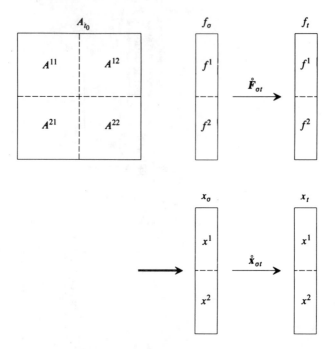

Figure 7.2 A bi-regional input–output growth rate model for Groningen
Notes: 1 = Groningen
         2 = rest of the country

$$x_\sigma = (I - A_{t_0})^{-1} f_\sigma \tag{7.4}$$

$$x_t = (I - A_{t_0})^{-1} f_t \tag{7.5}$$

$$\mathring{x}_{\sigma t} = (x_t - x_\sigma)/x_\sigma \tag{7.6}$$

$$\mathring{e}_{\sigma t} = (1 + \mathring{x}_{\sigma t})/(1 + \mathring{\rho}_{\sigma t}) - 1 \tag{7.7}$$

in which

t_0 is the table construction year (at the moment $t_0 = 1986$),
σ is the first year of the forecasting period,
t is the last year of the forecasting period,
A is the $2i \times 2j$ bi-regional matrix of input coefficients ($i = j = 59$),
x is the $2i$ bi-regional vector of output,
f is the $2i$ bi-regional vector of total final demand,
F is the $2i \times k$ matrix of final demand (k final demand categories),
$\mathring{F}_{\sigma t}$ is the $2i \times k$ matrix of final demand growth rates,
$\mathring{x}_{\sigma t}$ is the $2i$ bi-regional vector of output growth rates,
$\mathring{e}_{\sigma t}$ is the $2i$ vector of employment growth rates,

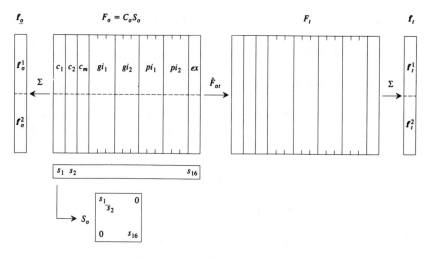

Figure 7.3 The bi-regional final demand matrix in ISAM

Notes: c_i is household consumption in region i
c_m is consumption due to net migration in region 1
gi_i is government investment in region i for three categories
pi_i is private investment in region i for three categories
ex is foreign exports

$\rho^{\circ}_{\sigma t}$ is the $2i$ vector of labour productivity growth rates and ι is a vector of 1s.

The final demand vectors f_σ and f_t are calculated as horizontal aggregates of the $2i \times k$ matrices F_σ and F_t, which contain k different final demand categories. F_t is derived by combining an estimated F_σ with an exogenous matrix of final demand growth rates $\mathring{F}_{\sigma t}$. As is shown in figure 7.3, the matrices F_σ, F_t and $\mathring{F}_{\sigma t}$ contain sixteen different columns: for household consumption in regions 1 and 2, migrant consumption in region 1, public and private investment in regions 1 and 2 and foreign exports. In its turn, F_σ is derived from a final demand coefficient matrix C_σ and a diagonal matrix $S\Lambda_\sigma$ with the k totals of each category of final demand on its diagonal ($F_\sigma = C_\sigma S\Lambda_\sigma$).

The structure of F as shown in figure 7.3 serves merely as an illustration. The way in which f is disaggregated into categories depends on the desired disaggregation of F_σ on the one hand and that of $\mathring{F}_{\sigma t}$ on the other hand. For example, in F_σ in ISAM, the column structure of c_1 is identical to c_m, which means that incoming and outgoing migrants are assumed to have the same consumption pattern as the resident population of Groningen. In $\mathring{F}_{\sigma t}$, however, there is a separate growth rate for c_m, which comes from the migration forecast, implying that $\mathring{c}_l \neq c_m$. For some investment categories the situation is the other way around, with identical growth rates in $\mathring{F}_{ot}$ for columns that are different in F_o. In both cases, the disaggregation has an influence on the resulting f_o and f_t.

The main consistency problem in the interregional input–output block is the treatment of feedback effects from the regional to the national level. As both regions sum to the national economy, ISAM implicitly produces national growth rates for production and employment, $\mathring{x}_{ot}$ and $\mathring{e}_{ot}$,[3] which are usually different from the ones that are forecast by the (exogenous) national CPB model. The major cause of these deviations presumably is the demand oriented bias in the ISAM predictions which is due to the absence of any explicit modelling of supply effects on production levels. These deviations, however, are small because all national final demand growth rates are correct by definition. Only in agriculture, which is a typically supply-driven sector, are occasionally substantial deviations to be found.

Our solution to this problem has been to rescale the implicit national growth rates to the exogenous CPB values. The correction on each entry j of $\mathring{x}_{ot}$ is then applied to the two entries j of the interregional vector $\mathring{x}_{ot}$ for Groningen and the rest of the country. This procedure requires that the implicit national forecast $\mathring{x}_{ot}$ be made exogenous and that the corrected regional forecast $\mathring{x}_{ot}$ is only endogenous in the sense that it indicates the regional deviation from the national growth rates for each entry j.

The necessary theoretical assumption behind this solution is that each industry j in the region in question (Groningen in our example) does not differ from its national counterpart in its demand/supply orientation. If this is not true, some Groningen industries will be overcorrected and others undercorrected. We have not yet been able empirically to verify this rather complicated assumption.

Finally, the question may be asked as to whether or not the above solution of the consistency problem reduces the interregional input–output model to a mere shift–and–share model. This is true to a certain extent when the model is specified as entirely top-down, i.e., when each entry in $\mathring{F}_{ot}$ is the same for region 1 and region 2. In figure 7.3, the top half of $\mathring{F}_{ot}$ would then be identical to the bottom half. In such an application, only national final demand growth rates would be used. The regional differences in $\mathring{x}_{ot}$ would only occur as a result of the regional differences in production technology, final demand structure and interregional trade coefficients, which would be equivalent to the outcome of a shift–and–share approach (although a very sophisticated one).

In a partially bottom-up application, however, at least some final

---

[3] The national vectors and matrices $\mathbf{x}, \mathbf{f}, \mathbf{F}, \mathbf{e}$ etc. are denoted in non-italics to distinguish them from their interregional counterparts x, f, F, e etc.

demand growth rates are estimated separately for region 1.[4] After correcting for consistency with the national $\mathring{x}_{ot}$, in this case, the regional forecast $\mathring{x}_{ot}$ will still have a bottom-up character.

4 The supply side of the labour market

The supply side of the labour market in ISAM consists of three blocks: population, migration and labour market participation. Only the participation block uses exogenous national CPB forecasts which makes the bottom-up content of the supply side of ISAM more substantial than that of the demand side.

The national forecasts of the labour supply by the CPB are implicit and not well documented. Partly for this reason, we have developed our own national population model in which a population forecast is made for each northern province and for the Netherlands as a whole using standard cohort-survival methods with regional and national birth and mortality rates.

The cohort survival method is well known and will not be described here (see, e.g., Rogers, 1975). We will restrict ourselves to discussing the way in which the migration effects are incorporated into the forecast of the potential labour force. If we denote region with suffix r, and $\sigma \rightarrow t$ is again the forecasting period, the regional population forecast is made in the following way

$$k_t^r = (B^r + V^r)^{t-\sigma} k_\sigma^r + \sum_{\tau=\sigma+1,t} (V^r)^{t-\tau} m_\tau^r \tag{7.8}$$

with

k_t^r is a $2a$ vector of population per age/sex group (a = number of age groups),
B^r is a $2a \times 2a$ matrix of birth rates,
V^r is a $2a \times 2a$ matrix of survival rates and
m_τ^r is a $2a$ vector of net migration.

The first term of (7.8) describes the standard cohort survival forecast of the resident population from σ to t. The second term is a little more complicated and refers to the net migration effect generated by m_τ^r that has to be added to the resident population k_τ in each year subsequent to the starting year σ.

The national population forecast uses the same specification as (7.8) where m_τ^r refers only to foreign net migration. Both forecasts lead to an

---

[4] To guarantee consistency with the national $\mathring{F}_{ot}$ in this case the final demand growth rates for region 2 may be calculated as a residual.

implicit forecast for region 2 (the rest of the country) which means that there is no consistency problem between the regional and the national levels.[5] However, the implicit population forecast for region 2 is not used, as our main policy interest is the comparison of the national economy with the regional economy.

The remaining consistency problem is therefore a possible difference between our own national population forecast and the one produced by the national CBP model. With respect to the natural population growth there is no problem as both models use the same birth and mortality rates, from the Central Bureau of Statistics (CBS, 1990). A minor actual consistency problem is related to foreign migration, which is forecast yearly by the CPB on a more or less *ad hoc* basis. For the three northern provinces, foreign net migration is small because it tends to be concentrated mainly in urban agglomerations in the western part of The Netherlands. Hence, this effect is simply estimated by applying the average regional share in national foreign net migration of the last quinquennium to the national yearly forecast.

Net *domestic migration* is modelled directly without separate estimates of the incoming and outgoing flows. Separate estimates were tried in earlier versions of ISAM and recently a renewed attempt was made for the present version. The results were fairly satisfactory for the flows themselves, but, not surprisingly, the implicit prediction of net migration failed. As our main interest is in the effects of net migration on the regional labour market we decided to model it directly. From a theoretical point of view this is not consistent at the micro level because 'there is no such thing as a net migrant' (Rogers, 1990). In our view, however, at the macro level regional net migration can be seen as an indicator of the relative attractiveness of a region with respect to labour market and housing market conditions. Therefore, we tried to use only independent variables that express this relative attractiveness. We will not describe the migration model in detail (see Stelder, 1991), but its general form is as follows

$$m_t^r = \psi_0^r + \psi_1^r \Delta h_{t-1}^r + \psi_2^r \mathring{e}_{t-1}^r - \psi_3^r (u_t^r / l_t^r - u_t^n / l_t^n) \tag{7.9}$$

where

Δh is the absolute increase in housing stock,
$\mathring{e}$ is the employment growth rate,
u is the number of unemployed,
l is the total labour supply,
ψ_i^r are regression coefficients (different for each entry of m_t^r) and
r and n refer to region and nation respectively.

---

[5] In the input–output model this problem is caused by the fact that an implicit national result is produced by the explicit forecasts for regions 1 and 2.

It is clear from (7.9) that only the last term is a relative indicator (the difference between regional and national unemployment). The employment and housing indicators simply did not work as relative indicators, which is clearly inconsistent with our theoretical considerations. At the moment our tentative explanation is that the net migration model *de facto* models out-migration because in-migration in Groningen and Friesland has been following national trends, while out-migration started to diverge from the national pattern from 1982 onwards.

Another interesting point to note is that (7.9) reveals inconsistencies between the three regions and between different age groups. As is shown in figure 7.4, the situation in Drenthe is substantially different from that in Groningen and Friesland, while the age structure of net migration in Friesland is also different from Groningen. It turned out that labour market indicators were especially relevant for the age group twenty-five to thirty-nine and that housing market indicators were more relevant for the age group forty to sixty-four. These findings reflect the life-cycle theory in migration research which predicts that job migration diminishes as people become older, with housing factors becoming more important. For the province of Drenthe, however, no significant labour market effect could be identified, and only housing market factors were found to be relevant.

It is clear that the population model in (7.8) needs a very detailed age/sex-specific forecast of net migration, especially when the forecasting period becomes longer. The migration relations found and used in ISAM, however, relate to a much more aggregated level of only three age groups (15–24, 25–39 and 40–64) with no specification by gender. This inconsistency in aggregation level is solved in a two-step procedure. First, we disaggregate the three migration groups into 10×2 age/sex groups using the assumption that the forecast net migration may be divided among these subgroups according to historical net migration data. Secondly, the resulting net migration for these twenty age/sex groups is disaggregated further into $a = 15 \ldots 64$, assuming that the age structure within each of the twenty groups is the same as that for the corresponding resident population.

Labour participation is modelled quite simply. The participation rate for females in The Netherlands increased by as much as 20 per cent between 1971 and 1990, whereas that of males decreased by 4 per cent. Regional percentage differences in these rates per age/sex group are very stable (Stelder, 1992). Hence, regional participation rates per age/sex group are assumed to follow the national projection by the CPB (Manders, 1989) in the following way

$$lf_t^r = lf_a^r + \Delta lf_{at}^n \tag{7.10}$$

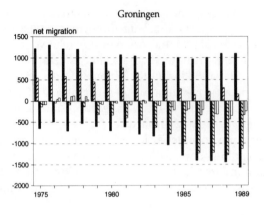

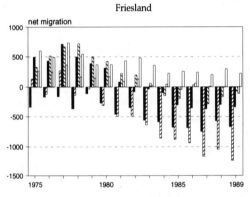

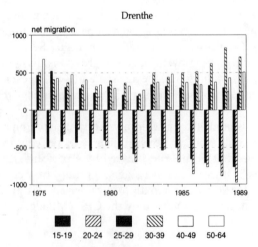

Figure 7.4 Net migration by age group

where

lf_t^r is a $2a$ vector with participation rates per age/sex group and
$\Delta lf_{\sigma t}^n$ is a 2a vector with percentage changes of national participation
rates per age/sex group over the period $\sigma \to t$.

Here again, a minor aggregation problem occurs. The population/migration model has cohorts for one year, while the (survey) information on participation rates only allows projections for five-year cohorts. Consistency is secured by aggregating the outcomes of the population projection to five-year cohorts.

Finally, *commuting* needs to be considered. Evers and van der Veen (1984) strongly argue in favour of a simultaneous approach to migration and commuting. They distinguish complementary commuting that results from residential migration without job mobility, and substitution commuting that results from the opposite mix. The present data, however, are insufficient to repeat their analysis for the 1980s, which has forced us to use simple extrapolation methods. The commuting balance between Groningen and Drenthe is assumed to change slowly in favour of Groningen, while the other relatively small commuting flows between the northern regions are assumed to remain constant. Total labour supply may now simply be estimated as follows

$$l_t^r = (lf_t^r)' k_t^r + \Delta com_{\sigma t}^r \qquad (7.11)$$

where

$\Delta com_{\sigma t}^r$ is the change in net commuting into region r over the period $\sigma \to t$.

5 Demo-economic interaction and global model consistency

The supply and the demand side of ISAM meet in the projection of the principal policy variable, the total number of unemployed people u_t^r, by means of (7.7) and (7.11)

$$u_t^r = (\mathring{e}_{\sigma t}^r)' \mathring{e}_\sigma^r - l_t^r \qquad (7.12)$$

where

$\mathring{e}_{\sigma t}^r$ is the i vector of employment growth rates for region r (the 'upper half' of $\mathring{e}_{\sigma t}$ in (7.7)) and
$\mathring{e}_\sigma^r$ is the i vector of employment in region r in the starting year σ.

The question arises whether the entire model may be solved in the way in which the majority of demo-economic models are solved, i.e., by means of the reduced form of a linear activity analysis solution (see, e.g., Oosterhaven and Dewhurst, 1990). The answer is negative because of the non-linear character of the last term of the migration equation (7.9). For Groningen and Friesland this third term is highly significant, while all linear specifications of the influence of unemployment on migration proved to be insignificant.

The solution to this essential non-linearity problem was found by means of iteration. Initially, the difference between regional and national unemployment is assumed to be constant, leading to a first estimate of migration with (7.9). Migration is then substituted into (7.8) which co-determines the first estimate of labour supply in (7.11), and migration influences population growth which is used to estimate consumption growth in (7.1), that in turn co-determines the growth of labour demand in (7.7). Labour supply and demand are then used to reach a first endogenous estimate of unemployment in (7.12). After this first iteration the same cycle starts again and convergence is reached after three to four iterations when the difference in unemployment between iterations becomes less than 0.1 per cent.

At present, global consistency is only reached by means of aggregating both labour demand and labour supply to their respective totals in (7.12). Regional data on employment per sector are not disaggregated into, for example, age/sex groups, while regional labour supply data are not disaggregated sectorally. An early attempt to make a qualitative projection of supply and demand according to levels of schooling produced extremely implausible outcomes (FNEI, 1978). At present, the quality of the data does not offer much better possibilities. Consequently, any plausibility check has to restrict itself to the global outcomes for total unemployment and its determining factors themselves.

6 Conclusion

The description of the ISAM demo-economic model shows that consistency problems are very data specific. Their nature, however, has some general aspects. First, we have aggregation and disaggregation problems. Focussing on age/sex groups enables the solution of part of these problems. The national/regional aggregation problem proves to be soluble by shifting from bottom-up to top-down approaches in a flexible way. Secondly, there are classification consistency problems, especially between the supply and demand sides of the labour market. Here, unfortunately, the only solution appears to be to aggregate to the common denominator of total supply and total demand. Obviously, a clear need for a more sophisticated approach is apparent. Finally, the solution technique depends crucially upon the functional form of the equations. In our case, the simultaneous solution to the standard linear activity description of demo-economic models could not be used. The essentially non-linear character of migration requires an iterative solution. An appropriate choice of starting values appears to be important in order to achieve a rapid convergence.

8 A CGE solution to the household rigidity problem in extended input–output models

ANDREW B. TRIGG AND MOSS MADDEN

1 Introduction

One of the important areas of recent development in the field of input–output analysis has been the modelling, in a regional context, of linkages between industrial output and household activity. Household consumption has been shown to be a very important component of the demographic-economic system (see, e.g., Hewings, 1986; Batey and Madden, 1981) and one which is rarely accorded the attention it deserves in terms of resources devoted to analysis and data collection. The linkages between industrial activity and household activity are traditionally modelled in input–output analysis by treating households as an ordinary industry which consumes industrial products and produces labour services. Additional rows and columns are added to the interindustry flows matrix in what has come to be called the extended input–output model. A core problem in applications of this model to the regional context has been how to model the impact of newly employed workers on a regional economy. Morrison (1973), for example, treated new workers as in-migrants attracted to the new town of Peterborough in the UK during the early 1970s. Since then, however, the world economy has suffered from two major recessions, and attention has become focussed on the pool of unemployed workers which now exists in many intra-national regions. The so called type IV input–output model has been developed in an attempt to capture explicitly the consumption profiles of employed and unemployed workers (see, e.g., Batey and Madden, 1981; van Dijk and Oosterhaven, 1986).

Developments of the interface between household and industrial activity in regional input–output analysis have been paralleled in the field of social accounting. Since Richard Stone's *Input–Output and National Accounts* (1961b) a central feature of the social accounts approach has been the co-ordination of income and product accounts with input–output accounts. This co-ordination has also been pioneered by Stone (1961a) in a three-region version which remains a prototype regional accounting framework. Whilst this early work used the standard Leontief closed input–output model, a more recent contribution to social accounting methodology by Stone and Weale (1986) parallels developments in the extended input–output literature. A two-region social accounts framework is developed in which workers move between unemployed and employed states of activity. Trigg (1987) has shown that the multipliers derived from this model are the same as those derived from the type IV extended input–output model. This incorporation of the type IV model within a social accounts framework has since been applied by Madden and Trigg (1990) to the analysis of interregional migration.

Whilst the type IV model provides a more realistic treatment of consumption than its antecedents, there are two fundamental problems. First, crude consumption propensities are used which are calculated by taking average consumption per unit of income for the two separate groups of employed and unemployed workers. This is despite the development in the parallel field of social accounting of a much more sophisticated model of the income–expenditure linkage, namely, Stone's Linear Expenditure System (Stone and Brown 1962). Secondly, there have been a number of rigidity problems associated with the explicit treatment of household consumption in the type IV model. Since survey data on consumer expenditure is usually collected and organised on a household basis, whilst workers are hired and fired as individuals, some form of mapping is needed between individual and household activity. The extended input–output matrix has proved to be very difficult to adapt in this respect. Whilst Madden and Batey (1980) provide an early attempt to embody household structure in the type IV model, the severe rigidity problems which were involved in the modelling of household consumption led to the construction of a personal consumption framework (Batey and Madden, 1983).

In this chapter we develop a new modelling framework which both provides a solution to the household rigidity problem and facilitates the estimation of accurate consumption propensities. Building on the proposals of Trigg (1989), the income–expenditure interface is developed by using micro data on household expenditure and individual economic activity. Micro observations are argued to be much more flexible for the modelling of interactions between household and industrial activity than the aggregate rows and columns used in extended input–output matrices. This micro approach is made operational by using a Computable General Equilibrium (CGE) model. Data are provided for 1984 by the UK Family Expenditure Survey (FES) and the UK input–output tables.

The first part of the chapter briefly introduces the structure of the type IV input–output model and explains how it relates to a social accounting framework. The household rigidity problem is examined, and a review is provided of recent literature on the subject. In the second part of the chapter two alternative micro procedures are considered for developing a mechanism by which jobs can be matched with individual workers and their households. A procedure which identifies productivity using a micro-econometric wage equation is decided upon in favour of the logit limited dependent variable model. In the final part of the chapter the micro job-matching mechanism is conjoined with the input–output model as part of a CGE model. A set of Jacobian multipliers derived from this model is reported.

2 The type IV consumption framework

Stone and Weale (1986) developed a set of two-region multipliers which relates to a two-region social accounts matrix (SAM). Following Trigg (1987) we capture the structure of this model in a one-region format. The usual Leontief equation is adapted such that

$$X = A.X + \beta^c.l_d.X + a^c.(l - l_d.X) + f, \tag{8.1}$$

where:

$X =$ a column vector of gross outputs,
$A =$ a square matrix of interindustry coefficients,
$f =$ a column vector of industrial final demand,
$\beta^c =$ a column vector of consumption rates per employed worker,
$a^c =$ a column vector of consumption rates per unemployed worker,
$l_d =$ a row vector of labour coefficients per unit of output, and
$l =$ a scalar representing total labour supply.

Gross output is directed to intermediate demand $(A.X)$, the consumption of employed workers $(\beta^c.l_d.X)$, the consumption of unemployed workers $a^c.(l - l_d.X)$, and to final demand (f). The number of unemployed workers is calculated as the residual left after subtracting the number of employed workers $(l_d.X)$ from total labour supply (l). The elements of this equation can be related to the first row of a schematic social accounts matrix (SAM) (see figure 8.1).

The typical element T_{ij} shows money flow from account j to account i. This provides a measure of the real flow of commodities flowing in the opposite direction. For example, T_{13} shows the flow of money from the unemployed to the production account – it measures the flow of commodities directed from the production account to the unemployed. Each of the four elements in the top row of this SAM can be modelled using the four components of equation (8.1). The intermediate commodity flows (T_{11}) can

| | Expenditures | | | |
Receipts	1	2	3	4
1 Production	T_{11}	T_{12}	T_{13}	T_{14}
2 Employed	T_{21}			
3 Unemployed				T_{34}
4 Final demand		T_{42}		

Figure 8.1 A schematic social accounts matrix

be related to gross output via the technical coefficients (A); whilst the sensitivity of flows of consumption goods $(T_{12}$ and $T_{13})$ to gross output are measured using labour demand coefficients (l_d) and consumption propensities $(\beta^c$ and $\alpha^c)$. The final demand for commodities (T_{14}), which includes categories such as investment and government spending, is represented by the exogenous component f.

The one-region version of the Stone–Weale equations shown in equation (8.1) can be re-written as three interconnected equations

$$(I-A).X-\beta^c.e-\alpha^c.u=f \tag{8.2}$$

$$e=l_d.X \tag{8.3}$$

$$u=l-e \tag{8.4}$$

where

$e=$ a scalar representing employment, and
$u=$ a scalar representing the stock of unemployed workers.

Collecting these terms together in a block matrix format yields

$$\begin{bmatrix} (I-A) & -\beta^c & -\alpha^c \\ -l_d & 1 & 0 \\ 0 & 1 & 1 \end{bmatrix} \cdot \begin{bmatrix} X \\ e \\ u \end{bmatrix} = \begin{bmatrix} f \\ 0 \\ l \end{bmatrix} \tag{8.5}$$

which is the same as the type IV input–output model developed by Batey and Madden (1983). The left-hand block matrix can be inverted to derive the type IV multiplier matrix.

This demonstration of the linkage between the block matrix type IV model and the social accounts approach of Stone and Weale (1986) has provided the basis for applications by Trigg (1987) to the evaluation of the impacts of defence spending, and for the work of Madden and Trigg (1990) on the sensitivity of interregional migration to economic activity. Both these applications, however, make use of crude consumption coefficients.

In particular, these consumption coefficients relate to individual employed and unemployed workers but are derived from *household* information contained in the Family Expenditure Survey (FES).

There have been several attempts to model household expenditure explicitly in the type IV framework. An early attempt by Madden and Batey (1980) involved the disaggregation of households into two categories: households with employed heads and unemployed heads. Due to rigidity problems it was replaced by the personal consumption framework shown in equation (8.5). A reformulation of the household consumption framework was later suggested by Madden and Batey (1986) in which households are classified according to whether they have any unemployed workers. An alternative model is also suggested by Hynes and Jackson (1988) in which households are disaggregated according to the number of employed workers in each type of household. For simplicity we shall examine the Madden–Batey (1986) version in order to demonstrate the rigidity problems associated with this suite of models.

The Madden and Batey (1986) version of the type IV input–output model has the following structure

$$
\begin{bmatrix} (I-A) & -\beta_h^c & -\alpha_h^c \\ -L_d & W & O \\ O & I & I \end{bmatrix} \cdot \begin{bmatrix} X \\ hh^e \\ hh^u \end{bmatrix} = \begin{bmatrix} f \\ O \\ hh^t \end{bmatrix} \quad (8.6)
$$

where:

β_h^c = a matrix of consumption coefficients for employed households,

α_h^c = a matrix of consumption coefficients for unemployed households,

L_d = a diagonal matrix of labour demand coefficients expressing employment per unit of sectoral gross output,

W = a diagonal matrix containing ratios of workers to households, each ratio applying to workers in a particular sector,

hh^e = a vector containing the numbers of employed households associated with each sector,

hh^u = a vector containing the numbers of unemployed households associated with each sector,

hh^t = a vector representing numbers of households associated with each sector,

I = an identity matrix, and

O = a null matrix.

Other terms have already been defined.

Employed households are categorised as households which contain at least one employed worker, whilst unemployed households contain no employed workers. The mapping between jobs obtained by individuals and household consumption works through the matrix W. An increase in jobs generates an increase in the number of employed households according to the ratios contained in this matrix. The type IV mechanism then calculates the residual number of unemployed households which are left in the economy. There is an increase in consumption via the induced increase in the number of employed households, and a reduction in consumption via the reduction in the number of unemployed households.

A problem with this model is that the jobs are assumed to be taken only by unemployed workers resident in unemployed households. The model ignores the pool of unemployed workers which exist in employed households. Since to be defined as employed a household only needs one employed worker the model is too rigid to consider the unemployed workers which would be found in these households. The relaxation of this rigidity, so that unemployed workers are modelled in all types of households, generates severe operational problems for the type IV model. In the versions developed by Madden and Batey (1980) and Hynes and Jackson (1988) new jobs are allocated to different household types by assuming fixed proportions of unemployed workers in each category. The household type with the largest proportion of unemployed receives the largest number of newly created jobs. There are two main problems with this job matching mechanism. Firstly, as new jobs are created the proportions of unemployed in each household type will not remain fixed. There is no exogenous mechanism by which new jobs can be allocated to different household types. A second problem is that the proportions of unemployed in each household provide very crude indicators of which workers will take up new jobs. The job matching mechanism ignores differences in productivity and market suitability between workers by assuming that all unemployed workers constitute a homogeneous pool. Moreover, the allocation of jobs to households in this mechanism may provide results which conflict with reality. Households with the highest proportion of unemployed workers are assumed to command the highest proportion of new jobs, but a more accurate scenario might be that workers in households with a high proportion of unemployed workers may have characteristics which render them less productive and less likely to obtain employment than their counterparts in households with less unemployed workers.

In the next part of the chapter a more accurate job matching mechanism is developed which estimates employment probabilities for each worker in a sample of micro observations.

3 A micro job matching mechanism

Micro information on the individual characteristics of workers can be used to predict for each worker the probability that he or she will obtain employment. We shall consider two alternative procedures. In the first a limited dependent variable model is used, whilst the second procedure makes use of an ordinary least squares wage equation.

A limited dependent variable model

In the work of Blundell, Ham and Meghir (1988) employment probabilities are calculated in which ϕ_i is a dependent variable such that

$$\phi_i = \begin{cases} 1 \text{ if a worker is employed,} \\ 0 \text{ if a worker is seeking employment.} \end{cases}$$

A latent variable is assumed to exist which is not measured but which explains the employment probability

$$\phi_i^* = \chi_i'\theta + \xi_i \tag{8.7}$$

where

$\chi_i' = $ a row vector of observable characteristics for individual i^i,
$\theta = $ a column vector of parameters, and
$\xi_i = $ a scalar representing the unexplained disturbance term for individual i.

The latent variable and the dummy variable are related such that

if $\phi_i^* > 0$ then $\phi_i = 1$. We observe employment.
if $\phi_i^* < 0$ then $\phi_i = 0$. We observe search unemployment.

Therefore, the probability of obtaining employment is

$$p(\phi_i = 1) = p(\phi_i > 0) = p(\xi_i > -\chi_i'.\theta) \tag{8.8}$$

Two possible alternatives are for this probability to be estimated either by assuming that ξ_i has a normal distribution (the probit model), or by assuming that it has a logistic distribution (the logit model). For each model a likelihood expression is maximised in order to identify the parameters which provide the best predictors of employment probability. In practice the two models generate similar results.

In table 8.1 the parameters are reported from a logit model estimated for a sample of workers in the 1984 Family Expenditure Survey (see appendix 8.1 to this chapter). The problem with these parameters is that they tend to contradict a priori economic reasoning. For example, the education coefficient is negative, which suggests that the more educated a person is the less likely (s)he is to obtain employment. Economic reasoning is also confounded by the skill variables, which become more strongly negative as

Table 8.1 *A logit employment probability equation*

	Coefficient	T-ratio
Intercept	2.930	1.05
Age	−0.031	−0.95
Age squared	0.001	0.28
Education	−0.432	−1.53
Education squared	0.013	1.79
Semi-skilled manual	−0.422	−1.95
Skilled manual	−0.861	−3.96
Clerical	−1.202	−4.97
Professional	−1.761	−5.79
Married	−0.521	−3.36
Greater London	0.009	0.04
West Midlands	0.091	0.47
Female	−0.151	−1.03

Notes:
Number of workers = 4,900.
Number of seekers = 294.

a worker's skill increases. Thus, unskilled workers appear to be more likely to get work than skilled workers. Some of the other parameters seem reasonable, such as the positive effect on employment probability of living in Greater London, and the negative effect of female gender. The implausible signs of some of the core variables, however, cast doubt on the reliability of this model. An alternative to the logit model is considered below.

A productivity-based approach

An economically plausible approach would be to match jobs with workers according to their productivity and market wage. In neoclassical economic theory workers are employed up until the point where the value marginal product of their labour is equal to their market wage. By observing market wages, marginal productivities can be identified using a micro-econometric wage equation (see Trigg, 1993). In a simple linear form this equation has the structure

$$y_i^w = \mathbf{Z}_i^{np} . \psi^{np} + \mathbf{Z}_i^{p} . \psi^{p} + \xi_i, \tag{8.9}$$

Table 8.2 *A log wage equation*

	Coefficient	T-ratio
Ψ^{np}:		
Intercept	1.263	32.874
Female	−0.376	−27.584
Unemployment	−0.011	−5.695
Primary sector	0.058	3.459
Textiles sector	−0.116	−4.254
Distribution sector	−0.267	−20.476
Greater London	0.170	8.956
Midlands	−0.036	−2.652
Ψ^{p}:		
Age	0.048	8.713
Age squared	−0.061	−16.685
Education	0.349	4.958
Education squared	−0.101	−1.099
Semi-skilled manual	0.075	2.839
Skilled manual	0.181	6.994
Clerical	0.236	8.965
Professional	0.483	17.396
Married	0.111	7.738

Notes:
Number of workers = 4,900.
$R^2 = 0.512$.

where

y_i^w = the wage rate,
Z_i^{np} = a row vector of non-productivity related regressors (including the intercept), and
Z_i^p = a row vector of regressors which reflect productivity.

The component $Z_i^p . \psi^p$ relates to the proportion of earnings which reflect productivity, whilst $Z_i^{np} . \psi^{np}$ controls for non-productivity earnings. The coefficients ψ^{np} and ψ^p can be estimated using ordinary least squares regression across the sample of employed workers in the FES sample. Predictors Ψ^{np} and Ψ^p can be estimated for each of these sets of parameters respectively. This is demonstrated in table 8.2. Unlike the logit parameters, in this wage equation all the signs seem plausible. Age, education and skills, for example, have a positive effect on wages, whilst regional unemployment and female gender have a negative effect.

If we assume that employers are interested in employing workers with a high productivity and relatively low wage, then the following employment probability $p(E_i)$ can be estimated

$$p(E_i) = (Z_i^p . \Psi^p)/(Z_i^{np} . \Psi^{np} + Z_i^p . \Psi^p) \qquad (8.10)$$

By predicting the productivity related wage and the total wage for each unemployed worker in the FES sample, a set of employment probabilities can be derived. A problem with this model is that the wage equation may suffer from sample selection bias. Since the wages of unemployed workers are inferred from the wages of employed workers, it could be that the parameters suffer from a bias since they depend on the unobservable characteristics of the selected sample of employed workers (see Heckman, 1980). This problem is avoided by the logit model since sample selection provides the analytical core of the estimation procedure. Future research will examine the extent to which sample selection is a serious problem for this alternative productivity-based approach. In the next section the employment probabilities derived from the latter approach are fused together with the input–output equations in a CGE solution.

4 A CGE solution

A prototype modelling framework for a new, more flexible, type IV household consumption framework is illustrated in figure 8.2. Assuming that government spending is an exogenous impulse to the system, this generates increases in gross outputs via the input–output model, which can then be translated into additional jobs using the usual labour coefficients. These economy wide jobs are translated into an equivalent number of jobs generated in the micro sample of workers. The employment probability model is then used to decide which workers in the sample obtain these jobs – those workers with the highest employment probabilities. In the next stage the wage equation (8.9) is used to predict the wages of new workers, and a tax-benefit model calculates the withdrawal of taxes and lost benefits. The net incomes of these individual workers are then imputed to the households in which these workers reside. Some form of demand system, such as Stone's Linear Expenditure System, can then be used to calculate the consumption propensities of these households, and the outputs of expenditure are fed back to the input–output model.

This framework can be represented as a CGE model (see, e.g., Scarf and Shoven, 1984; Harrigan and McGregor, 1988a), the solution of which will present the equilibrium of the system between household consumption derived from the employment probability model, the tax-benefit model and

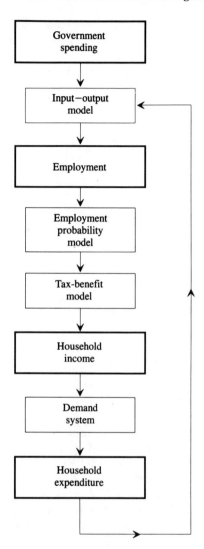

Figure 8.2 The interfaces between output, employment, income and expenditure

the demand system and household consumption derived from the accounts provided by the Leontief framework.

Different final demand injections into the system, positive or negative, will generate different initial household consumption from the accounting framework, and gross outputs of the system will adjust to ensure balance with the consumption derived from the micro-data model. Jacobian multipliers (see, e.g., Robinson and Roland-Holst, 1988) can be derived to establish the effects of different exogenous variable changes on the endogenous variables of the system.

The framework in figure 8.2 can be represented simply in the following simultaneous equation form

$$(I - A).X = f + gp + c_{hh}^e + c_{hh}^u \tag{8.11}$$

$$e = l_d.X \tag{8.12}$$

$$c_{hh}^e = \mathcal{F}(e, z) \tag{8.13}$$

$$c_{hh}^u = \mathcal{F}(u, z), \text{ and} \tag{8.14}$$

$$u = l - e \tag{8.15}$$

where

c_{hh}^e = household consumption of employed workers,
c_{hh}^u = household consumption of unemployed workers,
f = non-governmental final demand,
gp = government expenditure,
e = the number of employed workers,
u = the number of unemployed workers,
l = the total labour supply, and
z = the exogenous characteristics of households.

The framework may be solved as a CGE model, although the formulation, in contrast to most CGE models, does not involve a full specification of the economic system, as in, for example, the AMOS system (Harrigan *et al.*, 1991), or the classic work of Adelman and Robinson (1978).

For the preliminary version of the model reported upon in this chapter, we assume a fixed probability of employment for each of a set of workers with characteristics drawn from the Family Expenditure Survey (see section 3). As jobs are created in the system, workers are employed according to this probability. The actual number of jobs generated from gross outputs is modelled in equation (8.12); and the matching of these jobs with individual workers using the fixed employment probabilities is achieved as part of equation (8.13). This latter equation also models the consumption profiles of the households in which these individual workers are contained. These workers consume according to their household characteristics, based on a consumption profile generated from their FES reports. The usual type IV mechanism, by which the number of unemployed is derived as a residual, is shown in equation (8.15). The consumption of the households in which these unemployed workers are contained is modelled using equation (8.14). A CGE solution is established by modelling the impacts of final demand on industrial output and household

Table 8.3 *Industrial gross outputs*

Outputs in sector	Base year output (£m)	+ 100 million construction	− 100 million construction
1 Agriculture/fishing	23978.61	23981.35	23975.78
2 Energy/water	62000.52	62010.10	61986.31
3 Iron/steel	9410.53	9414.35	9406.31
4 Minerals	7884.61	7899.07	7869.64
5 Chemicals	20298.72	20302.20	20294.81
6 Metal/engineering	25446.55	25454.75	25437.28
7 Electrical engineering	18221.38	18223.25	18218.79
8 Transport manufacture	18099.23	18100.14	18095.62
9 Instrument engineering	1957.45	1957.59	1957.27
10 Food/tobacco	56964.47	56970.44	56957.62
11 Textiles	8693.05	8694.35	8691.23
12 Leather	865.27	865.35	865.18
13 Footwear/clothes	10493.44	10494.76	10491.34
14 Timber/furniture	6767.24	6770.64	6763.38
15 Paper/printing	18307.62	18311.34	18303.24
16 Rubber and other	10287.77	10290.11	10284.91
17 Construction	34935.92	35063.27	34806.83
18 Distribution	57020.19	57025.82	57013.05
19 Transport/communication	35062.04	35069.69	35051.26
20 Banking/finance	65089.79	65113.66	65062.47
21 Employment ('000)	14964.31	14970.81	14957.09

expenditure through a series of iterations. The balancing equation (8.11) provides the accounting constraint which must be satisfied.

It is also possible to compute Jacobian multiplier matrices for each scenario, which show the effects upon the economy of small changes in final demand in all sectors. These matrices are similar to the usual inverse matrices associated with SAMs or extended input–output models, but are not restricted by the rigidities of the SAM structure and in particular the rigidities of the household consumption areas of the SAM described earlier. In the next part of the chapter we show some results of the model response to certain exogenous (perhaps government-derived) shocks to the system via the final demand vector.

5 Empirical results

In the first column of figures in table 8.3 we show industrial and employment outputs of the system for the base-year. Industrial outputs are shown in millions of pounds sterling, and employment in thousands of jobs. Table

Table 8.4 *Selected entries from the Jacobian matrix for the base year solution*

Sector	1	2	5	6	10	13	17	18	19
1	1.2994	0.0457	0.0511	0.0474	0.4050	0.0521	0.0480	0.0675	0.0483
2	0.1777	1.4755	0.2596	0.1416	0.1506	0.1007	0.1335	0.1491	0.1725
5	0.1336	0.0273	1.2008	0.0380	0.0377	0.0430	0.0410	0.0328	0.0277
6	0.0476	0.0586	0.0633	1.2058	0.0760	0.0418	0.0895	0.0421	0.0307
10	0.3708	0.2276	0.1300	0.1213	1.3662	0.1273	0.1200	0.1719	0.1247
13	0.0114	0.0085	0.0086	0.0089	0.0095	1.0535	0.0101	0.0150	0.0111
17	0.0351	0.0247	0.0268	0.0294	0.0321	0.0283	1.2864	0.0395	0.0292
18	0.0654	0.0474	0.0606	0.1011	0.0754	0.0586	0.0644	1.0587	0.0652
19	0.0804	0.0645	0.1295	0.0830	0.0974	0.0603	0.0860	0.1137	1.1300

8.4 depicts selected entries from the Jacobian matrix derived from this base-year solution by applying incremental perturbations to each sector in turn, and re-solving the system. Each Jacobian entry represents the proportional change in output in each sector as a result of each perturbation, and can be interpreted in exactly the same way as each entry in a SAM inverse. Indeed, the structure of the matrix and the sign and relative sizes of the entries in table 8.4 are empirically very similar to those of a typical SAM inverse. In this particular case the largest entry, 1.4755, shows the effect that a unit injection in the energy/water sector would have upon itself. The largest interindustry linkage is the effect of changes in the food/tobacco sector on agriculture and fishing. The smallest entries are those in the footwear/clothing sector row.

Let us now investigate the effect of assuming a (government-inspired) increase in sales by the construction sector of 100 million pounds. The second column of table 8.3 shows the outputs. We can easily see that the effects of the extra injection into the construction sector have not followed the pattern predicted by the Jacobian multipliers for the base year. For example, the construction sector itself has expanded by a factor of 1.2735 rather than the larger 1.2864 suggested by the multiplier. Similarly, the energy/water sector has expanded by only 0.0958 rather than the multiplier value of 0.1335, whilst food/tobacco has experienced an expansion of 0.0597 compared with a multiplier of 0.1200.

The Jacobian for this new equilibrium solution shows some very interesting entries, a selection of which are reproduced in table 8.5. Perhaps the most intriguing aspects of this table are that the Jacobian entries are in all cases smaller than those for the base year, and indeed in two sectors – agriculture/fish and food/tobacco – are often negative. This means that

Table 8.5 *Selected Jacobian entries for the solution with a positive injection in the construction sector*

Sec	Sector								
	1	2	5	6	10	13	17	18	19
1	1.2596	−0.0041	0.0013	−0.0024	0.3552	0.0023	−0.0018	0.0177	−0.0015
2	0.1078	1.4056	0.1897	0.0717	0.0807	0.0308	0.0636	0.0792	0.1026
5	0.1160	0.0098	1.1832	0.0205	0.0502	0.0254	0.0234	0.0152	0.0101
6	0.0311	0.0420	0.0498	1.1893	0.0595	0.0253	0.0730	0.0255	0.0142
10	0.2532	−0.0100	0.0024	−0.0063	1.2386	−0.0003	−0.0076	0.0443	−0.0029
13	0.0040	0.0011	0.0012	0.0015	0.0021	1.0461	0.0028	0.0077	0.0037
17	0.0118	0.0014	0.0035	0.0061	0.0088	0.0050	1.2631	0.0162	0.0060
18	0.0377	0.0197	0.0329	0.0734	0.0477	0.0309	0.0367	1.310	0.0375
19	0.0549	0.0389	0.0575	0.0640	0.0718	0.0347	0.0604	0.0882	1.1045

incremental increases in sales to final demand by the sectors heading the columns in which the negative entries appear, would result in decreases in the output of these two sectors. The explanation of this must be that at the particular labour demand level achieved by this scenario, workers who consume more in some sectors when unemployed than when employed, are moving into employment, causing a decline in consumption in those sectors. This decline is manifested in negative multipliers for the two sectors identified, and reflects the effect of combining the micro-data approach, with its disaggregated and diverse set of household consumption patterns, with the input–output formulation.

The third column of figures in table 8.3 shows the effects upon outputs of a decrease in sales by construction to final demand of 100 million pounds. As we might expect, there is a non-linear relationship between columns 1, 2 and 3, with the decline in outputs resulting from a decrease in sales from construction to final demand being generally greater than the increase resulting from an increase in such sales. For example, the construction sector itself has declined by a factor of 1.2909 compared with the base-year Jacobian of 1.2864 and the corresponding increase factor, as a result of an increase in construction sales, of 1.2735. Energy/water declines by 0.1421, compared with a 0.0958 increase, and food/tobacco by 0.0685 compared with 0.0597.

We can also derive a new Jacobian matrix for this equilibrium, selections of which are shown in table 8.6. In this table, we see that all entries are bigger than those in table 8.5, and smaller than those in the base-year solution shown in table 8.4. There are few conclusions that can be drawn from these differences – they are derived from the consumption differences that occur as workers shift from unemployment to employment, in a hierarchy determined by the employment probabilities of the workers.

Each Jacobian matrix shows the effect of small changes in the final demand sales of the industrial sectors that occur simultaneously with the larger, government-inspired exogenous change that we are seeking to model. In this chapter we show only three of the possible Jacobians that can be calculated. In many cases, we might expect the Jacobian multipliers to be the same, as the same workers are drawn from unemployment into employment; in other cases, as in the three shown here, they will be different. It must be remembered, too, that the size of perturbation applied to each sector to calculate the Jacobians is instrumental in determining the Jacobian. Different sized perturbations will produce different multipliers.

Further empirical work will take advantage of the possibility of re-estimating the employment probabilities with each iteration of the model. This will of course greatly extend the solution time of each run, and will introduce further non-linearities that may be expected to produce counter-intuitive solutions.

Table 8.6 *Selected Jacobian entries for the solution with a negative injection in the construction sector*

	Sector								
Sec	1	2	5	6	10	13	17	18	19
1	1.2547	0.0010	0.0064	0.0027	0.3604	0.0074	0.0033	0.0229	0.0036
2	0.1130	1.4108	0.1949	0.0469	0.0856	0.0360	0.0688	0.0844	0.1078
5	0.1174	0.0111	1.1846	0.0219	0.0516	0.0268	0.0248	0.0166	0.0115
6	0.0325	0.0425	0.0513	1.1908	0.0610	0.0267	0.0745	0.0270	0.0157
10	0.2557	0.0025	0.0149	0.0062	1.2512	0.0123	0.0049	0.0568	0.0096
13	0.0044	0.0014	0.0016	0.0018	0.0025	1.0464	0.0031	0.0080	0.0039
17	0.0129	0.0025	0.0046	0.0072	0.0099	0.0061	1.2643	0.0173	0.0071
18	0.0399	0.0219	0.0351	0.0756	0.0499	0.0331	0.0389	1.0332	0.0397
19	0.0658	0.0408	0.0594	0.0659	0.0737	0.0366	0.0623	0.0901	1.1064

6 Conclusions

In this chapter a new procedure is developed for linking individual jobs to household expenditure in an input–output model. Unlike previous studies, which rely on the proportion of unemployed workers in households to model this linkage, this work estimates the productivity and market wage of each individual worker seeking employment. This is achieved using a micro sample of workers obtained from the UK Family Expenditure Survey. The productivity and market wage of each worker in the sample is predicted using a micro-econometric wage equation which is estimated using ordinary least squares regression. The employment probabilities of workers are estimated by taking the ratio of their estimated productivities relative to their market wage. Employers are assumed to be most likely to employ workers with a high ratio of productivity to market wage. The parameters estimated for this procedure are argued to be more economically feasible than those derived from the alternative logit limited dependent variable model.

A micro adaptation of the type IV input–output model is achieved using a CGE approach. The consumption of households is endogenised by conjoining micro data to the 1984 UK input–output tables. The impacts of an injection of final demand on industrial output and household consumption may be established in this model using a converging iterative routine. Jacobian multipliers may be generated for each solution of the model, which demonstrate, by analogy with SAM multiplier matrices, the effects upon the system of small perturbations in final demand sales of the industrial sectors of the economic–demographic system. In this chapter various injections in the construction sector are used to demonstrate the way in which the model behaves. We note that the non-linearities inherent in the model cause different multiplier matrices to be derived for different solutions.

The model developed in this chapter provides only a starting point for the development of a reliable impact assessment framework. In its present form the model suffers from a number of deficiencies which will be refined in future work. For example, the employment probabilities, which in this chapter are assumed to be fixed, are calculated from various characteristics which will doubtless change as economic activity changes. The consumption propensities are also assumed to be fixed and are derived as crude average coefficients. A demand system is required, such as the Linear Expenditure System developed by Richard Stone, in order to provide more accurate estimates of consumption propensities.

There is also a need to explore the stability and sensitivity of the model in response to changes in its parameters. For example, is the model more likely to be sensitive to changes in its input–output structure than it is to changes in the employment probabilities of individual workers? Sensitivity testing of this sort needs to be developed not just for this particular model but for CGE models in general.

Appendix 8.1

The UK input–output tables have been aggregated to a twenty-sector model which conforms with the industry classification in the Family Expenditure Survey (FES). Sample selections made for the FES sample involve the exclusion of all members of the armed forces, and any workers in the FES sectors 26 to 33. The normal gross wage code (007P) is used to calculate wage rates, whilst the education variable represents the age of leaving full-time education. The unemployment variable represents regional unemployment calculated from the Employment Gazette. The economy-wide number of individuals employed in each industrial sector has been calculated from the Census of Production (1984) and the Annual Abstract of Statistics (1986).

The disaggregation of jobs created in the economy to workers in the sample of micro data is achieved by relating the number of workers in the economy to the number of workers in the sample according to the relative sizes of each population. The sample is assumed to be representative of the economy as a whole. For the calculation of the net income of individual workers, a simple tax-benefit model is constructed which is limited to the coverage of unemployment benefit and supplementary benefit (now called income support). An average rate of taxation for all workers is assumed. This tax-benefit model will be expanded and refined in future work.

9 Operationalising a rural–urban general equilibrium model using a bi-regional SAM

MAUREEN KILKENNY

1 Introduction

Rural areas are often targeted for economic development. *Ex-ante* analysis of rural development policies is challenging because of the interdependencies between rural and urban areas which allow for 'leakages' of benefits through sales of urban products to rural consumers and through urban residents' ownership of rural land and capital. Conversely, the areas are not interdependent enough to assume a single market for goods, services and factors. Rural and urban markets are segmented because of the distances between them and/or because of habits or policies that restrict exchange. They are integrated to the extent that transport costs are not prohibitively high, and that rural and urban versions of the 'same' items are, in fact, substitutes. Thus, rural and urban areas should be modelled as separate but interdependent.

This chapter describes a rural–urban computable general equilibrium (CGE) model and the bi-regional social accounting matrix (SAM) needed to operationalise it. Three main steps are involved in the construction of any applied general equilibrium model. The first step is to formulate the theoretical general equilibrium model (see, for example, Dervis, deMelo and Robinson, 1982; Condon, Dahl and Devarajan, 1987). Second, develop a balanced SAM that exhaustively documents the observed flows of goods, factors, revenues and expenditures in the economic system of interest. Third, choose the functional forms and calibrate the parameters of the CGE model so that the solution for the base period replicates the data in the balanced, base-year SAM.

The focus of this chapter is on the second task: developing a balanced bi-regional SAM for a particular model. A basic rural–urban CGE model is discussed to illustrate this process. First, the structure of the model is presented. The act of determining the dimensions and types of transactions appropriate for the policy analysis model establishes the dimensions and accounts needed in the SAM database. The next part explains how national and urban data can be used to generate the bi-regional SAM, and how missing data on interregional transactions can be calibrated using other information. Finally, a new approach to balancing (any) model-specific SAM is presented.

A rural–urban CGE model

A CGE model is a set of equations representing the behaviour of agents interacting in an economy, market-clearing equations, and income/expenditure flows. CGE models are the n-dimensional analogues, solved using real-world data, of the neoclassical $2 \times 2 \times 2$ trade models by Heckscher–Ohlin–Samuelson (Jones, 1956).

In the rural–urban CGE model, agents are categorised as producing industries or consuming households by region; a national government; and the 'rest of the world'. The rural–urban CGE model solves for sectoral prices, quantities, employment, interregional trade and capital flows, wages, rents, income and consumption in each region; government budgets; trade flows and the exchange rate. The model framework is general enough to accommodate varying degrees of regional market segmentation and potential agglomeration economies. However, due to the nature of the regional delineation, it accounts for market segmentation but not distance.

This particular rural–urban model was developed to analyse the effects of changes in farm subsidies on regional income, non-farm industries, employment, and regional welfare in the United States (Kilkenny, 1993a). A minimum level of industry disaggregation is chosen to avoid proliferating data needs while still highlighting the key relationships between fundamentally different sectors. Six types of industries are distinguished in each region: agriculture, primary/extractives, agriculture-linked, manufacturing, business services and household services. This aggregation highlights the off-farm, rural community interindustry linkages with agriculture. It also highlights the pattern of regional specialisation.

At this degree of commodity aggregation all goods are traded internationally. Locally produced, other domestic and foreign versions are imperfect substitutes in demand and supply. Imperfect substitutability accounts for the observed interregional and international crosshauling. The apparent crosshauling also reflects the aggregation of different commodities over space, or of identical commodities over time. Thus, even though one region may supply a good at a lower price, all regions diversify. Since both domestic regions have all six industries there are twelve producer problems. By the same token, each region has its own commodity markets so there are twelve domestic commodity markets.

Labour and capital (and land in agriculture) are combined to produce output according to a simple Cobb–Douglas function.[1] Producer behaviour is represented by the first-order conditions for choice of inputs $(FD_{i,f,r})$, in which the arguments are prices, costs and the level of output

$$FD_{i,f,r} = [XD_{i,r} \cdot PVA_{i,r} \cdot a_{i,f,r}]/[FP_{f,r} \cdot \varpi_{i,f,r}] \qquad (9.1)$$

where $XD_{i,r}$ denotes output, $a_{i,f,r}$ is the share parameter in the Cobb–Douglas production function, $FP_{f,r}$ is the factor price in the regional market and $\varpi_{i,f,r}$ is the proportional difference between the regional industry and the average regional factor market-clearing price. (Subscript (i) denotes industry, (r) denotes region, and (f) denotes primary factor.)

Other inputs to production are considered perfect complements to the primary factors. Intermediate input demands are modelled using input–output data and Leontief functional forms. Regardless of whether or not interindustry demands are derived from Leontief or more flexible functional forms, input–output data are critical for parameterising the model.

For a model designed to analyse farm subsidy policies, it is important at this point to establish the mode by which the policies affect economic activity and income. There are two main modes of farm support in the US. One subsidises production, the other is direct income transfers. Farm production subsidies augment nominal value-added by raising the return per unit output. $PVA_{i,r}$ is the producer price $(PX_{i,r})$ gross of subsidies $(PIE_{i,r})$, and net of indirect taxes $(itax_{i,r})$ and the costs of intermediates $(\Sigma_j IO_{j,i} \cdot P_{j,r})$

$$PVA_{i,r} = PX_{i,r} \cdot (1 - itax_{i,r}) - (\Sigma_j IO_{j,i} \cdot P_{j,r}) + PIE_{i,r} \qquad (9.2)$$

---

[1] Any globally stable functional form or nest of functions is allowable (Perroni and Rutherford, 1989). For example, a constant elasticity of substitution (CES) functional form is also very useful because it is general enough to allow for varying returns to scale, according to the value of ϵ:

$$XD_{i,r} = \zeta_{i,r}[a_{i,r}K^{\rho ir} + (1 - a_{i,r})L^{\rho ir}]^{\epsilon ir/\rho ir}$$

where

K is capital,
ζ is the Cobb–Douglas Production shift term and
other variables and constants are defined elsewhere,

in which case the first-order conditions for factor demands are

$$K_{i,r}/L_{i,r} = [(W_{Lr} \cdot \omega_{Lir}/W_{Kr} \cdot \omega_{Kir}) \cdot ((1 - a_{i,r})/a_{i,r})]^{\sigma ir}$$

The scale coefficient ϵ can be specified as an endogenous function of the level of activity in an input supply industry, for example, to represent external agglomeration economies. For an application, see Kilkenny (1993b).

Subsidies on agriculture ($PIE_{AG,r}$) raise $PVA_{AG,r}$ and induce factor employment in agriculture according to (9.1). If the subsidy is removed, factors will either relocate to sectors stimulated by the change in the spending pattern, or, if no sectors are stimulated, lie idle (unemployed).

Factor market segmentation and regional income determination are modelled as follows. First, there are regional markets for labour, land and capital supplied by local households and by households in the other region. The short-run assumption is that commuting patterns are given. Local and commuter labour is mobile among sectors within a region, but not mobile between regions. In this way regional labour markets are insulated from each other, which means average wages may differ between regions. Second, following recently popular macroeconomic model assumptions, wages are assumed set by contracts (sticky) in the short run. Employment is entirely demand determined. Local labour supply is perfectly elastic at the wage, up to an assumed 108 per cent of the benchmark level of employment. If labour demand exceeds the full employment level, wage increases occur. The model estimates employment and the change relative to the benchmark that may arise regionally from a given policy change.

Factor prices vary by sector because of efficiency wage practices,[2] and by region ($FP_{f,r}$) because of regional constraints to factor mobility. The proportionality factor ($\varpi_{i,f,r}$) is calibrated to account for these variations, which are assumed invariant to the policy regime. Capital and crop land are modelled as sector and region-specific. Land supply is fixed in the short run and specific to the agricultural sector.

Household income (YH_{hh}) is factor income, net of factor taxes (factor supply $L_{hh,f,r}$ times net per unit factor income $NFY_{f,r}$), plus any non-distorting transfers (Tf)

$$YH_{hh} = \Sigma_{f,r} L_{hh,f,r} \cdot NFY_{f,r} + Tf_{hh} \qquad (9.3)$$

Thus, two ways that the government can directly raise a farm household's income are to subsidise the sector/region in which the household's labour, capital or land is employed or to increase transfers. The initial regional distribution of gains from farm subsidies will depend on which of these methods is used, and on the regional pattern of factor ownership.

Output subsidies provided to agriculture will accrue to owners of fixed factors of production: land- and sector-specific (immobile) farm capital. Under the short-run, sticky-wage assumptions, farm labour will continue to earn labour's opportunity cost in other sectors in the rural region. To the

---

[2] The 'efficiency wage hypothesis' is that industries may find it optimal to pay higher wages to elicit productivity rather than to pay monitoring costs; see Krueger and Summers (1988).

extent that farm land and capital is not owned exclusively by rural residents, farm production subsidies will immediately 'leak out' of the rural region. A second drain may be through the spending of subsidy income on items purchased from other regions. A tertiary drain of farm subsidy income is through urban household ownership of claims on rural non-farm capital-related income streams; for example, dividend income from variety chain stores that flow to metropolitan residents.

Households (indexed by the subscript hh) pay taxes (at rates $htax_{hh}$), save (at the rates mps_{hh}), and provide (or receive) trade credit to households in other regions (RS_{hh}). They purchase commodities ($C_{i,r}$) according to the observed budget shares ($\beta_{hh,i,r}$) out of disposable income

$$C_{i,r} \cdot P_{i,r} = \beta_{hh,i,r} \cdot (RS_{hh} + ((1 - mps_{hh}) \cdot (1 - htax_{hh}) \cdot YH_{hh})) \qquad (9.4)$$

Since consumer demand increases with disposable income, one impact of farm subsidies (whether coupled or in pure transfer form) is higher demand for all goods, particularly high budget share items purchased locally like household services. This is potentially one of the most important links between farm support programmes and the non-farm rural economy.

Aggregate demand in each regional market ($X_{i,r}$) is the sum of demands for intermediates ($INT_{i,r}$) by firms, for final goods by consumers ($C_{i,r}$), for the government ($GD_{i,r}$), and by investors ($INV_{i,r}$) and inventory/stocks ($DST_{i,r}$)

$$X_{i,r} = INT_{i,r} + C_{i,r} + GD_{i,r} + INV_{i,r} + DST_{i,r} \qquad (9.5)$$

Aggregate supplies in each region's market ($X_{i,r}$) are locally produced ($X_{i,r}^{L}$) or imported from non-local sources ($IM_{i,r}$); where non-local goods are crosshauled in from the other domestic regions ($X_{i,r}^{CH}$) or the rest of the world ($IM_{i,r}^{ROW}$). This 'nested' structure of the distribution of goods in regional markets is illustrated in figure 9.1. Preferences over the goods from different regions are given by constant elasticity of substitution functions at each level

$$X = AC1 \cdot [\delta 1 \cdot IM^{(-\rho 1)} + (1 - \delta 1) \cdot X^{L(-\rho 1)}]^{-1/\rho 1} \qquad (9.6)$$

$$IM = AC2 \cdot [\delta 2 \cdot IM^{ROW(-\rho 2)} + (1 - \delta 2) \cdot X^{CH(-\rho 2)}]^{-1/\rho 2} \qquad (9.7)$$

where $AC1$ and $AC2$ are preference shift terms.

Industry and region subscripts are dropped for readability in equations 9.6 to 9.10. The composition of each mix is determined to satisfy the first-order conditions for expenditure minimisation. Thus, the levels of local and non-local goods in the mix will vary as the local price (P^{L}) changes with relation to the alternative good price (P^{IM})

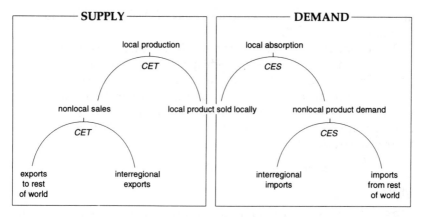

Figure 9.1 Destination structure on the SUPPLY side: sourcing structure on the DEMAND side

Note: *CES(T)* are constant elasticity of substitution (transformation) functions in two arguments

$$IM/X^L = [P^L/P^{IM} \cdot \delta 1/(1 - \delta 1)]^{\sigma 1} \tag{9.8}$$

The ratio on the left-hand side of this equation is the complement to the 'regional purchase coefficient', the portion of local demand met by locally produced supply $(1 - IM/X^L)$. An analogous equation describes how the mix of crosshauled or imported versions varies within the non-local bundle as relative prices change.

By the same token, supplies of local output (XD) are either sold within the region (X^L) or to non-local markets (EX); where non-local sales are exported to the rest of the world (EX^{ROW}) or crosshauled to the other region (EX^{CH}). Constant elasticity of transformation functions (9.9) and (9.10) represent the production possibility frontier between outputs destined for different markets; and the optimal mix is determined at each level with respect to relative prices by equations analogous to (9.6).

$$XD = AT1 \cdot [\gamma 1 \cdot EX^{(\eta 1)} + (1 - \gamma 1) \cdot X^{L(\eta 1)}]^{(1/\eta 1)} \tag{9.9}$$

$$EX = AT2 \cdot [\gamma 2 \cdot EX^{ROW \eta 2} + (1 - \gamma 2) \cdot EX^{CH(\eta 2)}]^{(1/\eta 2)} \tag{9.10}$$

where $AT1$ and $AT2$ are technological shift terms.

Market prices $(P_{i,r})$ are determined to clear each regional market

$$P_{i,r} \cdot X_{i,r} = P^L_{i,r} \cdot X^L_{i,r} + P^{IM}_{i,r} \cdot IM_{i,r} \tag{9.11}$$

Thus prices may differ between rural and urban markets and each regional price index reflects that. The economy-wide (or average) price level is held constant by implicit adjustments of the money supply. This assumption is innocuous since the system is homogenous of degree zero in prices and inflation has no real effects.

For subnational trading regions there is no nominal exchange rate to balance payments as there is for trading countries, and there is no reason why regional trade must balance. However, if there is a regional current account deficit there must be an equivalent regional capital account surplus. The inflow of regional savings (*rs*) required to allow a region to consume in excess of local production is determined endogenously to balance interregional payments

$$RS_{hh} = \Sigma_i PEX_{i,r}^{CH} \cdot EX_{i,r}^{CH} - \Sigma_i PX_{i,r}^{CH} \cdot X_{i,r}^{CH} \qquad (9.12)$$

where

$PEX_{i,r}^{CH}$ is the price of cross-hauled export good $EX_{i,r}^{CH}$ and
$PX_{i,r}^{CH}$ is the price of cross-hauled import good $X_{i,r}^{CH}$.

It is called 'trade credit' because it finances current consumption (not investment) and does not flow through the loanable funds market.

There are three other nominal flow accounts modelled. One pools household, enterprise, government and foreign savings to finance investment. The savings–investment identity equation is chosen to be the '*n*th' market in the simultaneous equation system and it remains implicit. If it clears in the solution of the rural–urban CGE model, we are assured that all transactions in the \$4 trillion economy have been correctly and completely accounted for and there are no leakages.

The second nominal flow account is the combined state and federal government account. Government savings are the residual of endogenous tax revenues (*GTAX*, calculated in a separate summation equation) over spending.

$$GSAV = GTAX - GTOT - \Sigma_{hh} Tf_{hh} - (\Sigma_{i,r} PIE_{i,r} \cdot XD_{i,r} + Tf_{i,r}^{ent})$$
$$- FBOR \cdot EXR \qquad (9.13)$$

where

$Tf_{i,r}^{ent}$ is transfers to enterprises,
$FBOR$ is foreign borrowing and
EXR is the exchange rate.

Government demand for commodities is modelled as fixed budget shares of the total level of spending on goods (*GTOT*), which is usually set exogenously. Farm subsidies (*PIE·XD*) are endogenous. A reduction in spending on farm programmes lowers the deficit (raises *GSAV*).

The third nominal flow account balances international payments by requiring the current and capital accounts to equate at the exchange rate. In the short run the nominal exchange rate adjusts (in the long run the trade balance adjusts). Foreign savings are the net inflow of capital required to balance payments given the excess demand for traded goods. Since our problem concerns the short run during which asset markets but not interregional factor markets clear, the exchange rate is determined endogenously while the balance of payments is exogenous.

The SAM

A social accounting matrix (SAM) framework can be used to organise data for national, regional, multi-regional and interregional CGE models. In fact, a SAM is the most appropriate framework for interregional models because a social accounting matrix is articulated by definition. In any SAM, each transaction has an identifiable origin account and destination account.

The ideal interregional SAM further identifies the regional location of both the origin and destination accounts. The conventional approach is to structure a multiple region SAM as a system of subsystems, in the linear algebra tradition (Stone, 1961a). Within-region transactions are contained in diagonal blocks, and interregional transactions are in off-diagonal blocks. A bi-regional SAM is required to operationalise this rural–urban CGE model, and is shown in a slightly summarised version in table 9.1. The six-commodity and the six-industry accounts in each region are collapsed (in the figure) to one each. All the other accounts are presented separately. Note that the diagonal quadrants of the figure represent intra-regional transactions, that the top-right quadrant represents sales by the urban region to the rural region and that the bottom-left quadrant represents sales by the rural region to the urban region.

The interregional SAM in table 9.1 is similar to, but more articulated than, its multi-region precedents.[3] The difference between interregional and multi-regional is the extent of pooling. In multi-region SAMs, transboundary flows are not mapped directly from the regional source account to the regional final destination account. They are first pooled into a common intermediary account, e.g., Round (1986). Income is not mapped directly from the sector/region source to the ultimate household/region destination as it is in the interregional SAM of table 9.1.

The difference for the CGE modeller is not trivial. Pooling would only be

---

[3] In fact, the fully articulated SAM for multiple regions was introduced by Stone (Stone, 1961a) but immediately abandoned as a data-organising framework for lack of sufficiently detailed observations on within-region and interregional transactions. By corollary, this author argues that if interregional transactions are a critical part of the analysis, then the fully articulated SAM framework should be used to solve residually for that missing data.

Table 9.1 *A schematic bi-regional SAM*

	1	2	3	4	5	6	7	8	9	10	11	12	13	14	15	16	17
					by residence							by residence					
1 Urban commodities			Intermediate goods				Household consumption								Govt. demand	Capital formation & stocks	Exports
2 Urban Industries	Local output sold locally							Cross-hauled output							Subsidies		
3 Urban Value-Added		Value-added net of tax															
4 Urban Labour			Labour income														
5 Urban Capital			Capital income														
6 Urban Land			Land income														
7 Urban Households				Labour income	Capital income	Land income					Labour income	Capital income	Land income		Transfers		Income from Rest of World
8 Rural Commodities								Intermediate goods		Intermediate goods				House-hold consumption	Govt. demand	Capital formation & stocks	Exports
9 Rural Industries	Cross-hauled output							Local output sold locally							Subsidies		Exports

Social Accounting Matrix (accounts 10–17, rows). The column entries appear in two groups, each headed "by residence."

Account	Rural Value-Added	by residence (1)		Other entries	by residence (2)		Further entries
10 Rural Value-Added	Value-added net of tax						
11 Rural Labour	Labour income						
12 Rural Capital	Capital income					Transfers	Income from Rest of World
13 Rural Land	Land income						
14 Rural Households		Labour income · Capital income · Land income · Net trade credit	Earnings · Enterprise income · Farm taxes · Income taxes		Labour income · Capital income · Land income	Earnings · Enterprise income · Farm taxes · Income taxes	Transfers
15 National Government				Tariffs · Indirect taxes			Income taxes
16 Savings		Net household savings	Enterprise savings		Enterprise savings · Net household savings · Govt. savings		Foreign savings
17 Rest of World				Imports			Foreign borrowing

appropriate if there were in fact no differences between the factor services or factor employment possibilities across regions. Furthermore, in a multi-region SAM, the cell representing distributed value-added to households includes the returns to outside-region employment. The column or row totals for the value-added accounts are the sum of regional value added generated plus gross inflows of value added. Since not all regional value added generated stays within the region, it is a misleading sum. Further-more, the sum represents neither pure region product nor net region income, and such data are neither available nor useful as a control total in SAM balancing.

Partitioning national data for the bi-regional SAM

The most challenging part of the interregional modelling process is working around missing data on interregional transactions. First, there are no data on rural–urban crosshauling of goods and services. Second, there are little data on extra-regional labour market participation other than data on net labour earnings of non-metro residents employed in metro industries. Third, there are no data on the regional origin of capital-related income nor the magnitude of interregional flows of funds. The lack of data also compels the modeller to abstract from potentially relevant but unquantifiable relationships such as the transport costs of rural–urban trade and conges-tion cost gradients.

The rural–urban SAM was developed from US national data and data on metropolitan counties, solving for the non-metropolitan data residually. A balanced national SAM distinguishing the six sectors, three factors, and one household was obtained from the Economic Research Service of the US Department of Agriculture. The national SAM includes the input–output accounts and all other relevant national income and product account information (Hanson and Robinson, 1989).

The easiest data to disaggregate by region are the industry output and labour income by industry. Wage and salary disbursements and employ-ment data are available by industry and region (US Dept. of Commerce, Bureau of Economic Analysis, 1989). To reconcile them with the national data, the raw data were used to generate shares, and the shares applied to the national measures. By the same token, industrial output is available on a county basis (US Department of Commerce, Bureau of the Census, 1988b). Metropolitan county data were summed so that the 'urban' share of national output by industry could be calculated as the ratio of metropolitan to national output, with the residual forming the rural share.

The basis of regional factor-market segmentation is a mix of 'journey to work' and industry by residence data. The Department of Commerce

(1989) data also include a measure of the net commuter earnings of non-metro residents in the form of the 'adjustment for residence' data. In net terms, more labour income is generated in the metro regions than is received by metro residents. In addition, the 'industry by residence' data published by the Department of Commerce, Bureau of the Census, were used to fill out the matrix of labour supply by households in each region to industries in each region.

Unfortunately, only net receipt-side data on capital-related income are reported in the Department of Commerce (1988b) source. It is also impossible to share out the data in any empirically meaningful way since the pair of control equations defining household shares of capital earnings by region and region shares of economy-wide capital earnings are insufficient to span the space. Nor are there any direct estimates of gross capital-related income flows, since tracking capital ownership from producer by location to claim-holder by residence is almost prohibitively difficult. In lieu of data, the assumption of perfect interregional capital mobility is employed. This suggests that capital ownership by residence is completely diversified. However, rural residents are more likely to be retired recipients of social insurance programme funds, so the larger population share proportion (23.6 per cent) was used rather than the non-metropolitan share of aggregate dividends, interest and rent (19.6 per cent) or income share proportion (18.7 per cent) as suggested by the data in Department of Commerce (1988a).

The basis for regional goods market segmentation is the place of residence of households. Consumer demands by region were constructed as personal income shares of national consumer demands by industry, and imports from foreign sources were partitioned using personal income shares. Government demands by industry and region were constructed according to population shares, while intermediate good demands were partitioned according to output shares (thus imposing the same input–output structure on both regions). Investment goods demands, inventory, and depreciation by industry and region were constructed according to wage bill shares, as were exports to foreign markets.

The difference between industry output plus foreign imports in each region and the sum of consumer, government, investment, inventory and export demands facing each region gives a first cut estimate of the net crosshauling between the regions. As expected, the data do not reconcile across regions and accounts. Furthermore, this net approach results in estimates that regions either export or import a commodity, but not both (i.e., no domestic crosshauling).

Finally, despite the fact that a balanced national SAM is used for control totals and regional shares are used to partition all of the data, the initial bi-regional SAM is not balanced. The imbalances appear in the commodity and household accounts. This is anticipated due to the lack of data on crosshauling between industries in one region and commodity markets in the other, and the associated interregional savings flows that would be required to achieve an interregional balance of payments.

Balancing the model-specific SAM

If a CGE model is initialised with a set of data that do not comprise a balanced SAM, the system of behavioural equations will not satisfy the critical adding-up properties upon which Walras' law (income = expenditure and supply = demand in every account) is based. To overcome this data problem, the incompatibilities between the accounts can be reconciled using some algorithm to balance the SAM. The generic problem for balancing a matrix A (set of a_{ij}'s) is to find a matrix $\mathring{A}$ ($\mathring{a}_{ij}$'s) that is 'close' to A but also satisfies a given set of linear restrictions (Schneider and Zenios, 1989). For SAMs, the fundamental restriction is that row sums equal column sums. There are two basic approaches to balancing matrices: scaling (e.g., RAS, Bacharach, 1970) and optimisation.

The optimisation problem is to minimise the deviations of each $\mathring{a}_{ij}$ from a_{ij}, and the deviations between their corresponding marginal totals. Deviations are measured by a penalty function. A quadratic penalty function has a statistical interpretation as a generalised least-squares estimator. Furthermore, bounds can be imposed on the relatively unknown $\mathring{a}_{ij}$'s. In this case, rather than using a generic optimisation algorithm, a model-specific approach was pioneered to balance the bi-regional SAM for the rural–urban CGE model. The CGE model equations include all market-clearing equations, and these are the equivalent of the SAM row = column equality in each commodity account. Industry supply equations ensure balance in the industry accounts, with factor accounts balanced by income equations. In addition, the CGE model equations provide cell-to-cell restrictions. The household income equations explicitly equate household factor supplies to each region and region-specific wages to regional income, and consumer demand equations explicitly relate regional household income to regional consumer demands in regional commodity markets. Thus, the CGE model equations are the ideal set of restrictions to be used to balance the SAM.

Furthermore, this approach allows the modeller to write just one set of equations for both the CGE model and the SAM balancing programme. Only the first-order conditions in the CGE model are excluded from the SAM balancing programme, which instead must include a minimisation objective function. Also prices should be exogenous and normalised to unity in the balancing programme so that all flows will be expressed in real terms. Slack variables must be added to each of the twelve commodity balance equations (which were not balanced initially).

For the rural–urban CGE model to reflect the interdependence between regions arising from crosshauling, the initial net estimates of interregional commodity flows are inappropriate. Even if the two regions traded large amounts of the 'same' commodity, if the amounts in each direction were similar in magnitude, these flows would cancel out, suggesting little, if any, interdependence. To improve the estimates of crosshauling, regional purchase coefficients and their standard errors (from other studies) were used to set upper and lower bounds on estimates of gross region-to-region imports ($X_{i,r}^{CH}$). When imposed in conjunction with the regional industry market clearing and regional commodity market balance equations, this results in an estimated pattern of two-way regional crosshauling consistent with overall balance.

Finally, no additional bounds are imposed on the determination of the regional savings (RS) required to finance purchases by consumers in one region for products from the other. The estimates of RS are determined residually given the interregional balance of payments equation.

The objective in the bi-regional SAM balancing programme is to minimise the sum of squared slacks. The solution of this problem is the set of all variable levels in real terms which are as close as possible to the data but which also satisfy the model's market-clearing and income = expenditure restrictions. In particular, the levels of crosshauling and interregional trade credit consistent with the pattern of regional employment and output are determined residually in the process of balancing the interregional SAM. The resulting SAM replicates the pattern of metro/non-metro output, employment and personal income reported in the original data, while crosshauling, capital ownership and interregional trade credit are hypothetical. This approach to balancing the SAM for a CGE model is an innovation which makes it possible for any model to be constructed from national and regional data even though this initially results in unbalanced data; that is, the interregional modeller can balance his/her own data.

Finally, the solution of the SAM balancing programme is the set of input data required to initialise and calibrate the CGE model: levels of real output, employment, wage income, trade between regions and international trade, demands by agents and category, etc., and the set of prices in the benchmark period normalised to unity. To operationalise the CGE model, all that is required is to read in these data, and add behavioural parameters and parameter calibrating equations as needed (see Mansur and Whalley (1984) on calibration).

Summary

This chapter has demonstrated how easily policy-specific CGE models can be developed and implemented. Policy analysis is the main objective served by modelling regional economic systems. The first step in modelling a system is the determination of its boundary (what is endogenous, what is exogenous). Unfortunately, the appropriate boundary depends on the policy issue. Does this mean that a unique model must be developed for each policy analysis? Or, does this mean that the policy analysts should develop a single complex model with very wide scope capable of analysing a wide variety of policies? Given the ease of developing policy-specific models, the first alternative is more viable than ever.

For example, a model of interdependent but distinct rural and urban regions is required to analyse the effects of farm subsidies on the whole economy, since farm subsidies accrue to rural residents in the United States, but these injections of income seem to 'leak out' of rural areas. We also need to consider alternative uses of farm labour, land and capital, and all industries up- and downstream from agriculture, as well as industries supplying goods that farmers consume. Then we should include households working in the non-farm industries and should probably consider the budgetary consequences of such programmes. Thus a general equilibrium model of two regions, six sectors, three primary factors, two households, the government and the rest of the world can be prepared. Such a general equilibrium model cannot be solved analytically because there are far more endogenous variables than exogenous ones, but can be solved numerically. The numbers (data) appropriate for initialising such a model must, explicitly or implicitly, come from a balanced social accounting matrix (SAM).

Unfortunately, there are gaps in our regional databases. But we can solve for some missing data by using national totals and some regional data. We should not, however, use the multi-region SAM framework which was developed to display only available data. We should use the original interregional SAM framework introduced by Richard Stone (1961a), and marshall the available data to fill in the blanks. From this, we can balance the SAM without having to prepare a second numerical optimisation programme.

The technique for in-house, model-specific SAM balancing is to use the general equilibrium model equations (except for behavioural equations, which are functions of relative prices that remain normalised to unity) as the set of linear restrictions on the data from the unbalanced SAM. Slack variables and an objective function to minimise the sum of squared slacks must be added. This becomes a model-specific SAM balancing programme, of which the output is exactly the required input for the numerical general equilibrium (CGE) model.

This chapter has shown how such a series of steps can be used to construct a SAM-based CGE designed to model the effects of different policies across a two-region, urban/rural system, and has demonstrated the feasibility of estimating data that are inevitably, in a model such as this, missing.

10 Combatting demographic innumeracy with social accounting principles: heterogeneity, selection, and the dynamics of interdependent populations

ANDREI ROGERS

1 Introduction

Richard Stone's work teaches us the importance of identifying the proper intersectoral or interstate flows to enter as numerators in constant-coefficient social accounting models, and of relating these numerators to appropriate denominators measuring stocks. When applied in demographic definitional and structural equations, such procedures lead to correctly specified 'incidence' rates and the subpopulations 'at risk' of experiencing the changes brought about by these particular rates. In this context, models of the determinants and consequences of migration, for example, that rely on the 'net migration rate' are misspecified. So too are models of labour force activity that rely on the 'labour force participation rate'. In both instances the denominators of the rates do not correspond to the subpopulations that are at risk of experiencing the events represented in the numerators. The result is a confounding of relative propensities with relative population sizes. Demographic innumeracy produces a biased model.

This chapter focusses on demographic innumeracies committed in mathematical representations of demographic processes involving multiple interdependent populations and goes on to show how the demographic accounting principles advocated by Stone (1971) can be used to identify some of the misspecifications that are thereby introduced.

2 Heterogeneity, selection and the definition of rates

As a population composed of heterogeneous subgroups ages, the members with the highest risks of exit from the population leave first. This differential selection can produce exit patterns for the aggregate population that deviate from those of the constituent subpopulations. If no entries or re-entries are allowed, then it can be shown that the aggregate measure will always underestimate the exit rates to which the average individual will be subject (Keyfitz, 1985). But if entries and re-entries are allowed, then no such a priori conclusion can be made. In either case, subsequent observations on the surviving population will differ from those obtained from the initial population, and the dynamics at the aggregate level will deviate from the underlying dynamics at the subpopulation level (Vaupel and Yashin, 1985). All of this can be illustrated readily, without loss of generality, with a simple numerical example involving just two subpopulations.

Heterogeneity and selection in independent unistate populations

Imagine two subpopulations of unequal size that start out with *fixed* but unequal crude rates of mortality. It can be shown that over time the aggregate death rate will decline as members of the frailer of the two subpopulations die off more rapidly. For example, if at the outset a sixth of the population experiences a mortality rate d_1 of a fourth, say, and the rest a death rate d_2 of a half, and there are no more births, then after t years there will be $(1 - d_1)^t$ of the frailer persons left along with $(1 - d_2)^t$ of the more robust individuals. The aggregate death rate at that time will be

$$\frac{\frac{1}{6}(1 - d_1)^t d_1 + \frac{5}{6}(1 - d_2)^t d_2}{\frac{1}{6}(1 - d_1)^t + \frac{5}{6}(1 - d_2)^t} \tag{10.1}$$

and, as a consequence of the arithmetic–geometric inequality set out in Keyfitz (1985), this will always be less than the initial aggregate death rate of $(1/6)(d_1) + (5/6)(d_2)$ To illustrate this numerically, note that

$$\frac{\frac{1}{6}\left(1 - \frac{1}{4}\right)^t\left(\frac{1}{4}\right) + \frac{5}{6}\left(1 - \frac{1}{2}\right)^t\left(\frac{1}{2}\right)}{\frac{1}{6}\left(1 - \frac{1}{4}\right)^t + \frac{5}{6}\left(1 - \frac{1}{2}\right)^t} < \frac{1}{6}\left(\frac{1}{4}\right) + \frac{5}{6}\left(\frac{1}{2}\right) = 0.458 \tag{10.2}$$

and, for example, for $t = 2$,

$$\frac{\frac{1}{6}\left(\frac{3}{4}\right)^2\left(\frac{1}{4}\right) + \frac{5}{6}\left(\frac{1}{2}\right)^2\left(\frac{1}{2}\right)}{\frac{1}{6}\left(\frac{3}{4}\right)^2 + \frac{5}{6}\left(\frac{1}{2}\right)^2} = 0.422 < 0.458 \tag{10.3}$$

The above, then, is an illustration of the general conclusion that the selective effect of heterogeneity always acts to underestimate the rates to which an average member of the aggregate population will be subject (Keyfitz, 1985). We simply wish to underscore that it applies only to *independent* unistate populations that experience only decrements. The guaranteed underestimate does not apply to *interdependent* multi-state populations that experience increments as well as decrements.

Heterogeneity and selection in interdependent multi-state population dynamics

To continue the above illustration in the context of a multi-state population, it is necessary to change the demographic process from a non-recurrent to a recurrent event, from mortality to, say, migration. If no in-migration is permitted, then out-migration, like death, becomes a non-recurrent event as far as each origin population is concerned and the above analysis does not need modification. But if the decrements of one subpopulation are recognised as increments to the other, then the above relationships are altered, and equation (10.1) becomes transformed into an expression that is simpler to understand in its matrix equivalent form. The numerator of equation (10.1) in matrix form can be expressed as

$$[1 \quad 1] \begin{bmatrix} d_1 & 0 \\ 0 & d_2 \end{bmatrix} \begin{bmatrix} 1-d_1 & 0 \\ 0 & 1-d_2 \end{bmatrix}^t \begin{bmatrix} 1/6 \\ 5/6 \end{bmatrix}$$

and the denominator as the above matrix product without the $d_1 - d_2$ matrix. The acknowledgement of increments in the multi-state perspective requires that the zeroes in the powered matrix be replaced by d_1 and d_2, respectively. The numerator then becomes

$$[1 \quad 1] \begin{bmatrix} d_1 & 0 \\ 0 & d_2 \end{bmatrix} \begin{bmatrix} 1-d_1 & d_2 \\ d_1 & 1-d_2 \end{bmatrix}^t \begin{bmatrix} 1/6 \\ 5/6 \end{bmatrix}$$

and the denominator, once again, is the above without the $d_1 - d_2$ matrix. Thus to find the aggregate migration rate for $t = 2$, we first calculate

$$[1 \quad 1] \begin{bmatrix} 1/4 & 0 \\ 0 & 1/2 \end{bmatrix} \begin{bmatrix} 3/4 & 1/2 \\ 1/4 & 1/2 \end{bmatrix}^2 \begin{bmatrix} 1/6 \\ 5/6 \end{bmatrix}$$

to find the numerator

$$\frac{131}{384} = 0.341$$

then compute

$$[1 \quad 1]\begin{bmatrix} 3/4 & 1/2 \\ 1/4 & 1/2 \end{bmatrix}^2 \begin{bmatrix} 1/6 \\ 5/6 \end{bmatrix}$$

to obtain the denominator of unity. The quotient 0.341 is the aggregate migration rate. Notice that it too is an underestimate, since it is smaller than the corresponding starting rate of 11/24 (0.458). However, observe that if we apply the same migration regime to a different starting population distribution, this inequality can be reversed. For example, if we reverse the 1/6 versus 5/6 initial distribution, then

$$[1 \quad 1]\begin{bmatrix} 1/4 & 0 \\ 0 & 1/2 \end{bmatrix}\begin{bmatrix} 3/4 & 1/2 \\ 1/4 & 1/2 \end{bmatrix}^2 \begin{bmatrix} 5/6 \\ 1/6 \end{bmatrix}$$

yields a numerator of $127/384 = 0.331$, and

$$[1 \quad 1]\begin{bmatrix} 3/4 & 1/2 \\ 1/4 & 1/2 \end{bmatrix}^2 \begin{bmatrix} 5/6 \\ 1/6 \end{bmatrix}$$

once again gives a denominator of unity. The quotient is 0.331, and this value is greater than the corresponding starting value of $7/24 = 0.292$.

The importance of the starting and ultimate distributions

The importance of the relative weightings imparted by the two alternative starting distributions in the multi-state illustration can be clarified by comparing them to the stable distribution. For the particular numerical illustration, the zero-growth regime defined by the matrix

$$\begin{bmatrix} 3/4 & 1/2 \\ 1/4 & 1/2 \end{bmatrix}$$

ultimately allocates a half of the total population to each subgroup. As the first starting distribution of 1/6 and 5/6 moves towards this stable state, it weights the higher out-migration rate less and less, and the aggregate rate declines from its initial value of 11/24 to its ultimate stable growth value of 3/8. Conversely, as the second starting distribution of 5/6 and 1/6 moves towards stability, it weights the higher out-migration rate more and more, and the aggregate rate increases from its starting value of 7/24 to the same ultimate stable growth value of 3/8. In the former case, the aggregate migration rate underestimates the rate to which the average individual will be subject; in the latter case it overestimates that same rate. The selective effect does not always act in the same direction.

Rates that are not incidence rates

Demographers, biostatisticians and actuaries define an incidence rate to be the rate at which a new event or outflow occurs in a population. Counts of occurrences of the event or flow in question appear in the numerator and levels of exposure to such events or flows, usually measured in person-years of observation, appear in the denominator. Thus such rates sometimes are also called occurrence-exposure rates. An individual contributes a person-year to the denominator each year he or she is included in the population at risk of experiencing the event or flow. We have seen how the selection effects of heterogeneity act to bias aggregate rates of incidence.

The biases introduced by heterogeneity's selective effects become even more problematic when rates are defined inappropriately, for example, when the denominator includes persons not exposed to the risk of experiencing the event or flow counted by the numerator. Two prominent examples of such rates are *prevalence rates* and *net rates*.

Prevalence rates measure the fraction of population that has a particular attribute, for example, an illness. The index has no dimension or units and, by definition, all of its possible values lie between zero and one.

Net rates are defined as the difference between a prevalence rate and an incidence rate. The latter defines the rate of exit from a population and the former, defined with respect to the same population, identifies the fraction who entered the population during the same interval of time. An example of a net rate is a net migration rate, which is the difference between an in-migration rate and the corresponding out-migration rate.

Notice that both prevalence and net rates include in their denominators persons who are not at risk of experiencing the event or flow included in the numerator.

3 Prevalence rates: what does the labour force participation rate measure?

Textbooks on labour economics typically define the labour force participation rate in terms that resemble the following definition:

The proportion of a group who participate in the labor force at any moment in time is the labor force participation rate ... the labor force participation *rate* of a group is thus analogous to the *probability* that an individual member of the group can be expected to participate in the labor force at any moment in time. (Fleischer, 1970)

The labour force participation rate is a prevalence measure. Changes in the numerical value of this measure over time are examined and form the subject of inquiry of scores of diverse studies. For example, Durand (1975) used the measure in his global study of the factors and processes underlying

Table 10.1 *Civilian labour force participation rates by age and sex, annual averages, 1970 and 1977*

Age group	1970	1977	Men change 1970–7	1970	1977	Women change 1970–7
16–19	56.1	61.0	4.9	44.0	51.4	7.4
20–24	83.3	85.7	2.4	57.7	66.5	8.8
25–34	96.4	95.4	− 1.0	45.0	59.5	14.5
35–44	96.9	95.7	− 1.2	51.1	59.6	8.5
45–54	94.2	91.2	− 3.0	54.4	55.8	1.4
55–59	89.5	83.2	− 6.3	49.0	48.0	− 1.0
60–64	75.0	62.9	− 12.1	36.1	32.9	− 3.2
65 and over ..	26.8	20.1	− 6.7	9.7	8.1	− 1.6

Source: Bureau of Labor Statistics (1982).

labour force changes that accompany economic development; Lebergott (1965) used it to develop the labour force component of the Brookings Quarterly Econometric Model of the United States; and a number of demographers and economists have used it to study the relationship between female employment and fertility (for example, Devaney, 1983; Gregory, 1982; Stokes and Hsieh, 1983).

But what does the labour force participation rate truly measure? What does it reveal about the labour force dynamics that produced it? Consider, for example, table 10.1, which presents age-specific labour force participation rates for males and females at two points in time. Referring to these data, the Bureau of Labor Statistics observed:

These patterns changed dramatically between 1970 and 1977 ... The single most striking change during this period involved young women. The participation rate of women 25 to 34 rose by 14.5 percentage points in just 7 years. Men 60 to 64 experienced a drop in participation which was nearly as large, 12.1 percentage points. (Bureau of Labor Statistics, 1982)

Can one conclude from such evidence that young women of that age were entering the labour force at increased propensities at the same time that the older men were leaving it in growing proportions? Apparently, the dynamics were more complicated than that:

Only a small portion of the net increase in accessions can be traced to a rise in gross entries ... For men 20 to 34, and for most women above the age of 20, the pace of entries actually slowed during this period. Instead the determining factor appears to have been a drop in gross labor force exits ... At the same time, the withdrawal process for persons 45 to 64 also became more efficient. An increase in the labor force separations of men outweighed ... a modest increase in labor force entries at this age. (Bureau of Labor Statistics, 1982).

Finally, not only do the net changes revealed by labour force participation rates hide the underlying changes in entries and exits, *they also confound propensities to enter and exit with the initial distribution of the working-age population across the two statuses: active and inactive.* Hence, the percentage changes are biassed. To see this more clearly, consider the following simple numerical illustration of labour force dynamics, which, despite its concocted nature, clearly illustrates our principal point.

Imagine a zero-growth working-age population (all those aged sixteen and over) of 900 individuals, that experiences a decrement due to the mortality of 150 persons every unit time period (that is, the death rate is one-sixth). For convenience, assume that this decrement is exactly offset by an increment of the same amount due to new entrants into the initial working-age of sixteen years (i.e., the 'births'). The model then is:

$$K(t+1) = 1 - dK(t) + b \tag{10.5}$$

where K is a vector of population and b a scalar of total births, or

$$900 = 5/6(900) + 150$$

Now assume that, initially, two-thirds of the population is in the labour force, and that one-sixth of that population exits the labour force during each time interval. To simplify matters, assume that the fraction leaving the inactive population to enter the labour force is also one-sixth. Finally, assume that one-fifth of the new entrants into the working-age population (the 'births') directly enter the labour force. This more detailed model then is:

$$\{K(t+1)\} = G\{K(t)\} + \{b\} \tag{10.6}$$

where G is a growth operator or

$$\begin{bmatrix} 420 \\ 480 \end{bmatrix} = \begin{bmatrix} 2/3 & 1/6 \\ 1/6 & 2/3 \end{bmatrix} \begin{bmatrix} 300 \\ 600 \end{bmatrix} + \begin{bmatrix} 120 \\ 30 \end{bmatrix} \tag{10.7}$$

If G and $\{b\}$ are held fixed, then it becomes a simple matter to determine the evolution of this process over time, because

$$\{K(t+n)\} = G^n\{K(t)\} + [G^{n-1} + G^{n-2} + \ldots I]\{b\} \tag{10.8}$$

where I is the identity matrix. Since G^n converges to zero as n is increased indefinitely, we conclude that (Rogers, 1971)

$$\lim_{n \to \infty} \{K(t+n)\} = (I - G)^{-1}\{b\} \tag{10.9}$$

Table 10.2 *Numerical example: the path to stability*

$n = 1$:

$$\begin{bmatrix} 420 \\ 480 \end{bmatrix} = \begin{bmatrix} 2/3 \ 1/6 \\ 1/6 \ 2/3 \end{bmatrix} \begin{bmatrix} 300 \\ 600 \end{bmatrix} + \begin{bmatrix} 120 \\ 30 \end{bmatrix}$$

$$lf = 0.667$$

$n = 2$:

$$\begin{bmatrix} 480 \\ 420 \end{bmatrix} = \begin{bmatrix} 2/3 \ 1/6 \\ 1/6 \ 2/3 \end{bmatrix} \begin{bmatrix} 420 \\ 480 \end{bmatrix} + \begin{bmatrix} 120 \\ 30 \end{bmatrix}$$

$$lf = 0.533$$

$n = 3$:

$$\begin{bmatrix} 510 \\ 390 \end{bmatrix} = \begin{bmatrix} 2/3 \ 1/6 \\ 1/6 \ 2/3 \end{bmatrix} \begin{bmatrix} 480 \\ 420 \end{bmatrix} + \begin{bmatrix} 120 \\ 30 \end{bmatrix}$$

$$lf = 0.467$$

$n = \infty$ *(stability)*:

$$\begin{bmatrix} 540 \\ 360 \end{bmatrix} = \begin{bmatrix} 2/3 \ 1/6 \\ 1/6 \ 2/3 \end{bmatrix} \begin{bmatrix} 540 \\ 360 \end{bmatrix} + \begin{bmatrix} 120 \\ 30 \end{bmatrix}$$

$$lf = 0.400$$

Table 10.2 presents the path to stability for the numerical example set out in equation (10.7). Observe that although the entry and exit propensities are held fixed, the labour force participation rates (lf) decline from their initial level of two-thirds to the equilibrium level of two-fifths. The decline arises not from changes in labour force accession and separation propensities, but is simply the consequence of the particular initial allocation of the working-age population across the two states: active and inactive. To see this more clearly consider the same regime of propensities applied to an initial population with the reversed allocation of population:

$$\begin{bmatrix} 570 \\ 330 \end{bmatrix} = \begin{bmatrix} 2/3 & 1/6 \\ 1/6 & 2/3 \end{bmatrix} \begin{bmatrix} 600 \\ 300 \end{bmatrix} + \begin{bmatrix} 120 \\ 30 \end{bmatrix} \tag{10.10}$$

Its ultimate equilibrium solution is the same as before, but now the labour force participation rate increases over time, from its initial value of one-third to its equilibrium value of two-fifths.

Another difficulty with interpreting the labour force participation rate arises from the fact that different regimes of labour force dynamics can give rise to identical activity rates. For example, consider the process defined by

$$\begin{bmatrix} 420 \\ 480 \end{bmatrix} = \begin{bmatrix} 1/2 & 1/4 \\ 1/2 & 1/2 \end{bmatrix} \begin{bmatrix} 300 \\ 600 \end{bmatrix} + \begin{bmatrix} 120 \\ 30 \end{bmatrix} \tag{10.11}$$

Here, as in equation (10.7), an initial labour force participation rate of two-thirds (0.667) becomes transformed to one of 0.533, after a unit time interval, but the underlying entry and exit proportions in equation (10.11) are totally different from those in equation (10.7): the fraction leaving the inactive population in the former equation is twice the fraction leaving the active population; in the latter equation the two fractions are equal. Moreover, the evolution of the latter process over time is different: its ultimate equilibrium solution yields a labour force participation rate of 0.526 instead of two-fifths.

The distribution of the population is not the only influence on the values taken on by the labour force participation rates; the particular age patterns of entry and exit rates also play an important role. Such age-specific rates are the natural inputs for the calculation of tables of working life.

4 Tables of working life

Tables of working life indicate the expected average number of working years remaining to a person attaining a given age. The conventional method for calculating such tables is spelt out in Shryock and Siegel (1971), for example, and it combines mortality rates at each age with labour force participation rates at that age. The procedure first calculates the normal life table stationary (zero-growth) population, by applying the age-specific mortality rates to a synthetic cohort, and then disaggregates that age-specific population according to the work status of the observed population, by applying the observed age-specific labour force participation rates of that population. Such tables are computed in many countries, and were regularly issued by the US Bureau of Labor Statistics until 1982, at which point they were replaced by a *multi-state* table of working life (Bureau of Labor Statistics, 1982).

Underlying the calculations of the conventional life table are a set of restrictive assumptions: a unimodal schedule of labour force participation (a shape often not followed by females), no exits from the labour force until the age of maximum labour force participation (except by death), and no new entrants into the labour force after that age.

Multi-state life tables are calculated using age-specific accession and separation rates and status specific regimes of mortality. Unlike conventional unistate life tables, therefore, they reflect the observed patterns of labour force entry and exit, independent of the age and labour force status composition of the population. In return for the extra input data, they free the life table model of the restrictive assumptions that are demanded by the conventional model.

They overcome many of the limitations of the conventional model which stem from its convenient but simplistic design. Although the conventional model rests on a set of readily accessible data – cross-sectional rates of labor force participation – these data are not really appropriate to the study of labor force mobility. Inferring flows from stocks of workers at each age can lead to misconceptions about current labor force behavior. (Bureau of Labor Statistics, 1982)

The principal input to the calculation of a multi-state life table is a matrix of transition probabilities for each age, developed from longitudinal records of labour force behaviour. The principal assumption underlying the calculations is the Markovian hypothesis that the age-specific transition probabilities are constant and that they depend solely on an individual's current age, sex and status; cumulative experiences in previous statuses are ignored.

The multi-state life table calculation procedure is straightforward. The Bureau of Labor Statistics reports that at exact age sixteen, according to 1977 data, the life table population for males included 70,539 inactive men and 27,059 who were in the labour force. Given the transition probabilities estimated from observed data, 70.3 per cent of those inactive at sixteen would remain so at exact age seventeen, 29.6 per cent would enter the labour force, and 0.1 per cent would have died before attaining the age of seventeen years. Thus 49,559 men would constitute the 'inactive to inactive' flow, and 20,889 the 'inactive to active' flow. An analogous calculation for those in the labour force at age sixteen produces corresponding totals of 19,898 and 7,125, respectively. Proceeding in this manner, age by age, one obtains the entire work life history of each starting cohort: the 70,539 persons who at sixteen years of age were inactive and the corresponding 27,059 who were in the labour force at that same age. Cumulating person-years lived active and inactive, backward from the oldest to the youngest ages in the life table in the usual manner, and dividing the resulting totals by the number of those initially active and inactive, gives rise to age- and status-specific life expectancies. For example, an inactive sixteen-year old could expect to live a total of 55.0 years, 38.1 of which would be spent in the labour force; an active sixteen-year old, on the other hand, could expect a total of 39.8 active years out of the same expected lifetime. Suitably aggregating the two together, gives the consolidated active life expectancy of 38.7 years (Bureau of Labor Statistics, 1982).

Table 10.3 sets out a numerical comparison of male working life expectancies at age sixteen obtained with the conventional and multi-state models. It focusses on two working life table measures: population-based and labour force-based life expectancies. The former reflects the average number of years in the labour force remaining to a person at a given age (in

Table 10.3 *A comparison of conventional and multi-state working life table expectancies for males aged* 16

	Working Life Expectancy		
	Population Based	Labour Force Based	Difference
Conventional Working Life Table for			
United States, 1972	40.7	44.8	4.1
United States, 1977	40.8	44.5	3.7
Denmark, 1972–4	42.8	47.5	4.7
Multistate Working Life Table for			
United States, 1972	39.3	40.3	1.0
United States, 1977	38.7	39.8	1.1
Denmark, 1972–4	42.0	43.25	1.25
Difference			
United States, 1972	1.4	4.5	
United States, 1977	2.1	4.7	
Denmark, 1972–4	0.8	4.25	

Sources: Schoen and Woodrow (1980) and Bureau of Labor Statistics (1982).

our case, sixteen years); the latter indicates the average number of years in the labour force remaining to a person at a given age, *who is in the labour force at that age.* In all three illustrations presented in table 10.3, the multi-state measures are lower than their conventionally calculated counterparts and their differences within each life table – i.e., between labour force-based and population-based measures – are much lower.

5 Net rates: how a net migration model can bias projected population totals

Inadequate data on interregional migration has led demographers and economists to focus on inadequate measures of geographical mobility. Foremost among such inadequate measures are indices based on the notion of *net* migration (Foot and Milne, 1984; Greenwood, Hunt and McDowell, 1986; Tabuchi, 1988), a component of demographic change that can be crudely estimated in the absence of migration flow data by assuming that it is approximately equal to the difference between an observed population and the corresponding population projected to that date with zero migration. Such a 'residual' method of inferring migration is a well-known technique of the demographer's mathematical apparatus. But it comes at a price, because it introduces a specification bias into the analysis.

For an empirical illustration of how net migration rates can bias projected population totals, consider past patterns of urbanisation in India and in the former Soviet Union (Rogers, 1985). The urban population of India around 1970 was growing by about 3.9 per cent a year, an outcome of a birthrate of 30 per 1,000, a death rate of 10 per 1,000, an in-migration rate of 29 per 1,000, and an out-migration rate of 10 per 1,000. Expressing these rates on a per-person basis gives rise to the demographic identity

$$r_u = b_u - d_u + m_u^i - m_u^o$$
$$= 0.030 - 0.010 + 0.029 - 0.010$$
$$= 0.039$$

The corresponding identity for the rural population is

$$r_r = 0.039 - 0.017 + 0.002 - 0.007$$
$$= 0.017$$

India's total national population in 1970 was about 548 million, 109 million of which lived in urban areas. A bi-regional model based on these data yields the projected evolution summarised in table 10.4. For purposes of comparison, we also include the corresponding projected evolution of the urban–rural population of the former Soviet Union, for which the corresponding demographic identities are

$$r_u = 0.017 - 0.008 + 0.027 - 0.011 = 0.025$$
$$r_r = 0.019 - 0.009 + 0.014 - 0.035 = -0.011$$

Both India and the former Soviet Union were urbanising populations around 1970. Consequently, the projected evolution of their principal indices follow the expected pattern of an urbanisation scenario. India's projected urbanisation, $U(t)$, grows from an initial level of about a fifth (19.9 per cent) toward an ultimate stable growth level of just over 38 per cent, while the former Soviet Union's projected urbanisation increases from about 56 per cent to just under 76 per cent. India's urban population growth rate declines from its initial level of 3.8 per cent a year towards an ultimate level of 2.1 per cent, while that of the former Soviet Union drops from 2.5 per cent to just under 1 per cent. The urban net migration rate, $m_u(t)$, declines over time in both illustrations, even though the two respective out-migration rates are fixed in each case. It depends on the initial allocation of the national population between urban and rural regions: *reversing that allocation would cause it to increase.*

Table 10.4 *Bi-regional models of urbanisation in India and in the former Soviet Union, 1970*

A India		B Soviet Union	

$$\begin{bmatrix} 113.16 \\ 446.68 \end{bmatrix} = \begin{bmatrix} 1.010 & 0.007 \\ 0.010 & 1.015 \end{bmatrix} \begin{bmatrix} 109 \\ 439 \end{bmatrix} \qquad \begin{bmatrix} 139.44 \\ 104.85 \end{bmatrix} = \begin{bmatrix} 0.998 & 0.035 \\ 0.011 & 0.975 \end{bmatrix} \begin{bmatrix} 136 \\ 106 \end{bmatrix}$$

$$\begin{bmatrix} 117.42 \\ 454.51 \end{bmatrix} = \begin{bmatrix} 1.010 & 0.007 \\ 0.010 & 1.015 \end{bmatrix} \begin{bmatrix} 113.16 \\ 446.68 \end{bmatrix} \qquad \begin{bmatrix} 142.83 \\ 103.76 \end{bmatrix} = \begin{bmatrix} 0.998 & 0.035 \\ 0.011 & 0.975 \end{bmatrix} \begin{bmatrix} 139.44 \\ 104.85 \end{bmatrix}$$

$$\vdots \qquad\qquad\qquad\qquad\qquad\qquad\qquad\qquad\qquad \vdots$$

Stable growth

$$\lambda_1 \begin{bmatrix} 0.377 \\ 0.623 \end{bmatrix} = \begin{bmatrix} 1.010 & 0.007 \\ 0.010 & 1.015 \end{bmatrix} \begin{bmatrix} 0.377 \\ 0.623 \end{bmatrix} \qquad \lambda_1 \begin{bmatrix} 0.753 \\ 0.247 \end{bmatrix} = \begin{bmatrix} 0.998 & 0.035 \\ 0.011 & 0.975 \end{bmatrix} \begin{bmatrix} 0.753 \\ 0.247 \end{bmatrix}$$

$$\lambda_1 = 1.021; \; r(\infty) = 0.021 \qquad\qquad \lambda_1 = 1.009; \; r(\infty) = 0.009$$
$$U(\infty) = 0.384 \qquad\qquad\qquad U(\infty) = 0.757$$

C Principal indices

India		Soviet Union	
$U(t) =$	$0.199, 0.202, \ldots, 0.384$	$U(t) =$	$0.562, 0.571, \ldots, 0.757$
$m_u(t) =$	$0.0182, 0.0176, \ldots, 0.00123$	$m_u(t) =$	$0.016, 0.015, \ldots, 0.00024$
$m_v(t) =$	$-0.005, -0.004, \ldots, -0.00077$	$m_v(t) =$	$-0.021, -0.020, \ldots, -0.00076$
$r_u(t) =$	$0.038, 0.038, \ldots, 0.021$	$r_u(t) =$	$0.025, 0.024, \ldots, 0.009$
$r_v(t) =$	$0.017, 0.018, \ldots, 0.021$	$r_v(t) =$	$-0.011, -0.010, \ldots, -0.009$

Now consider the corresponding evolutions that would arise under a model using *fixed net* migration rates instead of a fixed out-migration rate. Table 10.5 presents the net migration model counterpart of table 10.4. Notice that both projections ultimately stabilise at *total* (100 per cent) urbanisation and that the urban net migration rates for both countries are not too dissimilar despite their different sets of out-migration rates: 18 versus 16 per thousand. And observe that, relative to table 10.4, the projections shown for *urban* India and the former Soviet Union are both higher. This is because

Net migration is defined with respect to the particular population being projected. If that population is currently experiencing an excess of in-migrants over out-migrants, this feature will be built in as part of the projection process, and its effects will multiply and increase cumulatively over time. The converse applies, of course,

Table 10.5 *Uniregional models of urbanisation in India and in the former Soviet Union, 1970*

A India	B Soviet Union

$$\begin{bmatrix} 113.16 \\ 446.68 \end{bmatrix} = \begin{bmatrix} 1.0382 & 0 \\ 0 & 1.0175 \end{bmatrix} \begin{bmatrix} 109 \\ 439 \end{bmatrix} \qquad \begin{bmatrix} 139.44 \\ 104.85 \end{bmatrix} = \begin{bmatrix} 1.0253 & 0 \\ 0 & 0.9892 \end{bmatrix} \begin{bmatrix} 136 \\ 106 \end{bmatrix}$$

$$\begin{bmatrix} 117.48 \\ 454.49 \end{bmatrix} = \begin{bmatrix} 1.0382 & 0 \\ 0 & 1.0175 \end{bmatrix} \begin{bmatrix} 113.16 \\ 446.68 \end{bmatrix} \qquad \begin{bmatrix} 142.97 \\ 103.71 \end{bmatrix} = \begin{bmatrix} 1.0253 & 0 \\ 0 & 0.9892 \end{bmatrix} \begin{bmatrix} 139.44 \\ 104.85 \end{bmatrix}$$

$$\vdots \qquad\qquad\qquad\qquad\qquad\qquad\qquad \vdots$$

Stable growth

$\lambda_1 = 1.038;\ r(\infty) = 0.038$	$\lambda_1 = 1.025;\ r(\infty) = 0.025$
$U(\infty) = 1$	$U(\infty) = 1$

C Principal indices

India	Soviet Union
$U(t) = 0.199, 0.205, \ldots, 1$	$U(t) = 0.562, 0.580, \ldots, 1$
$m_u(t) = 0.018$ (fixed)	$m_u(t) = 0.016$ (fixed)
$m_v(t) = -0.005$ (fixed)	$m_v(t) = -0.021$ (fixed)
$r_u(t) = 0.038$ (fixed)	$r_u(t) = 0.025$ (fixed)
$r_v(t) = 0.017$ (fixed)	$r_v(t) = -0.011$ (fixed)

to regions experiencing net out-migration. In short, regional populations with a positive net migration rate are likely to be overprojected and those with a negative net migration rate are likely to be underprojected (Rogers, 1976).

6 Conclusion

When faced with the task of modelling the dynamics of two or more interdependent (multi-state) population subgroups, demographers, economists and sociologists have, until relatively recently, generally adopted one of two distinct approaches. They have either (1) examined each subpopulation apart from the others by appending to it a net migration rate to express its exchanges with the rest of the total population, or (2) disaggregated the total population into subgroups by means of a prevalence rate that ignored those exchanges and focussed only on their redistributional consequences (i.e., changes in relative shares of the total stock of individuals). The migration and spatial population dynamics literature adopted the first strategy (Rogers, 1990); the labour force participation and dynamics literature adopted the second (Bureau of Labor Statistics, 1982). Both approaches introduce population composition biases into the analysis of behaviour. With the development and diffusion of multi-state demographic methods, neither modelling strategy needs to be continued unless dictated by the unavailability of transition data.

Scores of studies continue to focus on the net migration rates as the dependent variable whose behaviour is to be explained, ignoring the biases that such a migration specification introduces into the modelled spatial population dynamics. For example, when Keyfitz (1985) asserts that aggregating the separate projections of the US and Mexican populations prior to projection will generate an underprojection relative to the aggregate of the separately projected totals, he is ignoring the fact that they are interacting populations and is implicitly adopting a *net* migration specification. The aggregation of interacting *multi-regional* populations prior to projection can produce *either* under- or overprojection; Keyfitz's proof of a guaranteed underprojection only holds if the populations are *non-interacting*.

If net migration rates are problematic, what about prevalence rates? For example, does a relatively large fraction of rural-born persons among urban residents *necessarily* imply high rural–to–urban migration rates? No, it does not. High rates of net urban in-migration produce high levels of urbanisation, with the consequence that urban areas account for increasingly larger fractions of national *births* over time and this results in natural increase being dominant. This, in turn, gives rise to a high fraction of natives in urban areas. Nevertheless, some migration analysts continue to use lifetime migration proportions as the independent variable to be explained.

This chapter has examined some of the ways in which different kinds of rates create biases in the distributional patterns that they generate. First, we examined the impacts of heterogeneity and selection on population dynamics. Second, we considered the prevalence rate and its problems. Then we focussed on the net rate and its biases. Our principal conclusion is that aggregate measures of multi-state population dynamics depend on initial conditions and therefore become increasingly biased as the effects of selection make themselves felt. This bias is especially problematic when inappropriately defined rates are used as the aggregate measures.

11 A micro-simulation approach to demographic and social accounting

MARTIN CLARKE

1 Introduction

In this chapter the problems of demographic and social accounting are addressed from an alternative perspective – that of micro-level analysis. We attempt to both review and describe how this alternative approach can be used to address some of the many and diverse problems that Richard Stone was concerned with during his long and distinguished academic career.

The attractions of accounts-based approaches are now well understood, particularly in the areas of economic modelling, especially in input–output analysis, and in population projection work. It is interesting to note that the theoretical and practical consistencies afforded by an accounts-based framework have been exploited by regional scientists adopting a mathematical as opposed to statistical modelling approach. The latter approach, however, has proved to be consistently more popular than the former, largely through the relative ease of model implementation as a result of widely available computer software (Clarke and Openshaw, 1987). Many enthusiastic users of these packages would do well to examine the accounting consistencies of their models before drawing too many conclusions from their results. Rogers, in chapter 10 of this volume, addresses some of the problems of consistency that can arise in implementing models without paying careful attention to the coefficients that these models include. Mathematical models with underpinning sets of accounts have inherent advantages over statistical methods despite the operational difficulties that can be encountered.

In this chapter we first address some of the issues faced in implementing account-based models and describe how the use of micro-analytical techniques can offer a potentially attractive alternative solution method. Next a brief overview of the development of micro-analytical simulation models is provided along with a description of some important applications. The following section attempts to illustrate some of the model-building design and implementation issues that are faced in a practical

195

application – that of small area demographic updating and projection. The application described concerns the development of a detailed household and individual projection model for the City of Leeds, where a full range of demographic and social processes were considered. We also highlight a number of extensions to this model that allow household income and expenditure patterns to be computed. The final section speculates on the future development of micro-simulation as a tool for policy analysis in regional science.

2 Issues in account-based modelling – the advantages and disadvantages of a micro-level approach

Issues in representation and analysis

A fundamental choice in any modelling exercise is specifying the form in which the system of interest is to be represented. In the majority of the work reported in this volume, the model designers have chosen to work with aggregate occupancy matrix representations of their system. Richard Stone, too, used this approach in his varied model applications. The alternative approach, which occupies the majority of discussion in this chapter, is to adopt a micro-level approach where the system is specified at the level of the individual decision-making unit, whether this be an individual, a household, a firm or a bank. In much of the literature these two approaches are viewed as competing and much effort has been devoted to extolling the advantages of one over the other. However, as we shall discuss, both approaches have merits and drawbacks, and it is the nature of the application that will usually determine the suitability of adopting a particular approach.

The objective of most process modelling exercises is to specify how the state of a system at, say, time $t + 1$, is derived, given the state of the system at t. This can be formalised as a difference equation of the following form:

$$O_i(t+1) = O_i(t) + \sum_j O_{ji}(t, t+1) - \sum_j O_{ij}(t, t+1) \qquad (11.1)$$

where

O_i is the membership of state i and
O_{ji} is the flows from state j to state i.

Conventionally, this change process is expressed through the use of a transition matrix μ, such that equation (11.1) can be replaced by

$$O_i(t+1) = O_i(t) + \sum_j \mu_{ji} O_j(t) - \sum_j \mu_{ij} O_i(t) \qquad (11.2)$$

where μ_{ij} is a transition rates matrix containing the probability of moving from state i to state j during time period $(t, t+1)$.

Clearly, much research focusses on the estimation of the transition rates matrices, and Richard Stone's innovative work in this area has been well documented (e.g., Stone, 1971).

We note at this stage that most micro-simulation work is directed at solving the same problem, for even though the models are specified at a micro-level, model outputs are normally aggregated to produce summaries in occupancy matrix form. The fact that these can be produced in a more flexible way is an attractive feature of the micro-approach but it is not the most compelling.

The well-documented problem of occupancy matrix size is often stated as one of the strong attractions of micro-simulation. Simply stated, the size of an occupancy matrix is related to the number of variables defined and the number of attributes associated with each variable and can be expressed as follows

$$n = \prod_i l_i \tag{11.3}$$

where n is the number of cells in the occupancy matrix and i is the number of attribute classes of each variable l. This occupancy matrix problem often becomes particularly acute for spatial problems when the interactions between regions or zones within regions are of interest. For example, a problem with 100 origin zones, 100 destination zones, eight product categories, three mode types and four household categories results in an occupancy matrix consisting of 960,000 cells. Furthermore, in the extreme case, the transition matrix for solving the $(t-1, t)$ period problem will be $960,000^2$ in size. However, this is certainly exaggerating the situation, since most analysts can devise ways (usually through process models) of reducing the size of these transition matrices. Despite this, the attractions of specifying a list of individual actors and specifying their attributes are strong from a representational perspective.

Issues in heterogeneity, interdependence and aggregation

A traditional dilemma for the modeller centres on how to incorporate as much detail about the description of a system of interest without making the resultant model specification unwieldy. Operations research has long advocated the use of 'Occam's Razor' – that is the exclusion of variables from models unless they are absolutely essential. This provides a useful rule of thumb but in many policy relevant social science applications the analyst is often concerned with the distributional impacts of policies. It is thus important in such cases to retain a detailed description of the population with, typically, a large number of variables and a reasonable number of classes associated with each variable. It is at this point that the issue of representation comes to the fore. To capture the required level of heterogeneity within a population requires either the use of a disaggregate occupancy matrix (and the associated matrix size) or the use of list representation and the adoption of a micro-simulation approach.

The problem becomes more focussed when there is also interdependence between population variables and events. For example, in a household the birth of a child may have significant impacts with regard to the mother's participation in the labour market, household income and housing choice. If the analyst was concerned with the impacts of social security programmes on females in the labour market, it is precisely this interdependence that would have to be considered. Again, micro-simulation is well suited to this type of problem. Generally speaking, the greater the level of interdependency between variables, the stronger the case for micro-simulation.

Another issue that is often faced is that of generating classes for a particular variable – whether this be age, income, expenditure. In the occupancy matrix approach, distinct classes or categories have to be predefined (0–4 years, 5–9 years, etc.). However, micro-simulation allows for a continuous representation without the need for any a priori classification. This also leads to another advantage of the approach – it allows for flexible aggregation of model outputs. Any form of aggregation can be performed on variables stored in continuous forms; this is often useful in comparing alternative aggregation schemes.

Dynamics

As we have already discussed, the conventional approach to dynamics in the occupancy matrix context is through the specification of an appropriate, corresponding transition rate matrix. This identifies the rate at which members occupying any particular cell in the matrix make transitions to other cells over a specified time period. In micro-simulation a related approach is adopted: the specification of appropriate conditional probabilities for events occurring to eligible members of the population. The solution to equation (11.2) for the occupancy matrix approach is simple – a set of multiplications. In micro-simulation the approach adopted is to use Monte Carlo sampling to determine if eligible individuals perform a transition or experience an event. As a solution method, it should give rise to the equivalent solution to the transition matrix approach for an exactly equivalent problem (subject to sampling error). However as we have mentioned above, this list processing approach allows for the more elegant handling of interdependencies between individuals in the population.

Data availability

The theoretical advantages and disadvantages of one or another approach to modelling will become irrelevant if appropriate data are not available to operationalise a particular model. Data availability has long plagued regional scientists who have attempted to build regional or subregional versions of national accounts models. More generally, they have had to devise methods for estimating or deriving missing data, using a variety of techniques such as iterative proportional fitting, statistical methods and so on. It is clear that data availability, or unavailability, could have a major impact on model design.

In many cases this is where micro-simulation of spatial systems faces a major disadvantage. While public-use micro-data sets are often available at the national level, they seldom exist with a detailed geographical reference and where they do they tend to have resulted from one-off surveys as opposed to systematic and regular data capture exercises. To try to alleviate this problem methods have been developed that synthetically create micro-data sets from aggregate distributions. A full account of these methods can be found in Birkin and Clarke (1988). Similarly, data on transition rates or probabilities are rarely available in fully specified form and, for small areas, have often to be generated from data available for more aggregated units. We illustrate how this can be undertaken in section 4.

Computational Issues

List processing is a computationally intensive activity and this has been a major factor in preventing micro-simulation from being widely used. Orcutt (1986) welcomed the phenomenal increase in computer power enthusiastically, suggesting it would herald an era of inexpensive micro-simulation modelling. However, comparatively, list processing still involves a more resource consuming solution time than equivalent transition matrix approaches. As we shall demonstrate in section 4, the algorithms that need to be developed for micro-simulation model implementation are also often complex, in order to capture fully the interdependencies between attributes and between individuals.

Conclusions

The choice of a particular modelling style in any problem-solving context will be influenced by a variety of factors. Among these will be the experience, taste, resource availability and time scale of the researcher. In some cases a detailed checklist of advantages and drawbacks of alternative styles will be drawn up and a decision made, bearing in mind the objectives and constraints of the research project. As we have already discussed, it is probably the case that in those applications that wish to address the problems of interdependence and heterogeneity displayed within socio-economic systems micro-simulation will be a strong contender. Whether it is actually chosen or not may depend more on the data and computational restrictions in force, along with the experience of the researcher, than on theoretical advantages that may be evident. In section 3 we present a brief overview of some of the applications of the methodology where researchers were convinced, at least at the outset, of the merits of the approach.

3 Applications of micro-analytic simulation models

Introduction

It has been noted before (Clarke and Holm, 1987) that there does not exist a single, well-defined source of literature on the application of micro-simulation methods, and that the technique is rarely if ever reported in regional science journals. Many of the applications of micro-simulation have been reported in government agency publications and have escaped the notice of all but the most ardent devotees of the methodology. Most applications have also been aspatial in nature, largely undertaken by economists.

However, for those undertaking a literature review, life is made some-what easier through the important contribution made by Orcutt over the last thirty years. References to his seminal work abound and the determined sleuth can, by following these references, build up a comprehensive picture of the diverse set of applications. For the more impatient regional scientist a review of some of the important applications with a spatial focus can be found in Clarke and Holm (1987). What follows is an abridged but updated version of that review.

It is useful to attempt to classify applications into a number of broad categories:

(i) Dynamic economic micro-simulation models

This style of modelling is characterised by the work of Orcutt and colleagues and best exemplified through the development of DYNASIM (Dynamic Simulation of Income Model, Orcutt, *et al.*, 1976). DYNASIM, developed at the Urban Institute in Washington DC, is a true dynamic model that simulates the economic and social behaviour of households over time. A range of events was simulated and in each case a large number of determinant variables were included in the transition probability computation. For example, the probability of job change was taken as a function of age, race, sex, education, tenure and sector of employment. Applications of DYNASIM have mainly been concerned with the examination of the cost and distributional effects of transfer income policies. Typical of this was the work of Wertheimer and Zedlewski (1978) who examined the effect of the AFDC (Aid For Dependent Children) programme on household income.

More recently Caldwell (1991) has developed CORSIM, the Cornell Dynamic Microsimulation Model. CORSIM is a particularly well-documented model that also has the distinctive feature of being implemented on both a PC and a supercomputer. The most recent example of its application has been in capturing patterns of dental disease, dental service utilisation and dental expenditures for persons and families in the United States. The model currently runs over a time frame 1973–91 and captures an impressive level of detail concerning individual dental health characteristics.

(ii) Static economic simulation models

A related application to DYNASIM is the KGB model named after its developers (Betson, Greenberg and Kasten 1980). Again this model was directed at addressing federal policies in the Carter administration, notably the Program for Better Jobs and Income (PBJI) – a complex package of income and job distribution policies. The model worked in four steps, but was basically a cross-sectional model with no explicit consideration of the time dimension. First, the pre-reform socio-economic status of the population in the sample is characterised. Some of this information was derived by applying rules (e.g., for tax computation purposes) to the individual attribute set, and amounts of unemployment compensation in current transfer programmes were estimated.

Secondly, net wage and disposable income are adjusted to what they would be if the new policy were implemented if desired hours of work and earnings remained unchanged. Thirdly, labour supply response to the changed wage rates and incomes under the new programmes are calculated and from this the new disposable income is calculated. Finally, it is determined whether an individual will take a programme job whenever he is in the labour force, only when he is unemployed, or not at all. A similar dynamic micro-simulation approach has been adopted by Galler and Wagner (1986), although they have also developed a single cohort simulation model to test policy impacts over a whole lifetime (Hain and Helberger, 1986). Again the main focus was on testing federal policies relating to income distribution. None of these models devotes any substantial attention to geographical specification, since their focus is on testing federal (i.e., national) policies where any geographical variation in policy impact is largely ignored.

(iii) Dynamic models with a geographical focus

The number of micro-simulation applications with a distinct geographical focus is very small. Yet, on the face of it, the addition of a spatial label should generate advantages for the micro-simulation approach, especially given the representational issues discussed above. There is a downside however: attaching a spatial label effectively implies a significant increase in the sample size that needs to be addressed if the results are to be interpreted at the small area level. Most of the applications described so far have typically used sample populations of between 1,000 and 3,000 households. In applications with a spatial label it is often necessary to consider approaching this number of units per zone. This has imposed severe computational problems for the analyst, especially when dynamic simulation models are constructed. In fact, Caldwell (1991) suggests that it has been the computational demands of micro-simulation models that have been the single most important drawback to their wider use.

One of the best-known applications with a spatial dimension is the Harvard urban development simulation model (HUDS) developed by Kain and Apgar (1985). HUDS is a dynamic disaggregate disequilibrium model of a metropolitan system. The model was implemented for the period 1960–70 for Chicago and was specifically used for assessing the effects of spatially concentrated programmes such as CHIPS on housing and neighbourhood improvement. The model operated with an explicit spatial dimension – 200 residential districts were identified along with twenty workplace locations. A consequence of this quest for spatial detail was the need to operate with a sample size of 70,000 households. Other attempts to model housing markets with micro-simulation models have included Wegener's model of the Dortmund housing system (Wegener, 1981) and the work of Clarke, Longley and Williams (1989) who constructed a model to examine asset accumulation and subsidy in the UK housing market.

Building on the tradition of spatial micro-simulation modelling in Leeds, Rees et al. (1987) have developed the UPDATE model for demographic updating and projection (described in more detail in the next section) and Williamson (1991) has developed an approach that allows the needs of the elderly population to be quantified and the package of services required to meet these needs to be planned. In Holland there is also a tradition of developing demographic micro-simulation models. Interestingly, the motivation for developing this approach was the difficulty in specifying an aggregate model with the level of detail required for policy sensitive analysis. A good account of the latest developments in this work can be found in Hooimeijer (1991).

(iv) Event-based micro-simulation

The work of a group of Swedish geographers is of interest because they have attempted to extend the micro-simulation approach in a way that accounts for the interrelationships between individuals and between individuals and other spatial entities, such as workplace, school, residence and so on. While the underpinning approach relies on Monte Carlo sampling an account of any action or event on other individuals and households is also tracked. For example, the offer of employment in another town to a member of a household will have impacts on the other members, and the decision to migrate or not may depend on factors such as schooling, housing and so on. In some cases not every member of the household will move, with concomitant implications for housing and employment. The model, known as HOMSKE (Holm *et al.*, 1985) has to date only been developed as an experimental tool, but seems well equipped to take advantage of recent developments in computer science, such as object-oriented programming and rule-based methods.

(v) Other applications

There is a plethora of interesting micro-simulation applications that do not fall easily in to any broad categorisation. One interesting branch is an attempt to develop a micro-level alternative to conventional input–output analysis. The most well-developed example of this approach is contained in the work of Eliasson (1985) who has constructed a model of interfirm linkages at the micro level in the Swedish economy. The justification for this approach is once again found in the desire to represent the heterogeneity within the population of industries and firms that constitute the economy.

Another unusual application area has been in anthropology and historical demography. The appearance of two micro-simulation software packages – POPSIM and SOCSIM (Gisebrecht and Fiew, 1969) encouraged a number of workers to examine the interrelationships between constituent members of a population. This had particular appeal in areas such as the analysis of kinship relations in small communities and in reconstructing historical populations from known ones (Wrigley and Schofield, 1981).

In concluding this brief review section it is worth once again emphasising that micro-simulation remains a fragmented specialism that lacks the coherence of the more conventional discipline of economic and social accounts pioneered by Richard Stone.

4 An application of micro-simulation: demographic and household modelling

Introduction

To illustrate some of the ideas discussed above we now describe an application of the micro-simulation methodology in a little detail. The application discussed is concerned with updating the detailed characteristics of a population of individuals and households over time at the small area level. The relevance of this approach is fairly obvious – in the UK and most other countries, a full census of population is carried out only every ten years, and while it provides a wealth of information for policy makers the data collected has a relatively short shelf life. In the intervening years, planners still have to plan service delivery, allocate resources to meet needs and so on. To undertake these tasks they need better, contemporary information on their client base. The model described in this section, known as UPDATE, can satisfy this requirement.[1]

A full description of UPDATE can be found in Duley (1989) and accounts of its various components in Duley and Rees (1990) and Rees, Clarke and Duley (1987). In the following section we summarise the main components of UPDATE through focussing on an account of the way in which the main demographic processes were treated.

Demographic processes in UPDATE

As indicated above, the solution procedure adopted in UPDATE is known as list processing. This involves taking each household and its constituent individuals in turn and testing for eligibility for certain events and for those eligible individuals (or households) testing to determine if particular

---

[1] UPDATE uses a synthetically generated micro-level population of individuals and households. The absence of any public use micro-data from the UK Census has forced the adoption of this synthetic sampling approach, fully described in Birkin and Clarke (1988). The structure of the UPDATE simulation system is shown in figure 11.2. Essentially, the population in each postal sector (containing, on average, about 2,500 households and 7,000 individuals) is processed sequentially through a series of demographic processes that can be mapped on to individuals and households. These include death, birth, marriage/cohabitation, divorce/separation, migration, socio-economic change and ageing. Each postal sector is therefore treated as a single, isolated system receiving in-migrants and dispatching out-migrants. The number of in-migrants is dependent on events within the postal sector only, and not elsewhere as in a more traditional multi-regional model. This simplification made it feasible to produce an operational model, and to incorporate a number of interesting innovations. It also demonstrates that, in any practical model implementation, certain compromises have to be made to further progress, and in this respect micro-simulation is no different from other modelling styles.

transitions occur, through Monte Carlo sampling. Two issues have to be confronted at an early stage with this list-processing method. First, and this is also addressed in a somewhat different way by Trigg and Madden in chapter 8 of this volume, is the problem of interdependency between households and individuals. Trigg and Madden look at the problem of the consumption characteristics of individuals being structured by the characteristics of the households in which the individuals find themselves. Here, we concern ourselves with issues such as those of marriage and cohabitation. These are normally addressed by the creation of pools of 'supply' and 'demand' (Clarke, 1986). The second is the problem of ordering of events. In sequential list processing choosing to consider mortality before fertility may result in females being prevented from giving birth by dying in the simulation period. Three solutions to this problem are available: first reduce the simulation period from say a year to a month and so reduce the probability of multiple events; secondly, assign randomly a day on which the event is deemed to occur, test for all events and eliminate non-feasible combinations or thirdly obtain probabilities for the occurrence of multiple events. In UPDATE the main demographic processes are all considered and we now describe them in turn.

Mortality

The micro-simulation model uses mortality rates for each single year of age (period–cohort) transition and each sex. The rate is updated for each year. The target variable to be estimated is

$p(mo)_{a\,a+1}^{ws}(y)$, the probability that a person in ward w in age group a and of sex s at the start of year y dies in that year before attaining age $a+1$.

To estimate these mortality probabilities we have available national deaths by single years of age, ward deaths by eleven aggregate age groups (roughly ten-year age groups) and the corresponding populations at risk for the base year. National population estimates are produced for each mid year, as are district population estimates which are used to factor crudely the 1981 ward population. Thus, the variables available for the estimation are

$D_a^{ns}(y)$, the deaths in year y in England and Wales (nation n) by sex s and single year of age a,

$D_c^{ws}(y)$, the deaths in year y in ward w by sex s in coarse age group c, and

$k_b^{ws}(y)$, the population in year y in ward w by sex s in age group b.

The age classification is as follows: a = single years of age from 0–74, and 75 and over; b = single years of age 0–24, 5 year age groups 25–29, ..., 70–74 and 75 and over and $c = 0, 1–4, 5–14, …, 65–74, 75$ and over. Classification a is the target one for the UPDATE model, classification b is the best that can be achieved for ward population estimates, and classification c is the one used to report the ward deaths.

The estimation then proceeds as follows:

National death rates are computed for age disaggregation a

$$d_a^{ns}(y) = D_a^{ns}(y)/k_a^{ns}(y) \tag{11.4}$$

and age disaggregation b

$$d_b^{ns}(y) = \sum_{a \in b} D_a^{ns}(y)/\sum_{a \in b} k_a^{ns}(y) \tag{11.5}.$$

The ward-level death rates are then the national death rates adjusted to satisfy ward death figures:

$$d_a^{ws}(y) = d_a^{ns}(y) \, D_c^{ws}(y)/\sum_{b \in c} d_b^{ns}(y)k_b^{ws}(y) \tag{11.6}$$

The mortality probabilities are then computed, shifting the age time plan from period–age (used so far) to period–cohort (required in any demographic projection model)

$$p(mo)_{aa+1}^{ws}(y) = 1 - \left[(1 - 0.5 \, d_{a+1}^{ws}(y))(1 + 0.5 d_a^{ws}(y)) \right] \tag{11.7}$$

Slightly more complicated estimation procedures applying the same technique are required for the first two ages and the last two ages, and these are described in Duley (1989).

Given these mortality probabilities for wards we need to convert them to probabilities for postal sectors. This is achieved by assuming that the probabilities are constant over the constituent enumeration districts. The enumeration districts which comprise individual postal sectors are then determined and the mortality probability for the postal sector calculated as a weighted average of the constituent enumeration districts.

Maternity

In the model, women are exposed to the risk of giving birth in each year expressed as a maternity probability. New infants are introduced into the family and household by sampling from a probability distribution of the numbers of births per maternity. The probabilities are concentrated, of course, at one birth, but the model allows for twins, triplets, quadruplets and quintuplets to be born using a sharply declining probability function. Births are sexed using local probabilities of a male or female infant.

Maternity probabilities are dependent, like mortality, on sex and age, but also, rather critically, on marital status and ethnic origin. National information on the age and marital status classification of births and on the age and ethnic group classification of births is combined with district-level data on births by age, marital status and ethnic group, together with total births by ward.

A four step procedure is used to estimate the target variable, defined as $p(ma)^w(a, m, e)$, the probability of a female giving birth in ward w, given age, marital status and ethnic group.

Step 1 Computation of national birth rates

First, we derive the number of births at the national level to mothers in age group b, of marital status m and in ethnic group $e(B^n(b, m, e))$ by using iterative proportional fitting methods, given the marginals $B^n(b, m)$ and $B^n(e, m)$. This is then translated into single year age of mother (a) by

$$B^n(a, m, e) = \sum_b p^n(a/b, m, e) . B^n(b, m, e) \tag{11.8}$$

where $p^n(a/b, m, e)$ is the national estimate of the probability of a birth to a mother of age a given age group b, marital status m and ethnicity e.

This array is then translated into rates by dividing by the female population at risk

$$b^n(a, m, e) = B^n(a, m, e)/Fe^n(a, m, e) \tag{11.9}$$

where $Fe^n(a, m, e)$ is the number of females by age, marital status and ethnic group.

Step 2 Computation of district birth rates

An initial estimate of the number of births at district level by age group b, marital status m and ethnic group e is computed using conditional probabilities derived from the national estimation

$$B^d(b, m, e) = p^n(e/b, m) \ B^d(b, m) \tag{11.10}$$

where $p^n(e/b, m)$ is the national estimate of the probability of an 'ethnic' birth given age group b and marital status m. This initial estimate is then adjusted to known district marginals $B^d(b, m)$ and $B^d(e)$ using iterative proportional fitting (IPF) techniques. District populations at risk $Fe^d(b, m, e)$ are estimated from marginal arrays $Fe^d(b, m)$, $Fe^d(b, e)$ and $Fe^d(e, m)$ using IPF. The district birth rates can then be estimated as:

$$b^d(a, m, e) = b^n(a, m, e) . B^d(b, m, e)/(b^n(b, m, e) . Fe^d(b, m, e)) \tag{11.11}$$

Step 3 Computation of ward birth rates

IPF was again used to estimate the female population at risk, $Fe^w(b,m,e)$ from marginal arrays $Fe^w(b,m)$ and $Fe^w(e)$, so that the following estimate could be made of ward birth rates

$$b^w(a,m,e) = b^d(a,m,e) . B^w / \sum_b \sum_m \sum_e b^d(b,m,e) . Fe^w(b,m,e) \qquad (11.12)$$

Step 4 Conversion of ward birth rates to maternity probabilities

The national ratio of maternities by mother's age to births by mother's age was used to adjust ward birth rates:

$$ma^w(a,m,e) = b^w(a,m,e) . MA^n(a) / B^n(a) \qquad (11.13)$$

$$p(ma)^w(a,m,e) = 0.5(1 + V^w(a)) . ma^w(a,m,e) \qquad (11.14),$$

where $MA^n(a)$ is the total number of maternities nationally to mothers in a single year of age a, $B^n(a)$ is the total number of births nationally to mothers in a single year of age a and $V^w(a)$ is the survival probability for ward w by age a of women.

These probabilities are then used in the model. Because we are working at the postal-sector level it is necessary to weight the probabilities in such a way as to reflect the proportion of a ward in a given postal sector.

Marriage and cohabitation; divorce and separation

Marriage and cohabitation involve matching individuals and, in many cases, creating new households. A marriage model has been developed by Clarke (1986) and in the current UPDATE model this has been extended in two respects. First, cohabitation (a man and a woman living together as husband and wife without having married in a civil or religious ceremony) is incorporated. Secondly, the marriage market is an open one, in that individuals are free to attract a spouse or cohabit to the area or to migrate from the area to find a spouse. Therefore, marriage is in part coupled with migration. The algorithm for marriage and cohabitation is set out in figure 11.1 and is described in detail in Duley *et al.* (1988).

The modelling of pair dissolution is slightly more straightforward in that no matching algorithm is required, but the implications of dissolution are equally complex. Because of data limitations certain assumptions concerning the outcome of a divorce transition are made, such as (i) the former husband sets up a new single-person household; (ii) the former wife and any children remain in their present dwelling unit with updated attributes reflecting their new circumstances; and (iii) both former partners become immediately eligible for remarriage.

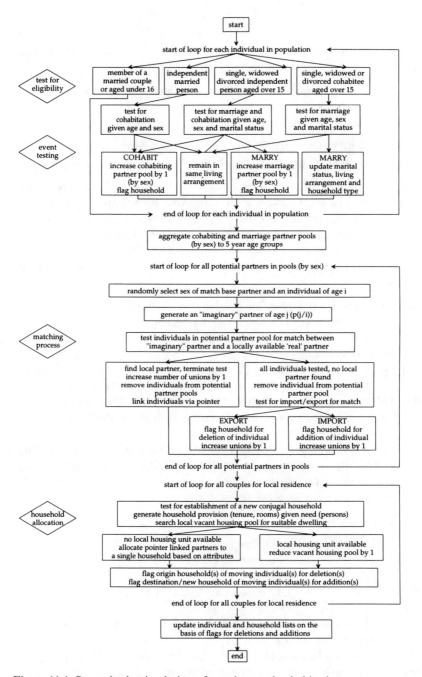

Figure 11.1 Stages in the simulation of marriage and cohabitation

Migration

Three main processes are addressed in the migration submodel. In turn these are:

(1) The estimation of mobility probabilities for wholly moving households:
The target variable to be estimated is as follows:

$p(hm)_s^{ta}(y)$, the probability that a household of type t with a head in age group a living in postal sector s migrates in year y.

By 'migrates' is meant 'makes a migration of the transition type over a single year'. The term 'mobility' indicates that no spatial boundaries are placed on the migrations involved: they can be moved within the area or out of it. The double classification by household type and age of head is used to capture two important influences on household mobility.

The steps undertaken to estimate household mobility probabilities are as follows.

 (i) **Initial district estimate.** The mobility probabilities for households in 1980–81 (the year prior to the Census), classified by type of household and age of head, are estimated for the district containing the postal sector of interest.
 (ii) **Spatial adjustment factor.** This mobility probability is adjusted up or down to reflect mobility in the particular postal sector of interest.
(iii) **Temporal adjustment factor**. This adjusted mobility probability is further adjusted up or down to reflect changes in mobility between 1980–1 and the current year of interest.
(iv) **Mobility probability due to demolition**. To this adjusted mobility probability is added an additional mobility probability reflecting moves forced on households as a result of housing demolitions in the particular postal sector of interest.

In other words

$$p(hm)_s^{ta}(y) = \text{initial district estimate}$$
$$\times \text{ spatial adjustment factor}$$
$$\times \text{ temporal adjustment factor}$$
$$+ \text{ mobility probability due to demolition} \qquad (11.15)$$

(2) The estimation of mobility probabilities for independently moving individuals
For each household that does not move as a whole, each eligible household member is exposed to a rate of moving as an individual or as part

Table 11.1 Destination selection: the division of movement within and without the small area, postal sectors in Leeds

sector	within	without	sector	within	without	sector	within	without
LS1 2	0.003	0.997	LS1 3	0.001	0.999	LS1 4	0.001	0.999
LS1 5	0.000	0.000	LS1 6	0.001	0.999	LS10 1	0.103	0.897
LS10 2	0.250	0.750	LS10 3	0.185	0.815	LS10 4	0.283	0.717
LS11 0	0.050	0.950	LS11 5	0.042	0.958	LS11 6	0.088	0.912
LS11 7	0.103	0.897	LS11 8	0.079	0.921	LS11 9	0.024	0.976
LS12 1	0.042	0.958	LS12 2	0.046	0.954	LS12 3	0.068	0.932
LS12 4	0.091	0.909	LS12 5	0.076	0.924	LS12 6	0.013	0.987
LS13 1	0.063	0.937	LS13 2	0.134	0.866	LS13 3	0.112	0.888
LS13 4	0.093	0.907	LS14 1	0.052	0.948	LS14 2	0.084	0.916
LS14 3	0.048	0.952	LS14 5	0.083	0.917	LS14 6	0.094	0.906
LS15 0	0.097	0.903	LS15 4	0.056	0.944	LS15 7	0.076	0.924
LS15 8	0.090	0.910	LS15 9	0.012	0.988	LS16 5	0.031	0.969
LS16 6	0.069	0.931	LS16 7	0.095	0.905	LS16 8	0.032	0.968
LS16 9	0.146	0.854	LS17 5	0.046	0.954	LS17 6	0.051	0.949
LS17 7	0.123	0.877	LS17 8	0.092	0.908	LS17 9	0.077	0.923
LS18 4	0.071	0.929	LS18 5	0.092	0.908	LS19 6	0.115	0.885
LS19 7	0.266	0.734	LS2 8	0.003	0.997	LS2 9	0.019	0.981
LS20 8	0.325	0.675	LS20 9	0.163	0.837	LS21 1	0.277	0.273
LS21 2	0.424	0.576	LS21 3	0.314	0.686	LS22 4	0.715	0.285
LS22 5	0.152	0.848	LS23 6	0.546	0.454	LS23 7	0.398	0.602

Table 11.1 *Destination selection: the division of movement within and without the small area, postal sectors in Leeds (cont.)*

sector	within	without	sector	within	without	sector	within	without
LS24 9	0.111	0.889	LS25 1	0.128	0.872	LS25 2	0.145	0.855
LS25 3	0.037	0.963	LS25 4	0.132	0.868	LS25 5	0.011	0.989
LS25 7	0.337	0.663	LS26 0	0.220	0.780	LS26 8	0.292	0.708
LS26 9	0.075	0.925	LS27 0	0.0225	0.775	LS27 7	0.077	0.923
LS27 8	0.108	0.892	LS27 9	0.109	0.891	LS28 5	0.164	0.836
LS28 6	0.129	0.871	LS28 7	0.122	0.878	LS28 8	0.116	0.884
LS28 9	0.058	0.942	LS29 6	0.014	0.986	LS3 1	0.018	0.982
LS4 2	0.047	0.952	LS5 3	0.043	0.957	LS6 1	0.135	0.865
LS6 2	0.050	0.950	LS6 3	0.076	0.924	LS6 4	0.049	0.951
LS7 1	0.017	0.983	LS7 2	0.040	0.960	LS7 3	0.067	0.933
LS8 1	0.051	0.949	LS8 2	0.048	0.952	LS8 3	0.057	0.943
LS8 4	0.087	0.913	LS8 5	0.058	0.942	LS9 0	0.115	0.885
LS9 6	0.073	0.927	LS9 7	0.083	0.917	LS9 8	0.068	0.932
LS9 9	0.035	0.965	LS7 4	0.042	0.958	BD10 0	0.000	0.000
BD11 1	0.110	0.890	BD3 7	0.029	0.971	BD4 8	0.073	0.927
WF10 2	0.202	0.798	WF2 0	0.034	0.966	WF3 1	0.144	0.856
WF3 2	0.127	0.873	WF3 3	0.167	0.833	WF3 4	0.054	0.946

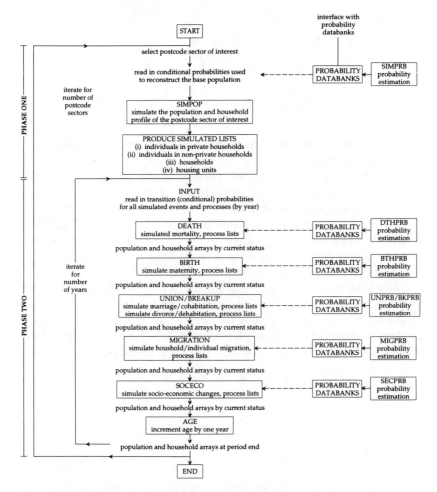

Figure 11.2 The structure of the UPDATE simulation system

of a unit smaller than a household. Eligibility for 'independent' mobility excludes children under sixteen and members of formal and informal couples, whose migration related to pair dissolution is modelled separately in the BREAKUP module (see figure 11.2).

Similar steps to those employed for wholly moving households are used to estimate individual mobility probabilities, with the exclusion of the housing stock component. The target variable to be estimated is

$p(im)_s^{agm}(y)$, the probability that an independent individual of age a, gender g and marital status m in postal sector s migrates in year y.

This probability is estimated as follows:

$$p(im)_s^{agm}(y) = \text{initial district estimate}$$
$$\times \text{spatial adjustment factor}$$
$$\times \text{temporal adjustment factor}$$
$$\times \text{reduction factor to reflect prior migration}$$
$$\text{in the pair formation and dissolution process} \quad (11.16)$$

(3) The estimation of the probabilities of staying in an area or out-migrating

The first pass through the list of simulated households generates a pool of moving households and fissioned part households (mainly individuals) which will search for suitable housing vacancies in the local housing market. To allocate migrants to housing units it is necessary to distinguish between moves within the area and moves to the outside world. The within-area movers compete for housing units in the small area, but movers out of the area release units for occupation by in-migrants.

Households and independent individuals for whom a migration has been simulated must therefore be allocated a destination inside or outside the small area of interest by sampling the appropriate probabilities of staying and leaving. If a matrix of intra- and interarea flows is known, probabilities of relocation within an area or outside it, given mobility, can be computed:

$$p(\text{staying}) = M_{ii} / \sum_j . M_{ij} \quad (11.17)$$

and

$$p(\text{leaving}) = \sum_{j \neq i} M_{ij} / \sum_j . M_{ij} \quad (11.18)$$

where M_{ij} is the number of migrants from origin i to destination j. However, such a matrix of interarea flows exists only for one set of areas, namely within-district wards. We need therefore to develop a method of using this information to make an estimate at a different spatial scale.

The method involves using a production-constrained spatial interaction model and comprises the following steps.

(1)   An origin-specific, production-constrained spatial interaction model (SIM) is fitted to the observed interward migration matrix (derived from OPCS's special migration statistics from the 1981 Census using the MATPAC programme). The model takes the form

$$M_{ij} = BF_i O_i W_j \exp(-\beta_i . d_{ij}) \quad (11.19)$$

where

$O_i = \sum_j M_{ij} = $ total migrants originating in ward i,

$W_j = \sum_i M_{ij} = $ attractiveness of ward j to migrants,

$\beta_i = $ a distance decay parameter for ward i,

$d_{ij} = $ the distance between ward i and ward j and

$BF_i = 1/\sum W_j \exp(-\beta_i . d_{ij}) = $ the balancing factor for ward i.

(2)   These ward β parameters are used to estimate the equivalent parameters for postal sectors by inputting the ward values to constituent enumeration districts and then computing a weighted average for enumeration districts lying within a postal sector, employing enumeration district populations as weights.

(3)   An intersector distance matrix is computed from knowledge of sector centroids and Pythagoras' theorem. Intra-sector distance is assumed to be

$$d_{ii} = (ha_i/\pi)^{0.5} \tag{11.20}$$

where ha_i is the area of postal sector i.

(4)   The production-constrained spatial interaction model is used to predict the share of out-migration from each sector to itself.

$$M_{ii}/O_i = W_i.\exp(-\beta_i . d_{ii})/\sum_j . W_j.\exp(-\beta_i d_{ij}) \tag{11.21}$$

where W_i and W_j are the attractiveness variables for postal sectors i and j which are set equal to the migration within or into the sector estimated by summing that variable available for enumeration districts.

(5)   The probability of staying in an area given mobility is computed by the left-hand side of equation (11.21), while the probability of leaving the area is 1 minus the probability of staying. Table 11.1 presents the within/without dichotomy for Leeds postal sectors. The variation is considerable, ranging from near negligible intra-area flows within LS 1 to large and in some cases dominant flows within peripheral postal sectors, those in LS 21 and LS 22, for example. Such a distribution can be explained broadly on the basis that migrants have further to travel to cross boundaries in the larger peripheral postal sectors. However, this relationship is constrained somewhat by local housing stock that increases the attractiveness of the destination sector, and intervening opportunities that reduce the distance of moves.

Within-area movers are then matched to vacant dwellings in the housing pool of the small area. Their successful matching is based on a probabilistic matching of their respective attributes: housing provision versus housing requirement (size of household–size of unit; disposable household income–purchase price/rental value). The mechanisms for such matching, the links between housing units, households and/or individuals are provided by pointers or common reference numbers.

Results

The UPDATE suite of programmes has been implemented for the 111 postal sectors of the Leeds Metropolitan District in the UK. The total population of Leeds M.D. in 1981 was approximately 750,000; therefore, each spatial unit was populated on average by some 7,000 persons. At the time of writing UPDATE has been run for the time period 1981–7 for all demographic events and in partial mode up to 1991. We present a limited set of results in this chapter; a full account of the methodology and outputs can be found in Duley (1989).

Figure 11.3 presents the age and sex pyramids for a selected number of postal sectors in the city for 1981 (actual census data) and 1987 (model output). In most examples we can observe evidence of increasing elderly persons (75+) between the two years. Figure 11.4 illustrates the changing household structure of the same postal sectors during the same period. It is when there is a need for more detailed distributions of variables to be output that the micro-simulation method comes into its own. This is demonstrated well in table 11.2 where we present the changes in living arrangements in two postal sectors of Leeds between 1981 and 1987. Note the decline in formally married couples and the increase in cohabiting couples for these two sectors.

Extensions

UPDATE represents one strand of micro-simulation work undertaken in Leeds in the 1980s. Very much related to this work is the objective of extending the attribute list for individuals and households beyond that which can be conventionally derived from traditional data sources. One area of interest has been in generating individual and household incomes at the small area level. Despite its collection and publication in the US census, in the UK the government has refused to collect and publish income data at anything other than national or crude regional levels. The results of the work published in Birkin and Clarke (1989) demonstrate how, using micro-simulation methods, it is possible synthetically to generate small area income distributions. Once these are available it is then relatively straight-forward to derive expenditure estimates for a wide variety of goods and services. This information has important applications in areas such as retail and health-care planning (see Clarke and Spowage, 1984).

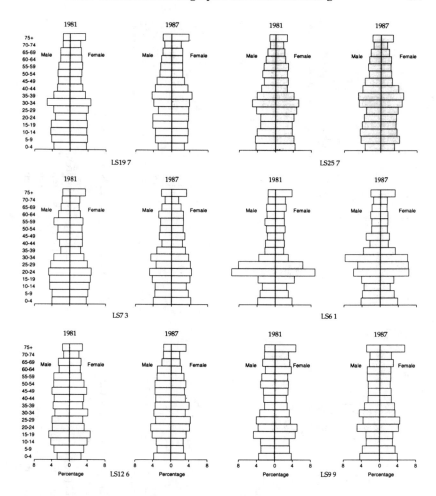

Figure 11.3 Ages and sex structure of the selected postal sectors in Leeds, 1981 and 1987

5 Conclusions

In this chapter we have attempted to demonstrate how an alternative methodology based on micro-simulation techniques can be used to solve demographic and social accounting problems of the type that Stone and other researchers generally approached at the macro level. It was argued that the attractions of the method over traditional occupancy matrix approaches are particularly strong in circumstances where heterogeneity and interdependence between and amongst individuals and their attribute sets are displayed.

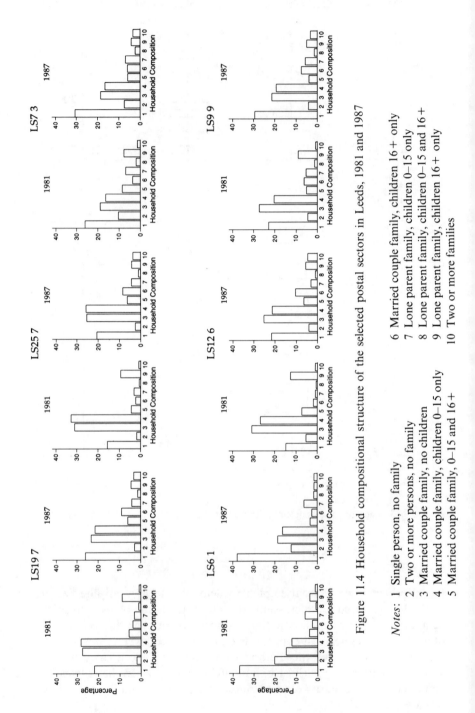

Figure 11.4 Household compositional structure of the selected postal sectors in Leeds, 1981 and 1987

Notes: 1 Single person, no family
        2 Two or more persons, no family
        3 Married couple family, no children
        4 Married couple family, children 0–15 only
        5 Married couple family, 0–15 and 16+

        6 Married couple family, children 16+ only
        7 Lone parent family, children 0–15 only
        8 Lone parent family, children 0–15 and 16+
        9 Lone parent family, children 16+ only
      10 Two or more families

Table 11.2 Changes in living arrangement in the 1980s: two test cases

| | independent | | | | married couple | | | | cohabiting couple | | | |
| | males | | females | | males | | females | | males | | females | |
age	1981	1987	1981	1987	1981	1987	1981	1987	1981	1987	1981	1987
16–19	440	414	446	392	3	7	13	12	1	4	2	20
20–24	373	342	325	259	84	95	145	144	6	46	10	54
25–29	216	216	158	121	196	157	227	264	9	45	8	46
30–34	111	124	90	127	232	302	220	242	6	32	4	22
35–39	46	81	64	81	149	230	172	221	2	15	3	10
40–44	59	50	67	61	164	152	209	182	3	7	2	5
45–49	75	73	68	87	197	193	202	205	3	8	3	5
50+	443	513	800	786	904	824	741	690	18	22	16	17
all ages	1763	1743	2018	1914	1929	1960	1929	1960	48	179	48	179
%1981	47.1		50.5		51.6		48.2		1.3		1.2	
%1987		44.9		47.2		50.5		48.4		4.6		4.4

Yeadon LS19 7

Table 11.2 *Changes in living arrangement in the 1980s: two test cases (cont.)*

| | independent | | | | married couple | | | | cohabiting couple | | | |
| | males | | females | | males | | females | | males | | females | |
age	1981	1987	1981	1987	1981	1987	1981	1987	1981	1987	1981	1987
16–19	510	529	468	427	6	5	17	11	0	6	0	18
20–24	249	381	203	267	150	108	251	150	1	51	3	64
25–29	106	126	80	103	337	208	435	350	2	42	2	37
30–34	84	87	67	97	544	410	523	406	2	21	1	15
35–39	55	73	61	80	393	469	367	494	2	12	2	9
40–44	43	62	40	74	306	393	313	385	0	9	0	6
45–49	30	65	41	65	292	341	261	297	2	5	1	3
50+	274	373	883	914	1295	1236	1156	1077	3	11	3	5
all ages	1351	1696	1843	2021	3323	3170	3323	3170	12	157	12	157
% 1981	28.8		35.5		71.0		64.2		0.2		0.2	
% 1987		33.8		37.8		63.0		59.3		3.1		2.9

Notes:
1981 and 1987 percentage figures presented by sex.
1981 and 1987 totals are the mean of 5 simulation runs.

However, as the review section illustrated, the number and frequency of applications of micro-simulation methods in regional science are small, and there remains a great deal of work to be done in this area compared with other methods such as input–output modelling, multi-regional population accounting models, spatial interaction models and most forms of spatial statistics. We have offered a number of explanations for this in earlier parts of the chapter and here stress again the point that the methodology is not new. It is some thirty years since the publication of Orcutt's first book (Orcutt *et al.*, 1962) and at least twenty years since the first spatial applications of the method. There is also no shortage of contemporary policy issues that would benefit from a micro-simulation approach. Current examples include work on the spatial diffusion of the HIV virus; the issue of asset accumulation and subsidy in the UK housing market and the problems associated with ageing and the elderly population. There is a wealth of potential for policy analysts in developing micro-simulation models in these and similar areas.

Bibliography

Adelman, I. and Robinson, S. 1978. *Income Distribution Policy in Developing Countries*. Oxford University Press

Airov, J. 1967. 'Fiscal policy theory in an interregional economy: general inter-regional multipliers and their application', *Papers of the Regional Science Association* 19: 83–108

Akita, T. 1992. 'Sources of regional economic growth in Japan: a case of Hokkaido Prefecture between 1970 and 1985', *Journal of Applied Input–Output Analysis* 1: 88–107

Allen, R. M. 1991. Personal communication

Anselin, L. and Madden, M. (eds.) 1990. *New Directions in Regional Analysis*. London: Belhaven Press

Bacharach, M. 1970. *Biproportional Matrices and Input Output Change*. Cambridge University Press

Barnard, J. R. 1969. 'A social accounting system for regional development planning', *Journal of Regional Science* 9: 109–15

Barnes, T. and Sheppard, E. 1984. 'Technical choice and reswitching in space economies', *Regional Science and Urban Economics* 14: 345–62

Batey, P. W. J. 1985. 'Input–output models for regional demographic-economic analysis: some structural comparisons', *Environment and Planning* A 17: 73–99

Batey, P. W. J. and Madden, M. 1981. 'Demographic-economic forecasting within an activity-commodity framework: some theoretical considerations and empirical results', *Environment and Planning A* 13: 1067–84

   1983. 'The modelling of demographic-economic change within the context of regional decline: analytical procedures and empirical results', *Socio-Economic Planning Sciences* 17: 315–28

Batey, P. W. J. and Weeks, M. J. 1987. 'An extended input–output model incorporating employed, unemployed, and in-migrant households', *Papers of the Regional Science Association* 62: 93–116

Batey, P. W. J., Madden, M. and Weeks, M. 1987. 'Household income and expenditure in extended input–output models: a comparative theoretical and empirical analysis', *Journal of Regional Science* 27: 341–56

Becker, C. and Mills, E. S. 1986. *Studies in Indian Urban Development*. Oxford University Press

Bell, C. L. G., Hazell, P. and Slade, R. 1982. *Project Evaluation in Regional*

Perspective. Baltimore: Johns Hopkins Press

Betson, D., Greenberg, D. and Kasten, R. 1980. 'A microsimulation model for analysing alternative welfare reform programs for better jobs and income', in Havemann, R. and Hollenbeck, K. (eds.) *Microeconomic Simulation Models for Public Policy Analysis.* New York: Academic Press

Bevan, D., Collier, P., Gunning, J., with Bigsten, A. and Horsnell, P. 1989. *Peasants and Government.* Oxford: Clarendon Press

Bigsten, A. 1980. *Regional Inequality and Development. A Case Study of Kenya.* Farnborough: Gower

1983. *Income Distribution and Development: Theory. Evidence and Policy.* London: Heinemann

1984. *Education and Income Determination in Kenya.* Aldershot: Gower

Bigsten, A. and Collier, P. forthcoming. 'Linkages from agricultural growth in Kenya', in Mellor, J. (ed.) *Agriculture on the Road to Industrialization.* Baltimore: John Hopkins University Press

Bigsten, A. and Ndungu, N. 1992. 'Kenya', in Duncan, A. and Howell, J. (eds.) *Structural Adjustment and the African Farmer.* London: Overseas Development Institute in association with James Currey

Birkin, M. and Clarke, M. 1987. 'SYNTHESIS: A synthetic spatial information system: methods and examples', *Environment and Planning* A20: 645–71

1989. 'The generation of individual and household incomes at the small area level using SYNTHESIS', *Regional Studies* 23: 535–48

Blundell, R. W., Ham, J. C. and Meghir, C. H. D. 1988. 'Unemployment, discouraged workers and female labour supply', Discussion Paper 88–19, London: University College London, Department of Economics

Bodkin, R. G., Klein, L. R. and Marwah, K. 1991. *A History of Macroeconometric Model-Building.* Vermont: Edward Elgar

Bröcker, J. 1988. 'Interregional trade and economic integration', *Regional Science and Urban Economics* 18: 261–81

Brooke, A., Kendrick, D. and Meeraus, A. 1988. *GAMS, A User's Guide.* Redwood City, CA: The Scientific Press

Bullard, C. W. and Sebald, A. V. 1977. 'Effects of parametric uncertainty and technological change in input–output models', *Review of Economics and Statistics* 59: 75–81

1988. 'Monte Carlo sensitivity analysis of input–output models', *Review of Economics and Statistics* 70: 705–12

Bureau of Labor Statistics 1982. 'Tables of working life: the Increment–decrement model', *Bulletin 2135.* Washington, DC: US Department of Labor

Caldwell, S. 1991. 'CORSIM: The Cornell dynamic microsimulation model', Paper presented to the International Symposium for Microsimulation, Stockholm, September 1991

Cambridge, Department of Applied Economics 1962. 'A social accounting matrix for 1960', *A Programme for Growth*, Vol. 2., Chapman and Hall

Carlino, G. and Lang, R. 1989. 'Interregional flows of funds as a measure of economic integration in the United States', *Journal of Urban Economics* 26: 20–9

CBS 1990. *Bevolkingsprognose voor Nederland 1990–2050*. Den Haag: Centraal Bureau voor de Statistiek

Chander, R., Gnasegarah, S., Pyatt, G. and Round, J. 1980. 'Social accounts and the distribution of income: the Malaysian economy in 1970', *Review of Income and Wealth* 26: 67–85

Chenery, H. B. 1960. 'Patterns of industrial growth', *American Economic Review* 50: 624–54

Chenery, H. B., Clark, P. G. and Cao-Pinna, V. 1953. *The Structure and Growth of the Italian Economy*, Rome: United States Mutual Security Agency

Clarke, M. 1986. 'Demographic processes and household dynamics: a microsimulation approach', in Woods, R. and Rees, P. H. (eds.) *Population Structures and Models: Developments in Spatial Demography*. London: Allen & Unwin, pp. 245–72

Clarke, M. and Holm, E. 1987. 'Micro-simulation models in human geography and planning: a review and further extensions', *Geografisk Annaler* 69 B: 145–64

Clarke, M., Longley, P. and Williams, H. C. W. L. 1989. 'Microanalysis and simulation of housing careers: subsidy and accumulation in the UK housing market', *Papers of the Regional Science Association* 66: 105–22

Clarke, M. and Openshaw, S. 1987. 'The AGW spatial interaction workstation', *Environment and Planning*, A 19: 1261–8

Clarke, M. and Spowage, M. 1984. 'Integrated models for public policy analysis: an example of the practical use of simulation models in health care planning', *Papers of the Regional Science Association* 55: 25–45

Collier, P. and Lal, D. 1980. 'Poverty and Growth in Kenya', World Bank Staff Working Paper No. 389, Washington DC

Condon, T., Dahl, H. and Devarajan, S. 1987. 'Implementing a computable general equilibrium model on GAMS: the Cameroon model', Discussion Paper: Report No. DRD290, World Bank Development Research Dept.

Conway, R. S. 1979. 'The simulation properties of a regional interindustry econometric model', *Papers of the Regional Science Association* 43: 45–57

Courbis, R. 1979. 'The REGINA model, a regional-national model for French planning', *Regional Science and Urban Economics* 9: 117–39

CPB 1991. *Macro Economische Verkenning 1992*. The Hague: Staatsuitgeverij

Crema, Y., Defourny, J. and Gazon J. 1984. 'Structural decomposition of multipliers in input–output or social accounting matrix analysis', *Economie Appliquée* 37: 215–22

Czamanski, S. 1973. *Regional and Interregional Social Accounting*. Lexington MA: Lexington Books

Defourny, J. and Thorbecke, E. 1984. 'Structural path analysis and multiplier decomposition within a social accounting matrix framework', *Economic Journal* 94: 111–36

Developing Countries, 'International monetary fund working paper', WP/89/95, Washington, DC

Dervis, K., de Melo, J. and Robinson, S. 1982. *General Equilibrium Models for Development Policy*. Cambridge University Press

Devaney, B. 1983. 'An analysis of variations in US fertility and female labour force participation trends', *Demography* 20(2): 147–61

Dewhurst, J. H. Ll. 1990. 'A decomposition of changes in input–output tables', Paper presented to the 37th North American Meeting of the Regional Science Association International, Boston, November 1990

Dewhurst, J. H. Ll. and Haggart, I. 1990. 'Consistent industry by industry input–output tables for Scotland 1973 and 1979', Dundee Discussion Papers in Economics No. 15, University of Dundee

Dewhurst, J. H. Ll. and West, G. R. 1990. 'An analysis of the tiered approach to the concept of fundamental economic structure', Dundee Discussion Papers in Economics No. 5, University of Dundee

van Dijk, J. and Oosterhaven, J. 1986. 'Regional impact of migrants expenditure: an input–output/vacancy chain approach', in Batey, P. W. J. and Madden, M. (eds.) *Integrated Analysis of Regional Systems*. London: Pion, pp. 122–47

Duley, C. J. 1989. 'Model for updating census-based household and population information for inter censal years', Unpublished PhD thesis, School of Geography, University of Leeds

Duley, C. J. and Rees, P. H. 1990. 'Incorporation of migration into simulation models', Working Paper 533, School of Geography, University of Leeds

Duley, C. J., Rees, P. H. and Clarke, M. 1988. 'A microsimulation model for updating households in small areas between censuses', Working Paper 515, School of Geography, University of Leeds

Durand, J. D. 1975. *The Labor Force in Economic Development*. Princeton, NJ: Princeton University Press

Elhance, A. P. 1992. 'Aggregation sensitivity testing for the maximal tendency procedure' (forthcoming), *Geographical Analysis*

Eliasson, G. 1985. *The Firm and Financial Markets in the Swedish Micro to Macro Model – Theory, Model and Verification*. Stockholm: Almgrist & Wiksell

Elkan, W. 1976. 'Is there a proletariat emerging in Nairobi?', *Economic Development and Cultural Change* 24

Erickson, R. 1980. 'Corporate organization and manufacturing branch plant closures in non-metropolitan areas', *Regional Studies* 14: 491–501

Eurostat 1979. *European System of Integrated Accounts (ESA)* (Second Edition), Luxembourg

1992. *National Accounts ESA, Detailed Tables by Sector 1970–1987*, Theme 2 Series C, Luxembourg

Evers, G. H. M. and van der Veen, A. 1984. 'A simultaneous non-linear model for labour migration and commuting', *Regional Studies* 19 (3): 217–29

Federal Reserve Board of Governors, 1980. 'Flow of Funds', *Annual Bulletin* Washington, DC

Feldman, S. J., McClain, D. and Palmer, K. 1987. 'Sources of structural change in the United States 1963–1978: an input–output perspective', *Review of Economics and Statistics* 69: 503–10

Feldstein, M. and Horioka, C. 1980. 'Domestic saving and international capital flows', *Economic Journal* 90: 314–29

Fleischer, B. M. 1970. *Labour Economics: Theory and Evidence*. Englewood Cliffs, NJ: Prentice-Hall

FNEI 1978. *De kwalitatieve structuur van de Noordelijke arbeidsmarkt: Een eerste kwantitatieve analyse.* Assen: Federatie van Noordelijke Economische Instituten

1986. *Integraal Sectorstructuur- en Arbeidsmarkt-Model voor Groningen, Friesland en Drenthe.* Groningen: Federatie van Noordelijke Economische Instituten

Foot, D. K. and Milne, W. J. 1984. 'Net migration estimation in an extended, multiregional gravity model', *Journal of Regional Science* 24: 119–33

Fraser of Allander Institute, Scottish Council Research Institute, and IBM UK Scientific Centre 1978. *Input–Output Tables for Scotland 1973.* Edinburgh: Scottish Academic Press

Galler, H. and Wagner, G. 1986. 'The microsimulation model of the SFb3 for the analysis of economic and social policies', in Orcutt, Merz and Quinke (eds.)

Gazel, R., Sonis, M. and Hewings, G. J. D. 1993. 'An examination of multi-regional structure: hierarchy, feedbacks and spatial linkages', Discussion Paper 93-T-11, Illinois: Regional Economics Applications Laboratory, University of Illinois

Gisebrecht, F. G. and Fiew, L. 1969. 'Demographic Micro-simulation Model POPSIM II Manual for Programs to Generate Vital Events', Technical Report No. 5 Project SV-285, Research Triangle Institute

Greenfield, C. C. 1985. 'A Social Accounting Matrix for Botswana, 1974–75', in Pyatt and Round (eds.)

Greenwood, M. J., Hunt, G. L. and McDowell J. M. 1986. 'Migration and employment change: empirical evidence on the spatial and empirical dimensions of the linkage', *Journal of Regional Science* 26: 223–34

Gregory, P. R. 1982. 'Fertility and labour force participation in the Soviet Union and Eastern Europe', *The Review of Economics and Statistics* 64(1): 18–31

Hain, W. and Helberger, C. 1986. 'Longitudinal microsimulation of life income', in Orcutt, Merz and Quinke (eds.)

Hanson, K. and Robinson, S. 1989. 'Data, Linkages, and Models: US National Income and Product Accounts in the Framework of a Social Accounting Matrix', ARED Staff Report No. AGES 89–5, US Department of Agriculture, Washington, DC

Harrigan, F. J., McGilvray, J. W. and McNicoll, I. H. 1980a. 'Simulating the structure of a regional economy', *Environment and Planning* A 12: 927–36

1980b. 'A comparison of regional and national technical structures', *Economic Journal* 90: 795–810

Harrigan, F. J. and McGregor, P. G. 1988a. *Recent Advances in Regional Economic Modelling.* London: Pion

1988b. 'Price and quantity interactions in regional economic models: the importance of "openness" and "closures"', in Harrigan and McGregor (eds.)

1989. 'Neoclassical and Keynesian perspectives on the regional macro-economy: a computable general equilibrium approach', *Journal of Regional Science* 29 (4): 555–73

Harrigan, F. J., McGregor, P. G., Dourmashkin, N., Perman, R., Swales, K. and Yin, Y. P. 1991. 'AMOS: a macro-micro model of Scotland', Strathclyde

Papers in Economics 91/1, University of Strathclyde, Glasgow

Harris, J. R. and Todaro, M. 1970. 'Migration, unemployment and development: a two-sector analysis', *American Economic Review* 60: 126–42

Hayden, C. and Round J. I. 1982. 'Developments in social accounting methods as applied to the analysis of income distribution and employment issues', *World Development* 10: 451–65

Heckman, J. J. 1980. 'Sample selection bias as a specification error', in Smith, J. (ed.) *Female Labour Supply*. Princeton NJ: Princeton University Press

Henderson, D., McGregor, P. G. and McNicoll, I. H. 1989. 'Measuring the effects of changing structure on employment generation potential', *International Regional Science Review*, 12 (1): 57–65

Hewings, G. J. D. 1986. 'Problems of integration in the modelling of regional systems', in Batey, P. W. J. and Madden, M. (eds.) *Integrated Analysis of Regional Systems*. London: Pion

1990. 'Death as final demand: Sir Richard Stone's social accounting frameworks and their application in regional science', in Gordon, I. (ed.) *Cambridge Economists and Regional Science*, London: Macmillan

Hewings, G. J. D. and Jensen, R. C. 1986. 'Regional, interregional and multiregional input–output analysis', in Nijkamp, P. and Mills, E. S. (eds.) *Handbook of Regional and Urban Economics*, Vol. 1. Amsterdam: North-Holland

1988. 'Emerging challenges in regional input–output analysis', *Annals of Regional Science* 22: 43–53

1989. 'Regional, interregional and multiregional input–output analysis', in Nijkamp, P. (ed.) *Handbook of Regional and Urban Economics*, Vol. 1

Hewings, G. J. D., Jensen, R. C. and West, G. R. 1987. 'Holistic matrix descriptors of regional input–output systems', Working Paper No. 60, Department of Economics, University of Queensland, Australia

Hewings, G. J. D., Jensen, R. C., West, G. R., Sonis, M. and Jackson, R. W. 1989. 'The spatial organization of production: an input–output perspective', *Socio-Economic Planning Sciences* 23: 67–86

Hewings, G. J. D. and Romanos, M. C. 1981. 'Simulating less developed regional economies under conditions of limited information', *Geographical Analysis* 13: 373–90

Hewings, G. J. D., Sonis, M., Jahan, S. and Lee, J. H. 1990. 'Alternative decompositions of social accounting matrices: an application to Bangladesh', unpublished paper, available from Regional Economics Applications Laboratory, Urbana, Illinios

Hirsch, W. Z. (ed.) 1964. *Elements of Regional Accounts*. Baltimore: Johns Hopkins Press

1966. *Regional Accounts for Policy Decisions*. Baltimore: Johns Hopkins Press

Hochwald, W. (ed.) 1961. *Design of Regional Accounts*. Baltimore: Johns Hopkins Press

Holm, E., Makila, K. and Oberg, S. 1985. 'Time geographic concepts and individual mobility behaviour', Paper presented to the Philadelphia RSA Meeting

Hooimeijer, P. 1991. 'URBIO: a life course approach to urban dynamics', Paper presented to the IGU Symposium on Microsimulation, Stockholm

Hughes, M. 1991. 'General equilibrium of a regional economy with a financial sector – Part I: An accounting framework with budget and balance sheet linkages', *Journal of Regional Science* 31: 385–96

1992. 'General equilibrium of a regional economy with a financial sector – Part II: A simple behavioral model', *Journal of Regional Science* 32: 19–37

Hughes, M. and Nagurney, A. 1990. 'A network model and algorithm for the analysis and estimation of financial flow of funds', mimeo, presented at the North American Regional Science Association Meetings, Boston, MA

Hulu, E., and Hewings, G. J. D. 1993. 'The development and use of interregional input–output tables for Indonesia, 1980, 1985', *Review of Urban & Regional Development Studies*, 5:

Hynes, M. and Jackson, R. W. 1988. 'Demographics in demographic-economic models: a note on the basic activity-commodity framework', *Environment and Planning A* 20: 1531–6

Industry Department for Scotland, 1984. *Scottish Input–Output Tables for 1979* (5 volumes), Edinburgh: HMSO

Internal Revenue Service 1988. *Source Book Statistics of Income, 1985: Corporation Income Tax Returns*. Washington DC: Publication 1053

1990. *Statistics of Income, 1987: Individual Income Tax Returns*. Washington DC: Publication 1304

Isard, W. 1960. *Methods of Regional Science*. Cambridge: MIT Press

Jahan, S. and Hewings, G. J. D. 1990. 'Spatial impacts of regional development programs in Bangladesh using a four-region social accounting system', Paper presented at the European Congress of the Regional Science Association, Istanbul, Turkey

1993. 'A four-region interregional social accounting matrix for Bangladesh: policy applications', Working Paper 93-T-1, Regional Economics Applications Laboratory, University of Illinois, Urbana

Jensen, R. C., Dewhurst, J. H. Ll., West, G. R. and Bayne, B. A. 1990a. 'The Gladstone study revisited: a reassessment/validation approach', Report to the Department of Manufacturing and Commerce, Department of Economics, University of Queensland

1990b. 'Combining shift–share analysis and input–output for a study of regional economic structural change', Paper to Regional Economic Modelling Conference, Newcastle, NSW

Jensen, R. C., Dewhurst, J. H. Ll., West G. R. and Hewings, G. J. D. 1991. 'On the concept of fundamental economic structure', in Dewhurst, J. H. Ll., Hewings, G. J. D. and Jensen, R. C. (eds.) *New Interpretations and Extensions of Regional Input–Output Modelling*, Avebury

Jensen, R. C., West, G. R. and Hewings, G. J. D. 1988. 'On the study of regional economic structure using input–output models', *Regional Studies* 22: 209–20

Johansen, L. 1985. 'Richard Stone's contributions to economics', *Scandinavian Journal of Economics* 87: 4–32

Jones, R. W. 1956. 'Factor proportions and the Heckscher–Ohlin theorem', *Review of Economic Studies* 24: 1–10

Kain, S. and Apgar, W. 1985. *Housing and Neighbourhood Dynamics: A Simulation*

Study. Cambridge, MA: Harvard University Press

Kenya (CBS) 1977. *Integrated Rural Survey 1974/75*. Nairobi

1980a. *Social Accounting Matrix 1976. A Preview*. Nairobi

1980b. *Urban Labour Force Survey 1977/8*. Nairobi

1981. *Social Accounting Matrix 1976*. Nairobi

Keyfitz, N. 1985. *Applied Mathematical Demography*, 2nd edition. New York: Springer-Verlag

Kilkenny, M. 1990. 'Transboundary capital flows in multi-region social accounting matrices', Working Paper 3–90–5, Department of Economics, The Pennsylvania State University

1993a. 'Rural/urban effects of terminating farm subsidies', *American Journal of Agricultural Economics*, 75(4): 968–80

1993b. 'Agricultural liberalization in segmented or integrated markets in the presence of scale economies', *Journal of Economic Integration*, 8(2): 201–18

Kilkenny, M. and Rose, A. 1994. 'Transboundary flows of capital-related income: an empirical assessment', Final report to the National Science Foundation

Ko, S. and Hewings, G. J. D. 1986. 'A regional computable general equilibrium model for Korea', *Korea Journal of Regional Science* 2: 4557

Krueger, A. B. and Summers, L. H. 1988. 'Efficiency wages and the interindustry wage structure', *Econometrica* 56 (2): 259–93

Kuznets, S. 1957. 'Quantitative aspects of the economic growth of nations, II: industrial distribution of national product and labor force', *Economic Development and Cultural Change* 5: 3–111

Lantner, R. 1974. *Théorie de la dominance économique*, Paris: Dunod

Lebergott, S. 1965. 'The labour force and marriages as endogenous factors', in Duesenberry, J. S., Fromm, G., Klein, L. R. and Kuh, E. (eds.) *The Brookings Quarterly Econometric Model of the United States*. Rand McNally, pp. 335–71

Leontief, W. 1953 (ed.) *Studies in the Structure of the American Economy*. New York: Oxford University Press

Leontief, W., Carter, A. P. and Petri, P. A. 1977. *The Future of the World Economy, A United Nations Study*. New York: Oxford University Press

Leontief, W. and Strout, A. 1966. 'Multiregional input–output analysis', in Leontief, W. (ed.) *Input–Output Economics*. Oxford University Press, pp. 223–57

Leven, C. L. 1958. 'A theory of regional social accounting', *Papers and Proceedings of the Regional Science Association* 4: 221–37

Madden, M. 1985. 'Demographic-economic analysis in a multi-zonal system: a case study of Nordrhein-Westfalen', *Regional Science and Urban Economics* 15: 517–40

Madden, M. and Batey, P. W. J. 1980. 'Achieving consistency in demographic-economic forecasting', *Papers of the Regional Science Association* 44: 91–106

1983. 'Linked population and economic models: some methodological issues in forecasting analysis and policy optimization', *Journal of Regional Science* 23: 141–64

1986. 'A demographic-economic model of a metropolis', in Woods, R. and Rees, P. D. (eds.) *Population Structures and Models*, pp. 273–95

Madden, M. and Trigg, A. B. 1990. 'Interregional migration in an extended input–output model', *International Regional Science Review* 13: 65–85

Malmberg, B. 1990. *The Effects of External Ownership – A Study of Linkages and Branch Plant Location.* Uppsala: Geografiska Region Studies

Manders, A. 1989. *Raming Arbeidsaanbod 1985–2000, Notitie nr. 35* Den Haag: Centraal Planbureau

Mansur, A. and Whalley, J. 1984. 'Numerical specification of applied general equilibrium models: estimation, calibration, and data', chapter 3 in Scarf and Shoven (eds.)

Miller, R. E. 1966. 'Interregional feedback effects in input–output models: some preliminary results', *Papers of the Regional Science Association* 17: 105–25

  1969. 'Interregional feedbacks in input–output models: some experimental results', *Western Economic Journal* 7: 57–70

  1986. 'Upper bounds on the sizes of interregional feedbacks in multiregional input–output models', *Journal of Regional Science* 26: 285–306

Miller, R. E. and Blair, P. D. 1985. *Input–Output Analysis: Foundations and Extensions.* Englewood Cliffs, NJ: Prentice Hall

Miyazawa, K. 1976. *Input–Output Analysis and the Structure of Income Distribution.* Berlin: Springer-Verlag

Morrison, W. I. 1973. 'The development of an urban inter-industry model: 1 Building the input–output accounts', *Environment and Planning* 5: 369–83

Mules, T. 1990. 'Economic change in a regional economy: the case of South Australia, 1980–81 to 1985–86', Paper to Regional Economic Modelling Conference, Newcastle, NSW

National Registry Publishing Company, 1988. *Directory of Corporate Affiliations,* Willmette, IL.

Oosterhaven, J. 1981. *Interregional Input–Output Analysis and Dutch Regional Policy Problems.* Aldershot: Gower

Oosterhaven, J. and Dewhurst, J. H. L. 1990. 'A prototype demo-economic model with an application to Queensland', *International Regional Science Review* 13 (1&2): 51–64

Oosterhaven, J. and Folmer, H. 1985. 'An interregional labour market model incorporating vacancy chains and social security', *Papers of the Regional Science Association* 58: 141–55

Orcutt, G. H. 1986. 'Views on microanalytic simulation modelling', in Orcutt, Merz and Quinke (eds.)

Orcutt, G. H., Caldwell, S. and Wertheimer, R. 1976. *Policy Exploration Microanalytic Simulation.* Washington DC: The Urban Institute

Orcutt, G. H., Greenberger, M., Korbel, S. and Rollin, A. 1962. *Microanalysis of Socioeconomic Systems: A Simulation Study.* New York: Harper & Row

Orcutt, G. H., Merz, J. and Quinke, H. (eds.) 1986. *Microanalytic Simulation Models to Support Social and Financial Policy.* Amsterdam: North Holland

Perroni, C. and Rutherford, T. 1989. 'A "Regularly Flexible" nested CES function for applied general equilibrium analysis', Paper presented at the 1989 NBER Conference on Applied General Equilibrium, San Diego, CA., 7–9 September,

1989; Mimeo, University of Western Ontario, London, Ontario, Canada

Polenske, K. R. 1970. 'A commentary on both models and their uses', *Growth and Change* 1: 39–40

1980. *The US Multiregional Input–Output Accounts and Model*. Lexington, MA: Lexington Books

Pyatt, G. 1988, 'A SAM approach to modelling', *Journal of Policy Modelling* 10(3): 327–52

1989. 'The method of apportionment and its application to multiplier models', *Journal of Policy Modelling* 11(1): 111–30

Pyatt, G. and Round, J. I. 1977. 'Social accounting matrices for development planning', *Review of Income and Wealth* Series 23

1979. 'Accounting and fixed-price multipliers in a SAM framework', *Economic Journal* 89: 850–73

1984. 'Improving the macroeconomic data base: a SAM for Malaysia, 1970', World Bank Staff Working Papers No. 646, World Bank, Washington DC

Pyatt, G. and Round, J. I. (eds.) 1985. *Social Accounting Matrices: A Basis for Development Planning*, World Bank

Pyatt G. and Thorbecke, E. 1976. *Planning Techniques for a Better Future*. Geneva: International Labour Office

Rees, P. H., Clarke, M. and Duley, C. J. 1987. 'A model for updating individual and household populations', Working Paper 486, School of Geography, University of Leeds

Rees, P. H. and Wilson, A. G. 1977. *Spatial Population Analysis*. London: Arnold

Robinson, S. and Roland-Holst, D. 1987. 'Macroeconomic structure and computable general equilibrium models', Paper presented at the American Economic Association Meeting, Chicago

1988. 'Macroeconomic structure and computable general equilibrium models', *Journal of Policy Making* 10(3): 353–75

Roe, A. R. 1985. 'The flow of funds as a tool of analysis in developing countries', in Pyatt, G. and Round, J. I. (eds.), *Social Accounting Matrices: A Basis for Planning*. Washington DC: World Bank

Rogers, A. 1971. *Matrix Methods in Urban and Regional Analysis*. San Francisco: Holden-Day

1975. *Introduction to Multiregional Mathematical Demography*. New York: Wiley

1976. 'Shrinking large-scale population-projection models by aggregation and decomposition', *Environment and Planning* A 8(6): 515–41

1985. *Regional Population Projection Models*. Beverly Hills: Sage

1990. 'Requiem for the net migrant', *Geographical Analysis* 22(4): 283–300

Romans, J. T. 1965. *Capital Exports and Growth Among US Regions*. Middletown, Conn.: Wesleyan University Press

Rose, A. and Miernyk, W. 1989. 'Input–output analysis: The first fifty years', *Economic Systems Research* 1(2): 229–71

Rose, A. and Stevens, B. H. 1991. 'Transboundary income and expenditure flows in regional input–output models', *Journal of Regional Science* 31: 253–72

Roson, R. 1992. 'The adjustment of interregional input–output coefficients under heterogenous price sensitivity: a survey and an application for Italy', *Annals of Regional Science*

Round, J. I. 1985. 'Decomposing multipliers for economic systems involving regional and world trade', *Economic Journal* 95: 383–99

1986. 'Social accounting for regional economic systems', in Batey, P. W. J. and Madden, M. (eds.) *Integrated Analysis of Regional Systems*. London: Pion, pp. 90–105

1988. 'Incorporating the international, regional and spatial dimension into a SAM: some methods and applications', in Harrigan and McGregor (eds.), pp. 24–45

1994. 'The structure of the European economy: a SAM perspective', in Round, J. I. (ed.) *The European Economy in Perspective: Essays in Honour of Edward Nevin*. Cardiff: University of Wales Press, pp. 59–83

Royal Swedish Academy of Sciences 1985. 'Nobel Memorial Prize in Economics, 1984', *Scandinavian Journal of Economics* 87: 1–3

Ruggles, R. and Ruggles, N. 1956. *National Income Accounts and Income Analysis* (2nd edn). New York: McGraw-Hill Book Co.

Scarf, H. E. and Shoven (eds.) 1984. *Applied General Equilibrium Analysis*. Cambridge University Press

Schinnar, A. P. 1976. 'A multidimensional accounting model for demographic and economic planning', *Environment and Planning* A 8: 455–75

Schneider, M. H. and Zenios, S. 1989. 'A comparative study of algorithms for matrix balancing', decisions sciences Working Paper 86-10-04 (Revised January 1989), The Wharton School, University of Pennsylvania, Philadelphia, PA

Schoen, R. and Woodrow, K. 1980. 'Labour force status life tables for the United States, 1972', *Demography* 17(3): 297–322

Scott, A. J. 1988. *Metropolis: From the Division of Labor to Urban Form*. Berkeley: University of California Press

Sherman, J. and Morrison W. J. 1949. 'Adjustment of an inverse matrix corresponding to changes in the elements of a given column or a given row of the original matrix', *Annals of Mathematical Statistics* 20: 621

1950. 'Adjustment of an inverse matrix corresponding to a change in an element of a given matrix', *Annals of Mathematical Statistics* 21: 124–7

Shryock, H. S. and Siegel, J. S. 1971. *The Methods and Materials of Demography, Vol. II*. Washington, DC: US Department of Commerce

Simpson, D. and Tsukui, J. 1965. 'The fundamental structure of input–output tables: an international comparison', *Review of Economics and Statistics* 47: 434–46

Skolka, J. 1989. 'Input–output structural decomposition analysis for Austria', *Journal of Policy Modelling*, 11(1): 45–66

Sohn, I. 1986. *Readings in Input–Output Analysis*. New York: Oxford University Press

Sonis, M. 1980. 'Locational push-pull analysis of migration streams', *Geographical Analysis* 12: 80–97

1982. 'The inverted problem of multiobjective programming', in Chiotis, G. P., Tsoukalas, D. A. and Louri, H. D. (eds.) *The Regions and the Enlargement of the European Economic Community*. Athens School of Economics and Business Science

1985. 'Hierarchical structure of central place systems – the barycentric calculus and decomposition principle', *Sistemi Urbani* 1: 3–28

1986. 'A contribution to central place theory: superimposed hierarchies, structural stability, structural changes and catastrophes in central place hierarchical dynamics', in Funck, R. H. and Kuklinski, A. (eds.) *Space-Structure-Economy: A Tribute to August Lösch*. Von Loeper: Karlsruhe

Sonis, M. and Hewings, G. J. D. 1988. 'Superposition and decomposition principles in hierarchical social accounting and input–output analysis', in Harrigan and McGregor (eds.) (1988a)

1989. 'Error and sensitivity input–output analysis: a new approach', in Miller, R. E., Polenske, K. R. and Rose, A. Z. (eds.) *Frontiers of Input–Output Analysis*. New York: Oxford University Press

1990. 'The "Matrioshka" principle in the hierarchical decomposition of multiregional social accounting systems', in Anselin and Madden (eds.)

1991. 'Fields of influence and extended input–output analysis: a theoretical account', in Dewhurst, J. J. Ll., Hewings, G. J. D. and Jensen, R. C. (eds.) *Regional Input–Output Modelling: New Developments and Interpretations*. Aldershot: Avebury

1992. 'Coefficient change in input–output models: theory and applications', *Economic Systems Research* 4: 143–57

Sonis, M., Hewings, G. J. D. and Lee, J. K. 1993. 'Interpreting spatial economic structure and spatial multipliers: three perspectives', *Geographical Analysis* (forthcoming)

Sonis, M., Oosterhaven, J. and Hewings, G. J. D. 1993. 'Spatial economic structure and structural change in the European Common Market: feedback loop input–output analysis', *Economic Systems Research* 5: 173–84

Sourrouille, J. V. 1976. 'Regional accounts: theoretical and practical problems encountered in the recent experience of Argentina', *Review of Income and Wealth* 22(1): 13–36

Sraffa, P. 1973. *Production of Commodities by Means of Commodities*. Cambridge University Press

Stelder, T. M. 1991. 'The annual economic outlook for the Northern Netherlands: An interregional implementation of the input–output growth rate model', Paper presented at the ERSA Congress, Lisbon, 27–30 August

1992. 'ISAM-2: Een nieuwe versie van het Integraal Sectorstructuur- en Arbeidsmarkt-Model voor Groningen, Friesland en Drenthe', Research memorandum nr. 451 Department of Economics, University of Groningen

Stokes, C. S. and Hsieh Y. S. 1983. 'Female employment and reproductive behaviour in Taiwan, 1980', *Demography* 20(3): 313–31

Stone, J. R. N. 1960. 'A comparison of economic structure of regions based on the concept of distance', *Journal of Regional Science* 2: 1–20

1961a. 'Social accounts at the regional level: a survey', in Isard, W. J. and
Cumberland, J. H. (eds.) *Regional Economic Planning*. Paris: OECD, pp.
263–95

1961b. *Input–output and national accounts*. Paris: OECD

1968. 'Input–output projections: consistents process and quantitative structures',
L'Industria 2

1970. 'Demographic input–output: an extension of social accounting', in Carter,
A. P. and Brody, A. (eds.) *Contributions to Input–Output Analysis*, Vol. 1,
Amsterdam. North-Holland, pp. 293–319

1971. *Demographic Accounting and Model-Building*. Paris: OECD

1985. 'The disaggregation of the household sector in the national accounts', in
Pyatt and Round (eds.)

1986. 'Social accounting: the state of play', *Scandinavian Journal of Economics* 88:
453–72

Stone, J. R. N. and Brown, A. 1962. *A computable model of economic growth, A
programme for growth I*. Cambridge: Chapman and Hall

Stone, J. R. N. and Croft-Murray, G. 1959. *Social Accounting and Economic
Models*. London: Bowes and Bowes

Stone, J. R. N. and Weale, M. 1986. 'Two populations and their economies', in
Batey, P. W. J. and Madden, M. (eds.) *Integrated analysis of regional systems.
London Papers in Regional Science 15*, pp. 74–89

Sundrum, R. M. 1990. *Income Distribution Analysis*. Routledge and Kegan Paul

Syrquin, M. and Chenery, H. B. 1989. 'Patterns of development, 1950–1983',
Discussion Paper No. 41, World Bank, Washington, DC

Tabuchi, T. 1988. 'Interregional income differentials and migration: their interrelationships', *Regional Studies* 22: 1–10

Trigg, A. B. 1987. 'The spatial and distributional impacts of public expenditure
programmes: a social accounts approach', *Papers of the Regional Science
Association* 61: 21–38

1989. 'Micro data and the household endogenous input–output model', *Proceedings of the International Meeting of Official Statistics*, pp. 55–69

1993. 'A micro solution to the labour reduction problem', unpublished

Vandemoortele, J. 1982. 'Income distribution and poverty in Kenya: a statistical
analysis', Discussion Paper No. 275, Institute for Development Studies,
University of Nairobi

1991. Personal communication

United Nations 1968. *A System of National Accounts*, Series F, No. 2, Rev. 3, New
York

US Department of Commerce, Bureau of Economic Analysis 1989. *Local Area
Personal Income*, Vol. 1, Summary 1982–7 (October 1989) US Government
Printing Office, Washington, DC 20402

US Department of Commerce, Bureau of the Census 1988a. County and City Data
Book, US Government Printing Office, Washington, DC 20402 (on diskette)

1988b. *Industry by Residence*, CPR Series p-20, No. 446; US Government
Printing Office, Washington, DC 20402

Vaupel, J. W. and Yashin, A. I. 1985. 'Heterogeneity's ruses: some surprising effects of selection on population dynamics,' *The American Statistician* 39(3): 176–85

Watts, H. D. 1981. *The Branch Plant Economy: A Study of External Control.* London: Longman

Wegener, M. 1981. 'The housing market in the Dortmund region: a microsimulation', in Voogd, H. (ed.) *Strategic Planning in a Dynamic Society.* Delft: Delft University Press

Wertheimer, R. and Zedlewski, S. R. 1978. The impact of demographic change on the distribution of earned income and the AFDC program: 1975–1985. Working Paper No. 985–1, The Urban Institute, Washington DC

West, G. R. 1981. 'An efficient approach to the estimation of input–output multipliers', *Environment and Planning* A 13: 857–67

West, G. R. and Jensen, R. C. 1980. 'Some reflections on input–output multipliers', *Annals of Regional Science* 14: 77–89

Williamson, O. E. 1981. 'The modern corporation: origins, evolution, attributes', *Journal of Economic Literature* 19: 1537–68

1985. *The Economic Institutions of Capitalism.* New York: Free Press

Williamson, P. 1991. 'Microsimulating information community care for the elderly', Paper presented at the IGU Symposium on Microsimulation, Stockholm, September 1991

World Bank 1988. 'Employment and growth in Kenya', mimeo Washington DC

1990. *World Development Report 1990: Poverty.* Oxford University Press

Wrigley, C. A. and Schofield, R. S. 1981. *The Population History of England 1541–1871: a reconstruction.* London: Edmund Arnold

Index